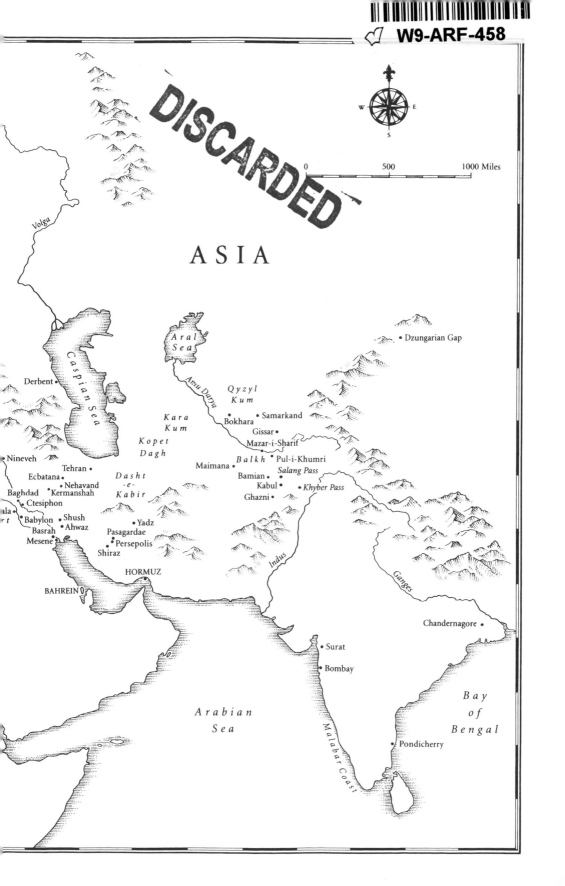

DISCARDED

ASIA

0   500   1000 Miles

Volga

Aral
Sea

Caspian Sea

Derbent

Qyzyl
Kum

Kara
Kum

Amu Darya

• Dzungarian Gap

Bokhara   • Samarkand
Gissar •
Mazar-i-Sharif

Kopet
Dagh

Nineveh

Balkh • Pul-i-Khumri
Maimana •   Salang Pass
Tehran •   Bamian •
Dasht   Kabul • • Khyber Pass
-e-   Ghazni •
Kabir

Ecbatana •
• Nehavand
Baghdad   • Kermanshah
• Ctesiphon

ala
t

• Babylon • Shush
Basrah • Ahwaz
Mesene •

• Yadz
Pasagardae •
• Persepolis
Shiraz

Indus

Ganges

HORMUZ

BAHREIN

Chandernagore •

• Surat

• Bombay

Arabian
Sea

Bay
of
Bengal

Malabar Coast

• Pondicherry

DATE DUE

In Search
of
Zarathustra

In Search
of
Zarathustra

*The First Prophet and
the Ideas That Changed the World*

PAUL KRIWACZEK

ALFRED A. KNOPF

NEW YORK

2003

Copyright © 2002 by Paul Kriwaczek

All rights reserved under International and Pan-American Copyright Conventions. Published in the United States by Alfred A. Knopf, a division of Random House, Inc., New York. Distributed by Random House, Inc., New York.

www.aaknopf.com

Originally published in Great Britain by Weidenfeld & Nicolson, London, in 2002.

Knopf, Borzoi Books, and the colophon are registered trademarks of Random House, Inc.

Library of Congress Cataloging-in-Publication Data
Kriwaczek, Paul.
In search of Zarathustra : the first prophet and the ideas that changed the world / Paul Kriwaczek.— 1st American ed.
p.   cm.
Originally published: London : Weidenfeld & Nicolson, 2002.
Includes bibliographical references and index.
ISBN 0-375-41528-9
1. Zoroaster—Influence. 2. Zoroastrianism—Influence. I. Title.
BL1555 .K75 2003
295—dc21   2002073015

Manufactured in the United States of America
Published February 11, 2003
Reprinted Twice
Fourth Printing, June 2003

With grateful thanks to Mandy Little and Toby Mundy,
who conspired to persuade me to bite off more than I
thought I could chew, and to Benjamin Buchan, who picked
up the baton and carried it to the finishing line

No, I don't sing anymore,
They say it's a sin!
In my ancient beautiful homeland,
Which is older than history itself,
Who decided that singing is a crime
Though Zarathustra fertilized this land with his songs?

(IRANIAN POPULAR SINGER GOOGOOSH)

Contents

Contents

Illustrations

Illustrations

CREDITS

The author and publishers would like to thank the following for their permission to reproduce pictures: Mary Evans Picture Library, 2; Hulton Archive, 3; Museum of Antiquities, Newcastle upon Tyne, 10; Weidenfeld Archives, 11, 17; Yassavoli Publications, Tehran, 15; Bildarchiv Steffens, Mainz/Dietmar Riemann, 19.

Introduction

Hello. I'm Paul Kriwaczek. Thanks for coming on this journey with me. I hope you'll find it an interesting and enjoyable trip.

I had been practising this little speech in Farsi—the modern Persian language—ready to deliver it to the young man who was to be my fixer, interpreter, language tutor, guide, travelling companion and friend on my whirlwind tour of Iran. As it happened, we missed each other in the crowded airport concourse, and I was ignominiously reduced to seeking out the help desk and asking for his name to be called over the public address system. The woman behind the grille, who was wearing the ubiquitous Iranian *chador,* the long black coverall which must leave no hair or indoor clothing visible, yet who disconcerted me with her impeccable English, made the announcement. As I waited for some anxious minutes, I looked around the arrival hall to catch a first impression of what difference the Ayatollahs had made to Iran since I had last been here more than thirty years ago.

There was surprisingly little change, I decided. Tehran's Mehrabad airport and the crowd that thronged it seemed, if anything, rather more modern, more Western even, than the equivalent in Moscow or Bucharest—let alone Istanbul or Tashkent. No family was sitting with mats spread out, picnicking on the floor. No traveller was sleeping in a corner, wrapped in blankets, walled in among piles of string-netted vegetables. No bearded ancient was trying to drag a goat through passport control. Only the occasional distinguished-looking clergyman in grey gown and round white turban, or the occasional woman preparing for a flight by donning a headscarf in place of a *chador,* suggested the religious dimension of the Islamic Republic of the year 2000.

Then suddenly there was Hossein, attended by his brother-in-law who was to be our driver, rushing up and greeting me effusively in his perfect American, banishing all opportunity for my carefully prepared Farsi greeting. As they swept me out of the terminal towards the clapped-out old Fiat in which we were to spend most of the following weeks, I began to feel a little guilty. I hadn't expected Hossein's enthusiasm and, concerned that interest in Persia's pre-Muslim past might not go down at all well among Iran's famously severe Islamists, I had not mentioned the real purpose of my trip during our preliminary telephone conversations, avoiding any mention of Zoroastrianism or its ancient Persian founder-prophet Zarathustra, and only saying that I wanted to explore Iran's cultural heritage. I needn't have worried. Iranians, as it turned out, are just as proud of what they were before they were Muslims, as they are passionate for their version of the Islamic faith. The very name of my entry-point was an auspicious sign. The ruling theocrats have done nothing to change it, even though Mehrabad, the name of the village whose site is now occupied by the airport, can be translated as "Founded by, or for, Mithra"—and Mithra is a very un-Islamic figure, an attendant of Ahura Mazda, the one and only God of the Prophet Zarathustra's teachings.

Of course, words and names nearly always lose their original associations over time. Just as few, if any, English speakers can be aware of naming the gods Woden or Thor when speaking of Wednesday or Thursday, so no modern Tehrani is likely to be conscious of invoking a pagan power when speaking of Mehrabad, or using any of the common words and expressions that hide within them the sacred name: *mehraban*, meaning "kind," for example, is literally "observant to Mithra." None the less, the Ayatollahs had thought nothing of trying to abolish the name of the city of Kermanshah just because they didn't like to hear the sound of the word Shah, and I had fully expected the airport, like so many other Iranian landmarks, to have been renamed for the revolution or its martyrs. Keeping the name Mehrabad was a signal that the Islamic rulers of today's Iran were not denying the link back to their pre-Islamic past.

This was to be my third journey to the Iranian world. I had spent time in Iran in the early 1960s, passing through in the days when the Shah still sat on the peacock throne and former premier Mossadegh, internationally vilified for turning up to public functions in what the Western press thought were pyjamas and carpet slippers, was still alive—though under house arrest. Having left Iran, a chance encounter in Kabul, capital of Iran's eastern neighbour Afghanistan, would lead to my living in that semi-feudal kingdom, as it still was then, for the next two years.

Decades later I again explored the region—this time Iran's northern neighbours in Central Asia, with their still strongly Iranian culture. We were shooting film for a television series about Islam, while the Soviet Union crumbled about our ears and its former republics teetered on the edge of civil war between disciples of Marx and followers of Muhammad.

Every country I had ever visited in the area was overwhelmingly Muslim—in the case of Afghanistan and Iran, Islam was the official state religion even back in the sixties. Yet nobody could have helped noticing an undercurrent of something else—hints and indications that behind the sincere dedication to the Qur'an there lay a hidden stratum of belief, something understood but never mentioned and certainly not to be admitted to an outsider—the spirit of Zarathustra, still powerful after thirteen hundred years of Islam.

In Search
of
Zarathustra

1

An Idea for Now

We bowled along the road into Uzbekistan from neighbouring Tajikistan, up and over a pass through the snowy Pamir mountains, with me intoning selected verses from Flecker's "The Golden Journey to Samarkand":

> *Away, for we are ready to a man!*
> *Our camels sniff the evening and are glad.*
> *Lead on, O Master of the Caravan:*
> *Lead on the Merchant-Princes of Bagdad.*
>
> *Have we not Indian carpets dark as wine,*
> *Turbans and sashes, gowns and bows and veils,*
> *And broideries of intricate design,*
> *And printed hangings in enormous bales?*
>
> *And we have manuscripts in peacock styles*
> *By Ali of Damascus; we have swords*
> *Engraved with storks and apes and crocodiles,*
> *And heavy beaten necklaces, for Lords.*
>
> *Sweet to ride forth at evening from the wells*
> *When shadows pass gigantic on the sand,*
> *And softly through the silence beat the bells*
> *Along the Golden Road to Samarkand . . .*

. . . and then we would suddenly hit a pothole with a crash. For the road was long and, in reality, far from golden—two hundred miles or so of cracked grey concrete slabs, each junction making our vehicle lurch violently enough to lift our stomachs into our mouths, the shoulder occasionally adorned with the burnt-out wreck of a truck lying on its side or even upside down. But arriving in Samarkand made the effort worth while. Here we were in one of the world's dream cities. Dusty, hot and tired, we stood in the central square and marvelled. It is said of the Taj Mahal that, however familiar the photograph, the reality is more breathtaking than one can possibly expect. So it is with Samarkand.

The Registan, the "place of sand," is one of the architectural wonders of the world. On the west end of a great plaza, where six radial roads, one from each of the ancient city gates, met in the hub of his capital, Khan Ulugh Beg, famed astronomer and grandson of the Mongol ruler Timur-i-leng, Timur the Lame or Tamerlaine, no stately pleasure dome decreed, but a jewel of a madraseh—an Islamic college. Its rectangular façade, pierced by a pointed entrance arch and flanked by stubby minarets like cannon tipped on end to fire prayers at heaven, glitters with sumptuous knotwork decoration, executed in brilliant shades of blue against a background the colour of pale sand, matching the Central Asian sky and the dusty earth. While far off in the West a fifteenth-century barbarian called Henry V of England was fighting the Battle of Agincourt, here, it is said, the noble and wise Khan himself gave classes in mathematics, astronomy and philosophy. A century later, Babur, founder of the Moghul Empire, mounted his command and control post for the defence of the city on the madraseh's roof.

Another hundred years on, the city governor—the resoundingly named General Alchin Yalangtush Bahadur—commanded the building of a further matching pair of colleges, one on the north and another on the east side of the stone-paved square. Now, though, the decoration was to be different. In the two hundred years which separated the first madraseh from its fellows, the ruling style had moved on. On the central building, which doubles as both madraseh and mosque, leaf and flower shapes in green and yellow are entwined into the crystalline geometry of its mosaic tilework. But it is the third madraseh, the *Sher-dar*, that catches the eye unawares. For above the entrance is what must be among the most extraordinary designs to be found on any Muslim religious building anywhere.

Sher-dar is Persian for "tiger-bearing." Over the grand archway through which the students would pass from blazing sunlight into the cool, dim, quiet interior, are depicted a symmetrical pair of tigers pursuing deer across a flower-strewn field. Over the back of each tiger rises an anthropomorphic sun, golden rays of light streaming out around a patently Mongol face. How astonishing on a building dedicated to educating the clergy of a religion which abhors the depiction of any living thing! The vision certainly perplexed our Pakistan-born Muslim anthropologist, the presenter of the series of films about Islam which had brought us and our television crew to Samarkand.

Standing in the middle of the square in trainers and trademark navy-blue *shalwar-kamiz*, Pakistani national dress, a short stocky figure dwarfed by the magnificence all around, he looked up at the images outraged and nonplussed, his piety affronted. How could decoration like this be applied to a madraseh of all places? Such pictures are strictly forbidden by Islamic law. It must be an error of some kind. Our local minder explained that the buildings had been restored in the 1920s and then again in the 1950s. Well then, the tigers and faces must have been added by the Soviet-era restorers: communist atheists who knew little and cared less about the principles of Islam; perhaps it was even done on purpose, to desecrate the sanctity of the architecture.

I was surprised that a man claiming the title Professor and nursing aspirations for high diplomatic office didn't recognise the device. For the sun rising over the back of a lion was the familiar symbol of both the nineteenth-century Qajar and the twentieth-century Pahlavi dynasties of Iran—not to mention the Mojahedin-e-Khalq terrorists of today. This version, with tigers for lions and faces on the suns, could only be an earlier expression of the same motif.

The images are certainly as old as the *Sher-dar* madraseh itself, the work of a certain Muhammad Abbas, whose signature peeps discreetly through the tilework tendrils, and whose praises are sung in the self-congratulatory dedication executed in stylised Arabic script around the archway. "The sky bit its finger in amazement," gushes the building of itself after a great deal more in the same vein, "thinking there was a new moon."

What the design actually means is another matter. Muslims and scholars disagree. Locals guess that the tiger and deer motif refer to the king's pursuit of his enemies or perhaps to some Samarkandi legend. The orthodox interpretation is that the tiger stands for a lion, a reference to the Caliph 'Ali, the "Lion of Islam"—the Prophet Muhammad's son-in-law and, in Shi'ite eyes, his only rightful successor—while the sun stands for the light of Islam.

But the sun-rayed face, seen on other buildings in the region too, actually belongs to another and older tradition than Islam. For the ever-rising and unconquered sun was always one of the symbols of Mithra, in Zoroastrian belief the intermediary between God and humanity, guarantor of contracts and fair dealing, who bestows the light of his grace on the lawful ruler. Tradition led Iranian kings and emperors down the ages to see themselves as Mithra's representatives on earth. In this tiger-and-sun design, the governor was glorifying his feudal master with the mandate of heaven. The *Sher-dar* madraseh is yet another sign that Islam in the Iranian world is like a woman's plain *chador* worn over party finery, a cloak that covers, disguises, or incorporates much traditionally Iranian, pre-Islamic, Zoroastrian belief. This time, General Alchin Yalangtush Bahadur had let the veil slip and revealed his real religious underwear.

To this day tiles decorated with elegant sun-rayed Mithra faces, not Mongolian now but Aryan, are on sale in Iranian markets. Ask what they represent and you will likely be told, as I was: "Just a face."

My two earlier journeys to the East had led me to stumble many times across the traces of the Persian prophet and the religious ideas developed by his later followers. Often dismissed by pious Muslims as mere folklore, or falsely condemned as foreign influence, or even blankly denied even in the face of overwhelming evidence, the traces of Zarathustra's teachings refuse to fade away. In spite of everything, Zarathustra lives.

Before travelling south to the Pamirs as the Soviet Union sulkily retreated into history—this was the beginning of the 1990s—we had spent time in Moscow, talking to experts on the region, acclimatising ourselves to both the culture of Central Asia and, as we quickly discovered, its climate. Moscow apartments in winter must be among some of the hottest places in the world; the Soviet high-rise housing blocks that line the Prospekts, the great grim thoroughfares leading out from the city centre through the suburbs, all stained cement and peeling plaster, don't allow you to adjust the savage central heating. But sitting sweating in shirtsleeves seemed an appropriate way to learn about life in the desert cities of the Soviet deep south; to hear Dr. Lazar Rempel, octogenarian Jewish architect and historian, give an outsider's view of Central Asia as he reminisced about his fifty-six years of exile in Bokhara and Samarkand.

Dr. Rempel's fate was not unusual in Stalin's USSR. Many of those unlucky enough to attract the attention of the Father of the International Proletariat found themselves expelled from home and condemned to live thousands of miles away, among people with a different language and a different culture. Most went back as soon as they could. My own uncle in Prague had been in the Czech army before the war and had led a band of Partisans into the Bohemian forest during the Nazi occupation. In 1946 he and his men were absorbed into the Red Army and sent to the steppelands of Soviet Kazakhstan, ostensibly to help guard a "disinfection station" to which victims of smallpox and other epidemic diseases were spirited away. One day a convoy of trucks arrived. Soldiers jumped out and began unloading bale upon bale of barbed wire.

"It seemed to me," my uncle told me long afterwards, "that when barbed wire starts going up, no good ever comes of it." So he ran away, to become, years later, a stalwart of the Czechoslovak military establishment.

But, unusually, Lazar Rempel had decided to stay in Central Asia. He had been sent to Uzbekistan in 1937, in the course of one of the great Soviet anti-Jewish purges. He was lucky to be alive. Stalin, who had once studied for the priesthood, had remembered his early Bible lessons well. The best way to make a nation like the Crimean Tatars or the Tribes of Israel disappear, he had learned from the ancient Assyrian despots, was to carry them off to faraway places, where they would eventually disappear into the general population.

Rempel made a new life for himself among the Muslims: "What did the prophet Jeremiah say? 'Build houses, plant gardens, take wives and beget children. For in the peace of the city where you are captive, you will find peace.' That was my way."

And how did the Jewish exiles get on with the locals? In all his fifty-six years of banishment, Rempel couldn't recall a single instance of being badly treated because of his race or religion.

"But then," he told me, "the Muslims of Central Asia are of a special kind; whatever they call themselves: Sunni, Shi'ah, Isma'ili, that is only on the surface. The first religion of these people was Zoroastrianism, the religion of Iran before Islam, and underneath they are still Zoroastrians through and through. If you don't believe me, go and look at their religious monuments. There are Zoroastrian symbols everywhere." He suddenly thought of something. "Wait, I will show you a picture."

Rempel jumped up and went rummaging among the piles of books, folders and papers which reduced the floor area of his flat to a rabbit run. He brought back a brown and faded photograph and waved it in front of me. "Look at this. Do you normally expect to see something like this in a mosque? I found it soon after I arrived in Bokhara. It was in the district of Juibar which, when I arrived, had just been emptied of its people—executed, expelled, I don't know. I happened to look through the gateway of an old mosque and there was this huge pile of rubbish, of manuscripts, just lying in the yard. At that time, in the late 1930s, it was too dangerous to possess even an ordinary document written in Arabic characters, let alone a religious text like the Qur'an. But people could not bring themselves to destroy the Holy Word, so they would secretly come and abandon their religious books in the courtyard of a mosque. I went through the top layers and set aside just the most interesting things I found. These are now preserved in the Tashkent museum. The rest, including manuscripts going back to the tenth and eleventh centuries, were all destroyed. And, you know, this happened in the very city about which the great philosopher Ibn-Sina had written that nowhere else in the world had he seen such books as he was able to read in the libraries of Bokhara."

Rempel's photograph showed a wall plaque bearing the icon of an Islamic saint, robed and turbaned, hands held out palm upwards, the Muslim gesture of prayer. The figure stood in front of a stylised Islamic cityscape of domes and crenellations. From around the head streamed rays of light. Whom did it represent? "Maybe the Prophet, maybe 'Ali. I am not sure. All I know is that this does not represent orthodox Islam. See the light rays? This is typically Zoroastrian. It is from this that Christian icon-painters first took the idea of the halo."

"Where is the original?"

"The mosque is long gone," Rempel admitted gloomily. Then he brightened up. "But the people haven't changed. The Soviets couldn't destroy their religion, only the evidence of their unorthodoxy, so the fundamentalists should really thank them for it. Go to Central Asia, see how the people still celebrate their marriages, how they mourn their dead. You will find their beliefs and rituals far richer, deeper and older than the Islam which conquered the area only in the seventh century."

Rempel's words were unexpectedly confirmed by another of our Moscow sources. Davlat Khodanazarov didn't look like the stereotype of an Islamist. He was rather handsome, clean-shaven with short dark hair, refined features, well dressed in a smart safari outfit and blue shirt—a film-maker as well as an Islamist politician. He made notes to himself as we talked, in meticulous handwriting. He had a sense of humour and knew how to play to the camera. When we commiserated with him for having only just failed to win the Tajikistan presidency for the Islamic party, he smiled wryly.

"You should congratulate me. I am relieved I lost." On the piece of paper in front of him he drew a stick man. "If I had won, I would have had to be assassinated." On the word assassinated, he heavily crossed the stick man out.

Given the support Khodanazarov had received from his country's Muslim parties, I was astonished to hear him say that Islam in Central Asia was strong because it was built on a firm foundation of Zoroastrianism.

"And this faith," he explained, "lives on into the present. Zoroastrianism is the ideology of the future. Do you know what Zoroastrians believe? That the world is a battleground between good and evil and it is the duty of everyone to foster good and fight evil. Zoroastrianism failed in the end because it came too early in history. It is an idea for now." He drew a globe on his paper, and then a ring around it. "The world has become a very small place. For the first time we really can speak of a world community. To secure our future we must find a humanist philosophy. And Islam, supported by the message of Zoroaster, offers that philosophy." He spoke the prophet's name as Zarathushtra, like the ancients did.

Amazing though it was to hear the name of the pre-Islamic prophet invoked with such respect by a Muslim politician courting the Muslim vote, the suggestion of a very complex Central Asian religious identity was hardly new to me. Listening to Khodanazarov's stirring speech, I was able to think back to many other times over the years when I had been offered hints and indications of something deeper going on behind the pious, sober and blank Muslim façade.

Central Asia lies on the outer periphery of the Islamic domain. Travel any further east and you find yourself entering a very different world, where Indian and Chinese culture preside. Here, on the edge, the three worlds blend. In the first centuries of the common era, for example, the territory of Gandhara, which linked Afghanistan with northwesternmost India, merged the Greek culture of Alexander the Great and his successors with Persian, Indian and Chinese elements. Under its Kushan rulers Gandhara became a world centre of Buddhist thought and art. The colossal third-century Buddhist statues of Bamian, now permanently destroyed by Afghanistan's temporary Taliban rulers, set a style for Buddhist iconography that proved to be definitive for the entire Orient. To this day, from India to Japan, statues of the Buddha are modelled, it is said, on the image of the god Apollo and draped in the flowing garment that the Greeks called the *chiton*.

So it is no great surprise to find that in Bokhara and Samarkand, so far from the Muslim mainstream, cut off by political and sectarian conflict from the centres of Islamic orthodoxy, the new religion should have been unable to wipe out every trace of the old. Even in Iran itself, part of the very heartland of Islam, the past can still burst out of its restraints and express itself forcefully in the present.

Most pious Muslims regard what happened before the time of the Prophet Muhammad's revelation as the period of *jahiliyya*, ignorance—best forgotten. Which is one thing for those like the Arabs, who first enter the full spotlight of history with the advent of Islam, but quite another for those to whom the Muslim conquest brought an end to a thousand years of spectacular achievement. Persians, particularly, could never forget what they once had been. The Persian national epic, Ferdowsi's *Shah-nameh*, written around the turn of the first millennium by a Muslim poet for a Muslim ruler, and still regularly recited in the Iran of the Ayatollahs, tells of the creation of the sacred Aryan land in ancient times, of the breakup of that Iranian world into the warring states of Iran and Turan and of their subsequent reunification. The Prophet Zoroaster (or Zarathushtra or Zardosht), his one supreme God Ahura Mazda, and Ahriman, the Power of Evil, all play a major part in the story:

> *Zardosht, the prophet of the Most High, appeared in the land.*
> *And he came before the Shah and instructed him.*
> *And he went out in all the land*
> *and showed the people a new faith.*
> *And he purged Iran of the power of Ahriman.*
> *He reared throughout the realm a tree with beautiful foliage,*
> *and men rested beneath its branches.*
> *And whoever ate of its leaves became learned*
> *in all that regards the life to come,*
> *but whoever ate of the branches*
> *became perfect in wisdom and faith.*
> *And Zardosht gave men the Zendavesta,*
> *and he bade them obey its precepts*
> *if they would attain everlasting life.*

Bald translation cannot convey the true flavour of the Persian verse, which Iranians declaim for the sheer pleasure of its sound as well as for its story.

Though the *Shah-nameh* is openly Zoroastrian in subject and treatment, somehow converting ancient history to myth and legend has purged nostalgia for the past of its apostasy. Even so, Iranian Islam, passionate as it is, has an uneasy quality about it, as if it could tip over at any moment into something older and much more complex than the simplicity of the Prophet's desert faith. "Underneath they are still Zoroastrians through and through," Lazar Rempel said of the Central Asians. And in Iran, too, pre-Islamic history lies very close to the surface, even though it was buried more than thirteen hundred years ago. How close it lies, and how threatening that proximity can be to the edifice of Iranian Islam built on top, became particularly clear to me as I observed, from a privileged vantage point, the Shah of Iran's extraordinary historical jamboree in October 1971.

THE GREATEST GATHERING IN HISTORY

In the early 1970s, Bush House, the headquarters of the BBC External Services in London's Strand, was a very unusual place. Developed, designed and decorated by Americans and dedicated to the "friendship of the English-speaking peoples," its imposing pillared portico sheltered dozens of groups of intelligent, articulate, often politically motivated expatriates and refugees from positively non-English-speaking peoples, who sat before the microphones of the BBC, representing to the world in dozens of languages the face of British post-colonial even-handedness and fair play. At the same time, and in the same serious spirit, many plotted and planned among themselves the confusion, if not the outright overthrow, of their governments. It was said that no other building on earth housed as large a number of would-be—and actual—revolutionaries and insurrectionists at the same time. Meeting in the canteen and debating and arguing for hour upon hour, day after day, they often seemed to be balanced just on the edge of action. Eventually plucking up the courage to jump after many false starts, they mostly came to a sad end. For weeks, a charismatic young man from northern Africa would hold daily court at a corner table. Suddenly he and his group were no longer there. Where were they? The word was that he had flown into his country hoping that the people would rise up to support him. They didn't. He was shot.

The Persian section of the Eastern Service, in which I worked at the time as a programme producer, was staffed by a mixture of archetypes. There were the elder statesmen, conservative and anglicised by long residence, who just wanted a quiet life. There were the young firebrands, usually Marxists, members of every possible expatriate opposition group. There were the ambitious hopefuls with their hearts set on America and movie or musical stardom. (Though we didn't know it at the time, we also had our proper complement of Iranian secret policemen.) Nobody overtly supported the Shah, but nor would any of the broadcasters have advocated, or foreseen, the creation of an Islamic state. They didn't all get on with each other, of course: small groups of expatriates who have to work together are always prone to petty jealousies, in-fighting and paranoia. The firebrands hated the elders for their dishonesty and their compromises; the elders accused the firebrands of ignorance, treason and terrorism. Each side considered the other fraudulent. But all were utterly astounded by what the Shah got up to in Persepolis.

Under Muhammad Reza Shah Pahlavi, Arya Mehr, son of the founder of the last Persian royal dynasty of our time, Reza Khan—who had begun his climb to power as an illiterate soldier from a northern province—the polity of Iran was entering a period of great social and political instability. The Shah's increasingly savage and crude efforts to suppress all opposition were proving ineffective. Protest spilled on to the streets, prisons filled with dissidents, there was an endless succession of executions, trials, disappearances, assassinations. In this inauspicious climate, teetering on the edge of revolution, the Shah seemed to believe that his only recourse was to assert his legitimacy by presenting his rule as a continuation of the Iranian imperial tradition. To this end, he decided to celebrate the 2,500th anniversary of the founding of the Achaemenid dynasty, whose empire had first brought fame and glory to the Persian nation.

The Achaemenid Empire is customarily regarded as having been founded by Cyrus II, known as "the Great," who was the first to unite the Iranian tribes of the Medes and the Persians. His reign began in 559 BC. Adding two and a half millennia to that date would bring one to the year 1941. The Shah seemed to feel that 1971 was close enough. But if the timing raised a few pedantic eyebrows, the proposed centrepiece of the celebrations, a pageant representing the march of Iranian national history and power, provoked a more cynical response. "When in trouble, play the nationalist card," snorted my closest Marxist colleague in his Hollywood-learned drawl, "but it'll do him no good. What the people want is a future, not the past."

In fact, the celebration was not intended to involve the people at all; they were kept outside an impenetrable ring of military steel. This performance was for foreign and media consumption only, as if the Shah hoped to cement his hold on the Iranian people by demonstrating the high esteem in which he was held everywhere but at home. Thus the main pageant took place before the representatives of sixty-nine countries, including twenty kings, five queens, twenty-one princes and princesses, sixteen presidents, four vice-presidents, three prime ministers and two foreign ministers. The occasion was, in the words of the Shah, "the greatest gathering of heads of state in history." Tens of millions watched it on television. The Persian section of the BBC ran live commentary from correspondents on the spot.

The show was truly spectacular, worthy of Cecil B. deMille at his most extravagant. In front of the ruins of Persepolis, Darius's sixth-century BC capital which Alexander the Great had personally torched, before the assembled dignitaries sheltering in air-conditioned tents furnished with Limoges china and Baccarat crystal, phalanx after phalanx of Persian soldiers from every period of Iranian antiquity marched in time to a fanfare of trumpets and a rolling of drums. Medes, Persians, Achaemenians, Seleucids, Parthians, Sassanians, Abbasids, Safavids and Turks, they flowed continuously on like a veritable river of history. Brightly clothed in authentic costume, cloaked, bearded, helmeted, shod and fully armed, all with meticulous attention to historical detail, a forest of spear-points, banners and glittering standards floated above their heads. Some travelled by chariot, others rode horses, the rest marched on foot. They seemed to have stepped straight from the bas-reliefs on the palace walls of ancient Susa, Persepolis or Ecbatana, Nineveh or Babylon. This is what the Assyrian cohorts must have looked like when they came down on Israel like a wolf on the fold.

It was a display set to confront thirteen hundred years of Iranian Islam. For at the high point of the ceremony, the Shah himself stood up before the shades of his adopted ancestors—though Cyrus's palace and tomb are actually forty miles away at Pasagardae—and spake thus:

> Cyrus, Great King. King of Kings. King of the Achaemenians, King of the land of Iran, I, the Shahanshah of Iran, offer salutations from me and from my nation.
>
> Cyrus, Great King of Kings, noblest of the noble, hero of the history of Iran and of the world, rest in peace. For we are awake. We will always stay awake!

While the guests at Persepolis concealed their embarrassment behind their glasses of chilled Piper-Heidsieck champagne, diplomatic observers abroad treated the event with the fond indulgence of elderly relatives observing the antics of a spoiled favourite nephew. Though we now know that the British Queen and Prince of Wales were advised not to attend on account of the event's vulgarity, a Foreign Office civil servant said to me at the time: "What's so wrong with putting on a show, anyway? After all, it doesn't really matter what the Persian people think. We can keep the Shah in power as long as is necessary."

A week later all Iranians were told to recite a prayer for the Shah which began with these words:

> Almighty God, Creator of the Universe and of mankind, bestower of intelligence, wisdom, and thought on humanity, who hast granted numberless blessings to our noble land, thou hast appointed the just Arya Mehr as custodian of the land of Iran.

In the Persian section of the BBC, even the firebrand Marxists were shocked. It was not just that Mohammed Reza Pahlavi had associated himself with Cyrus, the glorious founder of Persia's first empire—an emperor, moreover, who, quite unlike the cruel, vindictive and megalomaniac Shah, was famously generous and magnanimous to his defeated enemies. Now this monster was claiming to be the anointed of God! And, by implication, not the Prophet Muhammad's God, but the God of Cyrus, who was the God of Zoroaster.

"Perhaps," suggested one of the elder statesmen, rather apologetically, "he is only trying to show that after so many hundreds of years Iran has a Persian, rather than Turkish, ruling house again."

The firebrands exploded with contempt. "Our provinces are in the grip of famine and the police are torturing people to death, while he spends millions on this rubbish—and you're trying to find him an excuse?"

Now argument broke out about why the Shah had taken the title Arya Mehr. The elder statesmen claimed that in Farsi it simply meant "Light of the Aryans"; and that it was no more than deplorable self-aggrandisement.

"But Mehr," countered the philologists, "is a special word. Yes, by now it has come merely to mean light, or love, or friendship, but only because it derives from the name of Mithra, the helper of God."

I think this may have been the first time I had heard of Mithra, the rising and unconquered sun, the Zoroastrian immortal whose representative on earth was always the ruler on the throne of Iran. Could the Shahanshah of Iran be preparing to abandon Islam?

My closest Marxist colleague was mystified by this unexpected development. In his Manichaean world-view of progressive left and reactionary right, ruler and aristocracy ought to be natural allies of an obscurantist and backward-looking Muslim clergy. And for them, my colleague had no time and less respect. "Useless parasites. I'll rub shit in their beards," he would say, stroking his own clean-shaven chin with relish, dreaming of his proletarian revolution.

Throughout Islam's history the palace has often been challenged by the mosque. It is the pious Muslim's duty to oppose unjust rule, particularly in Shi'ite Iran. And everybody now knows how badly mistaken were both my closest Marxist colleague and his sworn enemy the American State Department, how badly they underestimated the power of religious conviction. It turned out that the Iranian masses weren't proletarians after all, but Muslims.

One evening nearly ten years later, my Marxist colleague was expected at dinner. Towards half past nine, when the other guests were becoming rather restive, he telephoned.

"I'm very sorry," he said. "But there's a revolution going on in my country and I have to be part of it. Wish me luck."

He has done very well in the Ayatollahs' Iran: he is politically influential—and bearded like the pard.

The Shah's error, like that of his British and American allies, was to misunderstand Iranian Islam. When the last Zoroastrian Shah's troops succumbed to the Muslim army at Nehavand in the year 641, it was to be for good. The defeat was so overwhelming that the entire Sassanian state and its religious establishment were completely swept out of existence. In any case, the old religion had been too tainted by association with a rigid, caste-bound and despotic monarchy, its priests too obsessed with enforcing the pettifogging details of correct observance. What Zoroaster had taught—"that the world is a battleground between good and evil and it is the duty of everyone to foster good and fight evil"—was entirely compatible with the Prophet Muhammad's new, simple and pure message. Yet though the Iranian state was incorporated into the Muslim world suddenly and by force, the Iranian people converted to Islam more slowly and largely by conviction—though heavy taxes must have played their part too.

New converts don't just give up their former spiritual and ethical world-view; they usually bring them along, transferring the old wine into the new bottle. Just as in Europe the Holy Roman Empire—"neither holy, nor Roman, nor an empire," said Voltaire—was actually a way for baptised German warlords to repackage their pagan traditions in Christian wrapping, so Iranian Islam came to incorporate Iranian national consciousness, Iranian national culture, Iranian national pride and, yes, Iranian Zoroastrian beliefs. But in this synthesis of old and new lies a danger: the incorporation of too many disparate elements into one religion risks making it too diverse to hold together. This is one danger that Ayatollah Khomeini and his successors have managed to avoid. But the conflict between different threads of Muslim belief has totally ruined Afghanistan and may be in the process of despoiling other Central Asian states too.

The Iranian clergy did not rouse the anger of the people with the cry that the Shah had "done evil in the sight of the Lord" by "whoring after other gods." Their pitch was simpler: Choose between Islam or a corrupt tyranny. But in the Central Asian borderlands, as elsewhere in Asia, the confrontation is within the faith itself: between a deep, rich and complex, Iranianised Islam and the severer puritan ways of the desert and mountain peoples surrounding them.

This is a conflict with many ancient precedents, and one whose biblical dimension became ever clearer as I watched the war-clouds gather over Afghanistan from a front-row seat. Ten years before the Shah's misguided Persepolis extravaganza, I was practising an earlier vocation as the only European dental surgeon in Kabul. The revolution that was to sweep away the entire Afghan *ancien régime* was still far in the future, but not even a young, naïve and ignorant outsider, never privy to the religious and political feelings of the citizenship, could be unaware of the tensions within Afghan society. Nor could I ever again believe in the fiction of a nation united by a single universal orthodox Muslim belief.

THE MULLAHS FORBID IT

By the beginning of the 1960s, the highway from Turkey through Iran to Afghanistan was a regular route for young travellers, principally Austrians, who bought Mercedes limousines cheaply in Germany and drove them all the way to India, where they could be sold at a handsome profit. Vienna to Delhi was normally a journey of no more than fourteen days for the car traders, but I and my friend were out to discover the world so we travelled at a far more leisurely pace, making detours to any spot on the map which attracted our interest. It was our first experience of Asia and we didn't know what to expect. But we were none the less astonished to find in Iran an atmosphere completely different from the one we had become used to in Jordan, Syria and other, Arab, parts of the Muslim Middle East. Iran was clearly a historic land with a way of life at the same time cultured, cynical, sophisticated, arrogant and wise. Much that we experienced seemed to remind us of something, but we weren't sure why or of what; even the unexpected seemed to have a familiar ring.

In 1963, we chanced to be in Tehran on Ashura, the tenth day of the Muslim month of Muharram, the anniversary of the martyrdom of the Prophet Muhammad's grandson Hussein, a day of great mourning in the Shi'ite world. "Passed a mosque," I wrote in my diary, "with a group of men inside, leaping, chanting and beating themselves with chains. Mediaeval Flagellants. Huge procession in the street. Men carrying giant, heavy decorated crosses on their backs like Christ to Golgotha."

Could it be that Christianity, which had once been widespread here in its Arian form, had strongly influenced Iranian Islam? (I have since learned that there are even Ayatollahs of that opinion.) Or were the resonances so clear simply because Iranians and Europeans are related peoples, both speakers of Indo-European languages, with a common ancestry and a common ancestral culture? I didn't realise back then how tightly Iran's Islamic, my Jewish, and Europe's Christian background would turn out to be connected.

Culture shock struck again some weeks later as we drove across the desert no man's land on Iran's eastern border with Afghanistan, a wide fan of dust spreading out into the shimmering air behind us, so that where we had come from was quickly lost to sight. Now we experienced a sudden lurch back in time.

Afghanistan, like other parts of Central Asia, belongs to the same cultural world as Persia. Though Iran is the only officially Shi'ite state among them, these are all historically Iranian lands, with a shared history and a common tradition. Yet while Iran itself, with all its problems—and its terrible roads—was obviously a modern nation, Afghanistan retained the appearance, manner and spirit of the Middle Ages—or perhaps of an even more distant era. As we were to discover, not only Kabul's social atmosphere but also its conflicts were reminiscent of the Bible.

While history doesn't really repeat itself, either as tragedy or farce, similar circumstances do give rise to similar outcomes. Compare modern

Afghanistan with the ancient Holy Land: a small weak state ground between the millstones of the mightiest powers of its day. In ancient Israel's case these were Egypt, Assyria and Babylon—and later Macedonia, Persia and Rome. Afghanistan's fate was to lie, in the nineteenth century, between the Russian Empire and the British Raj; in the late twentieth century between the USSR and America's then client-state, Pakistan.

Much of the story told in the Bible is an account of the clash between two attitudes to life. For faith and physical geography are always inextricably intertwined. Belief always takes on the face of its earthly environment. To the inhabitants of fertile and hospitable valleys and plains, every river and stream, every wood and forest, every hill and dale has its own, different, spiritual presence. Pure monotheisms, on the other hand, have always burst out of the desert, the mountains, the steppe, the waste places of the earth, where every spot is the same as every other and one God rules over all.

In the fertile agricultural north of the promised land of Canaan the peasant tribes of Israel practised a syncretistic faith, incorporating their ancient and traditional ways into the worship of YHWH, the God whose name must neither be fully written out nor pronounced, as well as assimilating the beliefs of other nations around them; in the words of the Prophet Jeremiah, they "walked after the imagination of their own heart, and after the Baalim, which their fathers taught them." By contrast, the desert pastoralists of the southern kingdom of Judah remained loyal to a severe, uncompromising, austere monotheism. The Jerusalem aristocracy with its Temple priesthood, trying to steer the course of their petty kingdom between the dangerous rocks of great-power politics, was loved by neither side and was seen by the biblical writers as mostly irredeemably corrupt.

Similarly, from Afghanistan's creation in the eighteenth century to the present time, a three-way war has continued between liberal traditionalists, fundamentalist purists and secular modernisers, with power swinging wildly from one party to another and, as in the ancient Holy Land, with ruler after ruler being deposed or assassinated by one side or another.

In the Kabul of the early 1960s, apart from Western expatriates, it was mainly the urbane aristocracy, including members of the king's own family, as well as the wealthier Farsi- and French-speaking bourgeoisie, who came for treatment to my surgery in their elegant Western clothes and smart karakul caps. Neither these sophisticated inheritors of Central Asia's Iranian tradition nor their simpler compatriots of the bazaar and the mosque, saw much threat from the rough, tough, bearded and turbaned Pushto-speaking Pathan tribesmen who came down from their Hindu Kush (Hindu killer) mountain strongholds, all slung about with rifles and shotguns and draped with ammunition bandoliers. To my patients, these wild men were a throwback to a gratefully discarded barbaric past, and culturally far closer to their brethren in the tribal areas of Pakistan than to their civilised Iranian mentors. Except, however, when they themselves wanted to buy rifles and shotguns, fake Beretta pistols and imitation Smith & Wesson revolvers; then they would mount expeditions to villages across the border, where such weaponry was skilfully constructed in the "no-go" North West Frontier Province on the Pakistan side of the Khyber Pass.

The Kabul government, which was really just the king and his court, had a plan for the Pathans. They supported the tribesmen's claim to a swathe of northern Pakistan, to be granted independence under Afghanistan's tutelage, and to go by the name of Pakhtunistan. In this way territory stolen from Afghanistan by the British would be restored to its rightful owners, and the restiveness of the mountain folk would be diverted away from Kabul and directed against those they openly despised as soft, unwarlike lentil-eaters to the south. They couldn't foresee that the lentil-eaters would eventually turn the tables and help Pakhtunistan come into being not on Pakistan territory but in Afghanistan itself. For the Taliban, who captured Kabul in 1996 and then overran almost all the rest of the country to found their Islamic Emirate, before, eventually, coming into conflict with America and her allies, were the military, political and religious expression of Pashtunwali, the Way of the Pathan, the austerely puritan tribal code of the armed mountain peoples, which views the sophisticated Farsi-speaking culture of Kabul and the other ancient Afghan cities with undisguised hatred, contempt and disgust.

At the start of the 1960s all this was in the future. Then the foreigner could revel in the medieval but hospitable atmosphere of the Kabul streets. I took it into my head to accommodate myself to local custom by commuting between home and surgery, not by car but on horseback. Khizr, my white stallion, was stabled in the large garden of the fine new German-built house which a group of us shared with two house-servants and a cook. The sight of a European riding out in the mornings was often too much for young mounted Kabuli bloods who would challenge me to race them through the streets of the city. I would demur but Khizr could never resist a challenge. There was nothing I could do—he would take charge and we would be off into another world.

We would career at full canter, weaving between motor traffic, horse-drawn carts, panniered donkeys, camels, flocks of fat-tailed sheep, and porters seeming to carry the contents of whole warehouses on their backs, with me hanging on to Khizr for dear life as he leapt over huge potholes and wide-open drains, along the great avenues with their multicoloured mosques, prisons and palaces, past modern hotels, Edwardian-era public buildings, ancient ruins and the fort on the ridge from which the noonday gun was fired. We would thunder across the bridges over the Kabul river, deep and thickly iced in winter, in summer no more than a sluggishly-flowing trickle, dammed into pools where young boys splashed and pelted each other with mud, along the lines of stalls and open-fronted shops whose displays of fruits, vegetables and spices spilled out on to the walkways, through the unpaved lanes, gullies and alleyways of the old quarters of town, where, jam-packed higgledy-piggledy as if huddling together for protection, khaki-coloured buildings of sun-dried brick climbed the steep hillsides towards the seven peaks around which the city had grown, pursued by a kaleidoscope of smells: of nose-tingling spices, of meat cooking over open fires, of sickly sweet fruit and rotting vegetables, of decomposing dog and donkey carcasses, and everywhere, but everywhere, the unmistakable stink of human excrement. As often as not, Khizr and I would at last find ourselves wildly lost, surrounded by high, blank, mute, mud-rendered walls with not a soul in sight. Then I would have to dismount and let my steaming and panting horse lead us slowly back, for his sense of direction and knowledge of the city were far greater than mine.

But such impromptu contests were limited to summer days and late-winter mornings. Once darkness fell, horse-riding was deemed highly dangerous. Not because of the lack of illumination—street-lighting there was, though sometimes the power dropped so low that one had to approach the light-bulb and peer at it closely to see if it was actually glowing. No, it was for another reason. Our cook, who in his fatherly way had taken it upon himself to instruct his group of innocent and ignorant foreigners in the ways of his country, counselled strongly against approaching any animal at night. After dark, horses, dogs, wolves and even birds could easily become the vehicle for *Divs*, malignant spirits or djinns. Back then I recognised the word, so close to the Latin for God, *Deus*. Now I realise that the *Divs* are the descendants of the *Daevas*, the ancient divine powers that Zoroastrianism demoted to the status of mere evil spirits, rather as Christianity reduced the old deities of Europe to no more than wicked demons.

Kabul was a proper city, the capital of the country, with modern buildings, an airport, hotels, restaurants and a university, used to hosting foreign travellers, well connected with the outside world. In such a place, orthodox Islam was the rule and the law. If even here the undercurrent of ancient superstition and belief couldn't be dammed up, how much more so must the inaccessible Afghan countryside belong to the past.

I suggested this to one of my patients, the director of the Kabul museum (now more or less completely destroyed, a tragedy for archaeologists and historians of the region). He enthusiastically agreed, but pointed out that although many pre-Islamic beliefs still survived, unlike in Iran, I wouldn't find anyone to admit to their Zoroastrian or pagan origin. In Afghanistan, he told me, every idea, no matter how outlandish, is always piously ascribed to the Muslim faith.

How true this was I discovered for myself when I and my friends set out for a week's exploration of the north of the country.

There were really only three main routes in Afghanistan—round the north, round the south and through the middle. My royal patients entertained themselves hugely with the antics of the two great powers, the USA and the Soviet Union, to whom had been awarded separate contracts for the engineering and surfacing of the principal strategic arteries across the country. On the southern leg, the Americans had started from the west and the Russians from the east, while the Afghans watched to see who would reach the centre first. Two of my palace friends would drive out to the end of the road-works to watch progress and cheer the workers on. Rarely in history can the digging of its own grave have occasioned such entertainment to the ruling order of a nation. They had forgotten that their country's nineteenth-century inviolability to British and Russian imperialism was largely based on the extreme difficulty of the terrain. Once good, modern roads pierced the wilderness and climbed the mountains, invasion was no longer too costly an enterprise for Afghanistan's rapacious neighbours. The clock began to tick for my royal friends on the day the roads were complete.

We drove up the northern route, over a ridge of the Hindu Kush Mountains via the Salang pass. It was spring and the road was easily passable—unlike in the winter season, when the Salang tunnel is spectacularly festooned with gigantic icicles more than twenty feet long and vehicles not infrequently slide off the icy road, to fall many hundreds of feet down the plunging ravine. After a hundred miles or so we came to the little town of Pul-i-Khumri (the bridge of the wine-pots). Here lie the remains of a great second-century Zoroastrian fire temple. We stopped at a nearby roadside teahouse to rest. It was late afternoon and the low sun cast long shadows across all that remained: a monumental staircase leading up four high terraces to where, archaeological excavation has disclosed, a Greek-style temple building once stood. We sat on *charpoy* string beds in front of a steaming blackened brass samovar, racks of brightly-coloured Japanese teapots and drinking bowls behind it, while an old white-bearded proprietor in a blue turban and striped *chapan* coat busied himself swilling out the chipped bowls on to the dirt floor with tea and then refilling them for us. We asked him to tell us what he knew about the archaeological remains.

He sat down, lit a china *chilim* water-pipe with a glowing lump of charcoal and over the next half-hour regaled us with a strange and complicated tale of witches and djinns, warriors and heroes. The cast of characters was impossible: Iskander—Alexander the Great—and the Prophet Muhammad, as well as 'Ali his son-in-law and the Great Khan of the Mongols. As the museum director had prophesied, history had been completely reworked to fit into a world which our Muslim teahouse-owner understood. If there was a slender thread of truth running through the tale, it was so twisted and extended as to be almost impossible to detect.

This, the old man explained, had been the site of a great mosque, where the king came every Friday to say his prayers. But the king was really a witch, although people didn't know it, and in his heart he hated Allah. He kept a great fire in the mosque and people had to walk through it to cleanse their feet. Then the *Shaitan,* the Devil, saw into his heart and knew that he was not a faithful believer, so he sent Iskander to kill him. The king sent for help from the Muslims in Medina and the Prophet sent 'Ali with four hundred warriors to help fight on his side. In turn Iskander sent his son to fetch the Khan of the Turks, who came with his war-band. The king decreed that the people who had come to fight should rest outside the mosque for three days and then the war should start. They camped under that tree over there. After three days, the war began. There was a great battle and one by one all the fighters were killed, the king ran off to India and the mosque was burned to the ground.

"That is the story," the old man said, "and it is all I know. The ruins have been as you see them ever since then, for holy 'Ali placed a curse upon them and populated them with *Divs* so nobody has dared to go near them after that time. But around here country people still light fires on their wedding day and walk through them in honour of that king—though the Mullahs forbid it."

The old teahouse-owner stood up from his pipe and looked over his shoulder as if hearing the call of the *muezzin*. We had heard nothing. "It is time for prayers now," he said, as if even mentioning such practices demanded instant repentance.

Many ancient sites of Afghanistan are said to be similarly haunted. In England, Roman cities were abandoned after the take-over by Anglo-Saxon settlers who, it is claimed, believed them to have been built by the giants of old and to be populated by the angry ghosts of the past. In Afghanistan too, and for much the same reasons, the remains of castles and towers, minarets and Buddhist stupas, palaces and Zoroastrian fire temples are left to decay, unpeopled and unmourned.

But some places gained such fame that they couldn't simply be forgotten. Balkh was once the greatest Afghan city of them all. North of the mountain country, close to the border with the former Soviet Union, people still speak proudly of the city that was founded in the Bronze Age, some one thousand years BC, and was for centuries the capital of Bactria and the centre of east Iranian civilisation. The ancients called Balkh the "mother of cities." The museum director had told me he believed this great city was probably the place where Zarathustra made his first conversions. More certainly, it saw the marriage of Alexander the Great to Princess Roxana; witnessed Abu Muslim raise the black banner of the Abbasid revolution that overthrew the first, Umayyad, dynasty of Islam; listened to the verses of Rabia, the foremost Muslim woman poet; and attended the original Barmecide feast, the imaginary banquet served in empty dishes to a starving man in *The Thousand and One Nights*. Balkh was destroyed in the Mongol invasion in the thirteenth century, rebuilt by Tamerlaine's son in the fifteenth and sacked again in the following centuries by Uzbeks and Turks.

Old Balkh now lies mostly in ruin. Yet its former greatness is proclaimed by the towering wall, stretching almost as far as the eye can see. Balkh's ancient citadel was huge. Like most Afghan constructions, the wall is built of sun-dried brick—of the earth itself—and is the colour of mud. So it is hard to detect where wall stops and earth starts, where human effort ends and nature begins. At certain times of day, like the late afternoon when the light catches the ancient brickwork at just the right angle, there are moments when the wall can look not so much as if it is crumbling away, but rather as if the process of raising it up out of the ground were not yet complete, as if the work has merely been suspended and is waiting for the builders to return to finish the job. Then it is possible to be convinced that you are standing on the very spot where, long ago, the prophet Zarathustra himself may once have gathered a crowd around him to hear his revolutionary message that there was only one true God.

Recollecting that magical afternoon before the walls of Balkh, and believing, as I do now, that the museum director may well have been right that the prophet found his first converts in just this part of the northeastern Iranian realm, I am struck again by the paradox of Zarathustra. His actual followers are a tiny religious minority, dispersed over a wide diaspora. The walls of his city of Balkh are returning to the earth from which they were raised. The fire temples once crowded with his devotees are now popularly imagined as occupied only by *Divs*, djinns and other evil spirits. He is never ever mentioned by the ordinary people of the Afghan lands to whom he probably first brought his mission.

It calls to mind a quatrain, a four-line verse, by Omar Khayyám about vanished glory, a sort of eleventh-century Persian forerunner of Shelley's "Ozymandias." It is, alas, untranslatable for it is based on a Persian pun. In Farsi the question "Where?" is pronounced "Coo." Khayyam writes of a ruined and deserted palace in the desert upon whose broken marble columns white doves perch, calling to one another: "Coo, coo, coo" (Where? where? where?).

Yet a prophet is not without honour, as Jesus said, save in his own country and among his own kin and in his own house. Zarathustra is far from forgotten in the modern world, where his name is not only still frequently invoked among philosophers, but is even known to many of the general public. For that we must thank Nietzsche, the German writer whose book title, as interpreted in music, brought the Persian prophet back to life both for me and for a whole new generation.

I was working on a series of television programmes about the history of music with a young conductor then new to the orchestral scene. She wanted to start with something both spectacular and familiar and chose the opening of Richard Strauss's tone poem *Also Sprach Zarathustra*, believing that it would be known to the audience from its use in Stanley Kubrick's film *2001: A Space Odyssey*. Our orchestra had 112 players—and a huge pipe organ; she wanted to point out the sheer excitement of hearing "all those musicians playing something at the same time." I asked her how much of the piece she would get the orchestra to perform. "Oh, just the well-known beginning," she said, perhaps a little ungraciously. "It's the only good bit in the whole thing."

The music begins with a pedal note from the organ, so low that it seems to come through the floor, entering the listener by the soles of the feet and spreading upwards to suspend the mind in a cradle of sound as first the brass comes in, then the strings, then the timpani. The same gesture is repeated and then repeated again before transforming itself into the final cadences of a musical introduction.

The shot was from a single camera, beginning with a very tight close-up on the organ pipes. As the music started, it slowly and smoothly tracked back in one continuous movement, including the brass in the picture just as they started to play, then the strings in their turn, then the percussionist as the timpani entered, until at the end, the whole orchestra was there on the screen playing away for all it was worth, with the conductor out in front, dwarfed by the perspective, beating time wildly with her baton. Once the move was rehearsed, there was no more for me to do and I indulged myself by leaving the outside-broadcast control truck and going to sit in the auditorium while the orchestra played.

The opening of Strauss's tone poem must surely be one of the most powerful orchestral fanfares ever composed. To hear it performed by a big orchestra in full spate, from a distance of no more than a few feet away, raises the hairs on the back of one's neck. Here was the last great composer in the Romantic tradition exercising total mastery of his craft.

The music stopped. The hall's reverberation faded. Orchestra and crew held their breath, waiting for the recording engineer to confirm a successful take. In the sudden silence the question posed itself to me. *Also Sprach Zarathustra, Thus Spake Zarathustra*—a title as dramatic as the music itself, but why that title? Presumably Strauss was an admirer of Friedrich Nietzsche and was paying homage to his idol's most famous work. I had attempted the book as a teenager in my "rebel without a cause" years, and secretly rehearsed passages to declaim, in a suitably theatrical manner, at girls I was trying to impress. I recalled that Zarathustra was supposed to have been thirty years old when he left his lake for a mountain hideaway where he would spend the next ten years, before coming down again to become the mouthpiece for the German philosopher's ideas and preach his message to the world—a message which would form the foundations upon which much modern philosophy would later be erected. What I didn't know was why Nietzsche had chosen an ancient Iranian prophet as his spokesman.

In itself, speaking with another's voice is not so unusual in literature—Nietzsche was following in a long tradition of preachers and pamphleteers who disguised themselves in the clothes of more illustrious or more ancient predecessors. Plato put much of his own philosophy into the mouth of his teacher Socrates, and the historian of Christian theology can list innumerable monks and prelates who wrote under the names of the great Fathers of the Church: the Pseudo-Jerome, the Pseudo-Augustine, the Pseudo-Methodius.

But the Pseudo-Methodius had only written what he or she thought was consistent with the real Methodius's views. Nietzsche's book, on the other hand, was a contribution to a very modern kind of European philosophy. Its contents could hardly claim to be consistent with the teachings of Zarathustra, who, as far as I knew, lived nearly three thousand years ago. However strong the pre-Islamic subtext to today's Iranian world, his actual followers, the Zoroastrians or Parsees (as they are called in India), are a small religious minority about whom the only thing most people know is that they are supposed to worship fire and to lay out their dead on towers for the birds to eat. It made me wonder whether either Nietzsche or Richard Strauss had really known anything about Zarathustra at all.

How strange, in any event, that such a remote figure should still be able to exert such a pull on the imagination. How odd that, while so few today follow the religion Zarathustra preached, there is yet an aura about his name, as of someone who once taught such great and important things that his reputation still resonates long after the teachings themselves have been forgotten.

One day, I thought to myself as I made my way back to the outside-broadcast control truck, it would be rewarding to find out what the name Zarathustra really did mean to Nietzsche and to Strauss. And, if that, then why not more? If Zarathustra is still remembered today, his memory must have been kept alive in people's hearts—or their heads—for nigh on three millennia. I wondered whether every intervening age saw what Zarathustra stood for in the same way, or whether he had represented one idea to Nietzsche, another to his medieval ancestors, yet another to the Romans and yet another again to the ancient Greeks. Was the foreign response different from that of the Persians themselves? And how, I asked myself, did his name and reputation pass from one nation to another?

In the meantime, there was a music programme to finish. It was to be many years before the project finally took shape: to trace Zarathustra's mark on people's minds back through the three thousand years of history that have passed since his death, not as a work of scholarship but as a voyage of personal discovery; to explore the many guises in which the teachings of the first, and greatest, sage of ancient times lived on after his earthly life was over. To go, in short, in search of Zarathustra.

2

The True Philosopher

On a summer afternoon a year before the start of the Great War, at a little railway station somewhere in Austria, a group of travellers sit at the tables of the platform buffet: a red-cheeked Dutch youth who seems to be able to do no more than giggle; an archetypically English, tongue-tied, newspaper-reading husband and wife; an impatient American tourist, strung about with field-glasses and camera; and a grey-haired German, stiff-figured, stiff-voiced and stiff-moustached, clearly once, if not now, a colonel. Nearby sit a peasant woman, with a crying baby wrapped in a black shawl, and a non-descript little man nursing a soft hat.

The little man politely orders a bottle of beer, calling the harassed waiter *Herr Ober*, Mr. Head Waiter, an honorific which offends both the American tourist's and the German ex-colonel's sense of social decorum. A conversation now strikes up between American and German on how best to treat waiters—or anybody else for that matter. Though they both believe that waiters should not be pandered to (the German: "If you treat them in this manner, at once they take liberties"; the American: "You've got to pinch those waiters some to make 'em skip")—in the tourist's case it is in the name of democracy, while in the ex-colonel's it is in the interest of authority. The American now invokes the name and ideals of Tolstoy.

"I take considerable stock in Leo Tolstoi myself. Grand man— grand-souled apparatus."

The German responds with a dogmatic declaration: "Tolstoi is senti-mentalisch. Nietzsche is the true philosopher, the only one."

. . .

The scene is from John Galsworthy's one-act satire *The Little Man,* published in 1915. I remember it so well because it was the centrepiece of a brilliant teachers' ruse employed by the English master at the school I attended in the 1950s. He had been trying, presumably unsuccessfully, to engage us with the nineteenth-century explosion of thought and literature that resulted from the publication of Darwin's *Origin of Species.*

Adolescent boys are not well-known for their interest in the history of philosophy, but our teacher understood his pupils perfectly. There was a limit to the number of times the same point could be made without driving the class to mutiny, but having observed our penchant for adopting catch-phrases, he knew that once such a phrase had been taken up, it was destined to be repeated ad nauseam in response to every possible cue. So he arranged for his pupils to mount a public performance of Galsworthy's play—directing it himself. Sure enough, long afterwards, whenever the occasion prompted, we would gleefully recite "Tolstoi is sentimentalisch. Nietzsche is the true philosopher, the only one," complete with heavy phoney German accent. Our English teacher's device had succeeded. And it was to have a lasting effect. Just before writing this, I telephoned an old friend who was with me in that class fifty years ago.

"If I were to say to you: 'Tolstoi is sentimentalisch,' " I asked, "what would your response be?"

Instantly the reply came back: "Nietzsche is the true philosopher, the only one."

Naturally enough, having been introduced to the only true philosopher's name, I went to the school library to find out what he had written. On the shelf I found a translation of something called *Also Sprach Zarathustra.*

For a work of literary philosophy, Nietzsche's masterpiece is not a difficult read even for a schoolboy, just rather bewildering. Here were no theories, no logical arguments. *Also Sprach Zarathustra* impressed me as an inspired prophetic outburst, couched in brilliant, powerful, almost biblical, poetry and prose—ideally suited to the mood of the upcoming Beat generation, perfect for impressing the girls and for browbeating parents, teachers and other authority figures. What it actually all meant was quite beyond me at that age. Moreover, I assumed that Zarathustra was a name that Nietzsche had made up. I would reach adulthood before learning that a prophet by that name had actually once lived.

After all, it's such an odd name, with its capital Z, as mysterious and archaic-sounding as Zachary, Zebedee, Zenobia or Zephaniah. Even the Greeks seem to have found it outlandish, for they reduced it to Zoroaster, though it is not obvious why they avoided the "th." The sound is common enough in Greek names too, and their alphabet has a perfectly good letter, called *theta*, to represent it. Perhaps, in their admiration for him, they wanted his name to end in their word for star: *aster*. (Strangely enough, even Zarathustra is an imperfect rendering of the original. In Old Persian, the prophet's own language, he was called Zarathushtra, which probably meant something like Rich in Camels. Nietzsche, with a superfluous and unpronounceable "z" in his own name, kept the "th"—though that combination can't be pronounced in German—but deprived the prophet of his "sh"—which can.)

Nietzsche's book, though well recognised by grammar-school students and philosophers, never managed to introduce Zarathustra's name to popular culture. For that, two other artists were largely responsible: the composer Richard Strauss and the film director Stanley Kubrick. Between them, they made it familiar to a whole generation of cinema-goers. Music is more accessible than philosophy, and movies are more popular than either.

Kubrick's *2001: A Space Odyssey* achieved instant success and popularity, particularly among the young, who took it to their hearts as emblematic of the "counter-culture"—and who would sometimes in those days fill the cinema with so much cannabis smoke that even highly respectable and law-abiding patrons would stagger out of the darkness unwittingly stoned. The introduction to Richard Strauss's tone poem *Also Sprach Zarathustra*, which features prominently in the film, quickly became its musical signature. Suddenly audiences who would normally much rather listen to the Beatles than to Brahms, or to the Moody Blues than to Mahler, now wanted to buy recordings of Strauss's work. A version by Brazilian jazz arranger Eumir Deodato even won the 1973 Grammy Award for Best Pop Instrumental and was itself featured on the big screen in Peter Sellers's last successful movie, *Being There*. Thanks to Kubrick's space epic, the name Zarathustra was widely heard again. But why had the great director chosen that particular piece of music? I was convinced that there was more to the use of Strauss's piece than mere chance appeal.

Until Kubrick, most film-makers had taken it for granted that science fiction must be accompanied by music that sounds self-consciously avant-garde and futuristic. *2001: A Space Odyssey* was based on an Arthur C. Clarke story: *The Sentinel*. Kubrick, I guessed, must have perceived a backward-looking element in Clarke's science fiction in spite of its futuristic setting—

a contemporary take on a nineteenth-century idea. Hence his use of music by two Victorian Strausses. Johann Strauss's "Blue Danube Waltz" accompanies the revolving space station, an obvious reference to the giant English-built Ferris wheel in the Vienna Prater gardens, made famous by its appearance in the film *The Third Man*. What the opening bars of Richard Strauss's tone poem *Also Sprach Zarathustra* referred to was more difficult to fathom.

Apart from the space adventures, did *2001: A Space Odyssey* have an underlying theme? In Kubrick's film a mysterious monolith first triggers the evolution of a group of apes into humans, and finally, far away across an abyss of psychedelic space, spurs the evolution of a man into something new: a "star child," whatever that may be. Human evolution was clearly involved, and not just from pre-humans to ourselves, but the next stage onwards too. Searching through Nietzsche's newly famous work, I found the following line, which seemed to sum up the film's message perfectly:

Man is a rope stretched between the animal and the Superman—a rope over an abyss.

Kubrick, far more cultivated than the usual run of Hollywood directors, had recognised in Arthur C. Clarke's theme an echo of one of the central notions of Nietzsche's philosophy as expressed through his Zarathustra: that it is human destiny to move beyond human nature—that our task is to transcend ourselves. Featuring Richard Strauss's *Also Sprach Zarathustra* in his film was Kubrick's nod to Nietzsche.

Yet neither Kubrick's film nor Galsworthy's play give any indication of why a nineteenth-century German philosopher should have chosen an obscure ancient Persian prophet as his mouthpiece. Looking among the mountain of books, papers and articles about Nietzsche that have accumulated like geological strata since his death, I found frequent reference to the philosopher's own justification. This was that Zarathustra had been "the first to see in the struggle between good and evil the essential wheel in the working of things," close enough to what Davlat Khodanazarov in Moscow described as the core of Zoroastrian belief: "the world is a battleground between good and evil." But of how Nietzsche had discovered this Zarathustrian connection, and when, not a word. To find the answer, I would have to delve much more deeply into Nietzsche's life-story. Luckily there are ample sources to explore.

Given his adult appearance, all piercing eyes and rampant moustache, it's hard to imagine Nietzsche as a baby. But even he started life that way—at about ten o'clock on the morning of 15 October 1844, in the little country town of Röcken bei Lützen near Leipzig in eastern Germany. Significantly, this is less than thirty miles from Wittenberg, where Martin Luther lit the blue touch-paper of the Protestant Reformation when he nailed his ninety-five theses to the door of All Saints' Church. The Nietzsche family was deeply religious; the baby's father, Karl Ludwig, was Röcken's Lutheran pastor. Owing his position to King Friedrich Wilhelm IV of Prussia, whose birthday it was that day, he rather ingratiatingly named his child Friedrich Wilhelm. He himself conducted the little boy's baptism, building his sermon upon the rhetorical question: "What will become of this child? Will it be good or will it be evil?"

So it was there from the very beginning, that issue of good and evil, both so Zoroastrian and so Protestant, touching so closely on the proposition that had divided Luther from the Catholic Church—that Christians are saved not through their own efforts but only by the gift of God's grace—an issue that would haunt baby Friedrich Wilhelm into maturity and beyond. The division of life, thought, word and deed into two opposing moral absolutes, positive and negative, a principle known as ethical dualism, was to be Nietzsche's central obsession—a cross that would burden the child as he grew up, and that would oppress the adult Friedrich Nietzsche to the end of his days. All his working life, the philosopher would struggle to escape those contrasting categories imposed upon him by his father; as he himself later put it: to pass beyond good and evil.

But for the present, little Friedrich—or Fritz, as they called him at home—seemed a happy child to all who knew him. He had a devoted mother. His father was "the perfect picture of a country parson; gifted in spirit and heart, adorned with all the virtues of a Christian, he lived a tranquil, simple, yet happy, life." Friedrich clearly adored his father. When he was two, a baby sister came along; when he was three a little brother joined them. It was a joyful family.

But the good times were not to last. In 1849, when Fritz was not yet five, his father died at the early age of thirty-six, after more than a year of suffering wretchedly from a progressive brain disease. Then, the very next year, his little brother Joseph died too. Nietzsche's carefree childhood was over.

The shock of bereavement was now compounded by what to young Fritz must have seemed like being sent into exile. The Nietzsches had to vacate the pastor-house near the church in Röcken, leave all their happy family memories behind, and move to rented rooms in the nearest larger town: Naumburg an der Saale. Today Naumburg is a small, light industrial town nestling on the grimy banks of a polluted east German waterway. In Nietzsche's day it was a centre of agricultural trade, great barges bringing the produce of the fertile valleys of Saxony up the Saale river, and famous throughout the region for its magnificent Romanesque and Gothic cathedral dedicated to Saints Peter and Paul.

There Friedrich lived for the next eight years entirely surrounded by women—his grandmother, his mother, two aunts and his younger sister Elisabeth. Did they try to smother the little boy with too much affection to make up for the loss of his father? Did they try too hard to mould their Fritz in his father's image—or in their own? One day Nietzsche's Zarathustra would advise, in a chapter significantly entitled "Old and Young Women":

Let man fear woman when she loves, then she makes every sacrifice; everything else she regards as worthless.

The warning was not to be taken lightly:

You go to women? Do not forget your whip.

Having previously been, by his own account, a normal, happy little boy, Friedrich now became quiet and withdrawn. "No longer wild and carefree," as he later wrote, he sought solitude and felt most at ease when alone. Like many another child faced with sudden loss, he couldn't understand why evil should be visited on such a good man as his father, or on such an innocent victim as his baby brother. Psychologists tell us that many children who suddenly lose a parent feel guilty, wondering whether they themselves were somehow to blame. And young Fritz's change of character does suggest a burden of guilt. At first he was sure that he would find the answer in religion. He studied the Bible assiduously, so much so that he was contemptuously known as "the little minister" among his friends. He worked hard at school and was rewarded with good reports: "Diligent and behaves well. Takes a lively interest in the teachings of Christianity."

It was, after all, the family tradition. The Nietzsches had produced some twenty ministers of the Church over five generations. One grand-father, a distinguished Protestant scholar, had been granted an honorary doctorate in 1796 for a work affirming the "everlasting survival of Christianity." It was taken for granted that Friedrich would follow in his forebears' footsteps and study theology, so at fourteen he was sent to prepare for university entrance at the nearby highly-regarded boarding school of Schulpforta. Meanwhile the family moved again, this time within Naumburg, to the big, white, corner house in the Weingarten, to which Friedrich would continue to return throughout his life. The house, first rented by Friedrich's mother, then bought by her twenty years later, is still there today, housing a Nietzsche museum.

So far, no Zarathustra. But that's hardly surprising. A pious young Christian like Friedrich would in any case have dismissed the Persian prophet as a benighted pagan, destined at best—like Dante's Virgil—for purgatory. However, times were changing. The mid-nineteenth century was a heady time for an adolescent boy growing up in Germany. That most adolescent of movements, German Romanticism, was surging towards its high tide in all the arts: music, painting, literature and philosophy too. The Enlightenment, the intellectual movement of the seventeenth and eighteenth centuries which stood for reason, order, restraint, harmony and the progressive acquisition of knowledge, had laid the foundations of our modern view of the world. But strong resistance had sprung up to oppose it.

Textbooks say that the Enlightenment ended with the death of the philosopher Immanuel Kant in 1804. In truth, its powerful influence continued to be felt throughout the century and still shapes many of our values even today. But by the beginning of the nineteenth century German Romanticism had begun to make a cult of the irrational, the mystical, the dissonant and the excessive.

Where a framework for interpreting how the world actually works had been painstakingly developed by Enlightenment thinkers and scientists, Romanticism cast doubt on the validity of all factual knowledge. Where technology was rapidly beginning to exercise mastery over nature, Romanticism delighted in humanity's insignificance in the face of the elements. Where the Enlightenment had stood for the victory of mind over body, Romantics emphasised the pre-eminence of the body over the mind. Where the Enlightenment had emphasised duty to the social order, Romantics passionately embraced freedom and liberty—even libertinism—for the individual. Where Enlightenment thought had been agnostic or simply opposed to religion, Romantics saw numinous, spiritual, forces at work all around them, though they had little tolerance for the sober organised religion of the conservative establishment.

All this may sound familiar to anyone who grew up in Europe or America during the reign of the "counter-culture" in the swinging 1960s. And indeed many social commentators have suggested that Romanticism never died, but was merely suppressed under the weight of more sober generations, only to burst out again almost exactly a century after young Friedrich started at high school. Perhaps society is always veering between the two extremes: what Nietzsche would later contrast as the Apollonian spirit, the spirit of measured restraint (after the classical Apollo, god of the sun, of balance, proportion, rationality), as opposed to the Dionysian spirit, the spirit of ecstatic excess (after Dionysos, god of nature, of drunkenness and sensuality). Nietzsche convinced himself that everything wrong with European civilisation was the result of a damaging emphasis of Apollo over Dionysos. The rot had set in, he believed, with the Greek philosopher Plato.

Hero-worship, too, was very much in the air. Where in the mid-twentieth century the well-known portrait of Che Guevara graced a hundred thousand student bedsitting rooms, their nineteenth-century ancestors were voraciously consuming Thomas Carlyle's *Heroes, Hero-Worship and the Heroic in History* and his idolisations of Cromwell and Frederick the Great. While our own beatniks and hippies read Allen Ginsberg, Jack Kerouac, William Burroughs and Richard Brautigan, and immersed themselves in the music of the Beatles, the Beach Boys and the Rolling Stones, Fritz Nietzsche, at home for the school holidays, set up a literature and music club called Germania, where they read the Romantic poetry of Hölderlin, the Romantic novels of Jean-Paul Richter, and discovered the music of Wagner through the club's subscription to the music journal *Zeitschrift für Musik*. They didn't play guitar but piano.

These heady days were, however, to be brought to a sudden end by an event which has no twentieth-century counterpart. It struck during Nietzsche's second year at Schulpforta, an intellectual bombshell which would smash the human self-image, and scatter established beliefs and attitudes to the wind. It was Charles Darwin's publication in 1859 of *On the Origin of Species by Means of Natural Selection*.

Darwin's theory of evolution didn't just contradict the teachings of the Book of Genesis, it was even more fundamental than that. While the passing of time had accustomed people to accept that the physical universe

worked according to a series of natural laws—laws that a genius like Newton could tease out, define and publicise without being accused of heresy or
apostasy—the living world remained the preserve of God's will. *On the
Origin of Species* was now suggesting that life, too, was law-driven, in the
same way as the physical world. In Darwin's picture, there was no room at
all left for divine intervention. Moreover, even though the origins of humanity were not included in his first book on evolution, the implications of
Darwin's thesis for human beings were clear from the start. If God had not
created each species separately, as the Book of Genesis told, then there was
no reason to believe that human beings had a different origin from the rest
of the living world. Where, then, did that leave humanity's superiority over
animals?

These were among the many questions that Darwin's publication
raised, stimulating debates that upturned the intellectual world of schoolboy Friedrich, aspirant minister of the Church and future prophetic vision-
ary, when, in 1864, at the age of twenty, he passed his final school examination
and enrolled as a student of theology and classical philology in the University of Bonn.

It is not unusual for devoted followers of a cause or religion to look for
desperately sought-after answers by delving ever deeper into the texts of
their creed—only to find nothing but further questions. Nor is it uncommon for such disappointed devotees to swing violently in the opposite
direction and come vehemently to oppose what they once revered. In our
time, many youthful communists have become right-wing ideologues in
middle age. Nietzsche seems to have had just such a reverse in his first year
at university. After a period of agonised soul-searching, he decided that he
now no longer counted himself a Christian.

Ever the dramatist, back home in Naumburg for the university vaca-
tion, he expressed his change of mind by creating a scandal: refusing to
accompany his mother and sister to Holy Communion on Easter Sunday
1865. There was now no possibility of his becoming a pastor like his father,
and no point in his continuing his study of theology. From here onwards,
he would devote himself full time to classical philology, the study of Latin
and Greek, the languages of ancient Greece and Rome.

As so many of the source documents of Christian theology are in
Greek, like the Gospels, or in Latin, like the writings of the Church
Fathers, this course was a normal part of a priest's or pastor's training. But
what interest could this field sustain for someone who had turned his back
on Christian teaching? What could its appeal have been to Nietzsche? I

thought that maybe some dramatic development in the study of language at this time might hold the answer, some new discovery that had grabbed the imagination of the young student. In seeking out the story of nineteenth-century philology, I found just such a revelation. But I also unexpectedly found more: I found the link to Zarathustra.

AN EVENT IN THE HISTORY OF LITERATURE

To pursue that link, we must temporarily leave the young Friedrich Nietzsche as he begins his second year at college, freezing him in suspended animation as he enters the doorway of the elegant eighteenth-century palace on the banks of the River Rhine that still today houses the University of Bonn. We will return to him later. But first we must make a detour, a long flashback in time, to explore the background to what European thinkers in young Nietzsche's day were making of the Persian prophet's ancient fame.

Zoroaster's reputation had been high in the classical world. Writers from the time of Xanthus of Lydia in the fifth century BC onwards had accorded him huge respect as "the greatest religious legislator of ancient times"—without, however, describing in detail what he had taught or relating what the texts preserved by his followers actually contained. To the classical world, Zarathustra was a mathematician, astrologer, wizard or magician. His influence was thought to have shaped the views of philosophers from Pythagoras to Plato. From his supposed devotees, the Magi, the Greeks gave us the word magic.

The rediscovery of the classics during the European Renaissance once again brought the Persian prophet's name to scholarly attention. Henceforth anyone writing about the history of civilisation or religion would metaphorically doff his cap to the memory of the Persian sage as a mark of respect. In 1700 Thomas Hyde, a professor at Oxford University (who coined the word cuneiform for the wedge-shaped writing of the ancient Middle East), collated every reference to Zoroaster that he could find in Greek, Latin, Hebrew and Arabic sources into his magisterial *Historia Religionis Veterum Persarum eorumque Magorum* (History of the Religion of the Ancient Persians and their Magi).

Zoroaster was now seen as the acceptable, even noble, face of pre-Christian religion. When, in the 1730s, the French composer Rameau was forbidden to stage his opera *Samson*, because the presentation of biblical figures was thought to be blasphemous, he was permitted to rework the piece under the title *Zoroastre*. The French writer and philosopher Voltaire included him among those who had transmitted God's natural law to humankind:

> *This sovereign law, in China, in Japan,*
> *Inspired Zoroaster, illuminated Solon.*
> *From one end of the world to the other, it cries:*
> *"Love one God, be just, and cherish your fatherland."*

And in *The Magic Flute*, Mozart disguised Zoroaster as the benevolent Sorastro, of whose two arias George Bernard Shaw once said that they were the only music he knew that would not sound out of place in the mouth of God.

But though Zarathustra had been honoured and celebrated by the intellectuals of three centuries, what he had actually taught still remained unknown. It seems to have occurred to nobody that, since there still survived—among the Zoroastrians or Parsees of Persia and India—devotees of the religion which followed his precepts and bore his name, it might be a worthwhile task to read the prophet's own words as preserved in their sacred texts.

Throughout the Middle Ages, European relations with Asia had been with ruling Muslim powers who weren't in the least interested in the scripture of an unbelieving, *kafir*, minority. Now Westerners, their empires expanding across the old world, became increasingly convinced of their intellectual, cultural and racial superiority over the swarming masses of the East. In such an atmosphere, asking Zoroastrians about their prophet was pointless and rather demeaning.

As Europeans tightened their colonial grip on Asia their contempt would only increase. By the nineteenth century, while there was still grudging respect given to Muslims and even Hindus, a certain Lady Callcott, supposedly a "first-rate authority," would pronounce the Parsees of India "vulgar in appearance." Further: "They do not possess either the elegant aristocratic forms of the Hindus, or the high breeding of the Mohammedans." In Persia, another nineteenth-century traveller, a Lady Shiel, would find that "the fire worshippers are the poorest, worst looking and stupidest of the whole population." Far from according any merit or value to the Zoroastrians' own knowledge of their religion, an English clergyman would write: "Certainly nothing can appear more irreverent than the mode in which the Parsees are to be seen at sunset on the shore of Bombay, jabbering over a ritual which they do not understand."

This was, after all, the era of Macaulay's famous and outrageous minute on Indian education with its dismissal of Indian culture as consisting of "medical doctrines, which would disgrace an English farrier,—Astronomy, which would move laughter in girls at an English boarding school,—History, abounding with kings thirty feet high, and reigns thirty thousand years long,—and Geography, made up of seas of treacle and seas of butter."

None the less, there were exceptions: those who went against the common grain and used the opportunity of easier access to the East, and ever closer contact with the indigenous populations in all their religious variety, to discover exotic cultural treasures and bring them home. In 1718 a certain Mr. Bourchier, a civil servant of the East India Company, brought back from the British factory at Surat on the Indian west coast, a precious copy of a Zoroastrian sacred book called the *Vendidad*. This he deposited in the Bodleian Library where it was kept, so it was said, on the end of a golden chain. Though nobody was able to decipher the document, it seems to have been regarded as something of a trophy. A copy of a few pages was carefully traced and sent to Paris, where it inspired a young student of Oriental languages attached to the Bibliothèque du Roi. Zarathustra's true legacy was now about to be rediscovered.

In a dusty book on the shelves of the University of London Library—the third volume of *Miscellanies of the Philosophical Society London 1856–7*—I found an article by a Member of Parliament of the day and former Calcutta judge, Sir Erskine Perry, called "Notice of Anquetil du Perron and the Fire Worshippers of India." As I sat there reading, trying hard not to interpret the old-fashioned letter "s" as an "f" in such phrases as "taking paffage on a veffel," the chipped table and gloomy library corridors rapidly retreated and I found myself swept up in the romantic life-story of one of the most colourful adventurers of eighteenth-century France.

Abraham Hyacynthe Anquetil du Perron was a Parisian grocer's son, a Catholic and the younger brother by eight years of a famous historian of the day. Rebellious and fiery by temperament, and probably envious of his elder brother's success in the pre-revolutionary French establishment, he had first chosen to study Hebrew—a field completely *passé* in France except among Protestants. He continued his studies in Utrecht where, with the support of the local bishop, he also applied himself to Persian and Arabic. Most graduates of Utrecht were aiming for employment as interpreters and dragomans in the Levant, but Abraham Hyacynthe had no interest at all in such a mundane occupation. Nor was he anxious to enter the Church to please his episcopal backer. So he returned to Paris, to the Bibliothèque du Roi, and waited for destiny to take a hand in his future.

He was twenty-three when fate pointed the way, when he saw those leaves copied from the *Vendidad* manuscript in the Bodleian Library and knew immediately what he had to do: to travel to the Indies, to Surat, where the manuscript had come from, and to make his name by being the first to decipher and translate it.

Easier said than done, however. In 1754 a seven-year colonial war was breaking out between France and Britain, a war which would rage across North America, the West Indies, Africa and India. Only troop transports were sailing to India that year. Nothing daunted, young Anquetil, who wished to be beholden to nobody and had therefore told nobody of his plans, packed two handkerchiefs, two shirts, two pairs of stockings, a set of mathematical instruments, a Hebrew Bible and a volume of Montaigne, enlisted as a private in one of the regiments destined for the East, and marched with his corps—otherwise largely composed of discharged convicts—to the port of embarkation. As soon as his Paris patrons discovered his plans, however, they insisted on his discharge from the ranks, arranged for an annuity to be paid him from the resources of the Bibliothèque, and secured his free passage on board the East Indiaman the *Duc d'Aquitaine* to Pondicherry on the east coast of India, headquarters of the French colony.

The voyage from France was a five-month-long nightmare. Du Perron suffered from constant seasickness and diarrhoea. Plague struck the ship and more than a hundred died, including even the captain. The young French scholar arrived in Pondicherry, sick, exhausted and stick-thin.

Today, Pondicherry is a small, quiet seaside tourist resort, part of a "Union Territory" made up of a number of formerly French enclaves widely scattered along the coast of southern India. As late as the 1960s when I last saw it—and maybe still today—French influence remained strong and obvious, not least among the local policemen whom I saw cycling along the early-morning streets in tall blue French-style *képi* caps, with long baguettes under their arms. But in the mid-eighteenth century this was the French capital in India and a bustling port, though with no harbour—ships had to anchor in the roadstead a mile or so offshore, from where small boats ferried passengers and freight to the quayside. This was the manner of Du Perron's arrival in India. He clambered ashore and immediately asked to be taken to the residence of the head of the French mission.

One can easily imagine him, a pale and haggard young man, his clothing stained and tattered, ushered in to the glorious presence of M. de Leyrit, the haughty Governor General of French India. The contrast between them must have been shocking. As Du Perron saw it:

> From the midst of a glittering retinue, there rose a man of nearly six feet in height, slim, in a white jacket, his head surmounted by a foot-high white head-dress.

What was this distinguished imperialist to make of the dishevelled youth who appeared before him, neither master nor servant, blathering on about inscriptions, manuscripts and undeciphered documents? The Governor General turned his back on his visitor with the eternal mantra of the mystified minister: "We'll have to see."

It took Abraham Hyacinthe nearly a year and a half to establish himself. Eventually his charm, erudition, quick wit and generous disposition won him a place in French colonial society—in spite of his fierce temper and tendency to express unwelcome, if honest, opinions. But his keenness to pursue his researches into the Zoroastrian canon was being thwarted. His grand ambition to be the first to translate the Parsee religious books could get no further in Pondicherry, which he found "too European." He tried joining a military expedition into the interior of the country but was back with a life-threatening fever within eight days.

After some weeks in the French hospital, he thought, oddly enough, that he might discover more about the ancient Persian tongue in Bengal. He took a sea passage to Chandernagore, the principal French settlement in Bengal, where he attached himself to the camp of the local military commander. But he was no better situated here than in Pondicherry. His fiery personality and readiness to speak his mind didn't endear him to the French officers, and he had no opportunity to learn anything other than a smattering of the Bengali language. He could also see clearly that the French territory was on the point of being lost to the British. There was nothing for it save to set his sights on Surat again.

But how to get there? Bengal is in the north-east of India, Surat a thousand miles away in the north-west. The obvious route was to cross the subcontinent. Du Perron duly embarked on a boat on the Ganges river, which he hoped would take him at least halfway, only to discover—this was February 1757—that the truce between France and Britain had ended and renewed hostilities now made an overland journey impossible. Moreover, the British had by now taken complete control of the seas in the Bay of Bengal, and even sailing back to Pondicherry was no longer safe. The only solution was to travel by land all the way south down the Indian east coast and all the way north up the west, half-circumnavigating the entire Indian subcontinent.

Anquetil du Perron's flight from French Bengal to Surat is the stuff of a Hollywood adventure yarn. Sir Erskine Perry summed it up in brief:

> Pondicherry was ten or twelve hundred miles, by land, from the French camp in Bengal; the route had never been traversed by a European; it was in May, the hottest month of the year; the intervening country was in great part jungle, well stocked with tigers; fierce hostilities were raging in parts of the route between the French and English; and Anquetil was nearly penniless; nevertheless, he determined to set out, and actually accomplished this adventurous journey, *on foot,* accompanied by one porter to carry his slender kit. He commenced his perilous march on the 5th of May, and reached Pondicherry on the 10th of August, having safely extricated himself from divers exciting adventures,—of hunger, robbery, imprisonment, and attempted assassination. At Pondicherry he found his brother, who had just been appointed second in command at the French factory at Surat, and they took sail together for that settlement. A. du Perron, however, landed at Maheé on the Malabar coast, and thence proceeded by land to the Jewish settlement at Cochin, to Goa, to Aurungabad, to the caves of Ellora, and through Kandésh to Surat.

The journey had taken two years.

Surat, however, was at first sight no more accommodating to the needs of a scholar and researcher than Bengal. Conflict raged on all sides, between the representatives of the European nations—two of them, France and Britain, in open warfare—and between the local rulers and the colonialists. Greed and envy promoted discord between factors and traders; even the Parsee community was split by theological disputes between reformers and traditionalists. Everyone was suspicious of the young Frenchman who had come all the way from Bengal with his odd requests. The head of the Por-tuguese mission wrote: "This gentleman demands many things, but one sees no sign of either money, or orders from his superiors."

But the turbulent situation, far from impeding Du Perron's quest, played into his hands. Though it took months of delicate negotiations, he finally contrived to get sight of the document he had been seeking for so long by skilfully exploiting the differences between the parties, and playing off one side against the other. In December 1758, he received by hand the following note from M. Taillefert, head of the Dutch mission:

Monsieur Du Perron,

The messenger bearing these presents will hand you a copy of the Book of Zoroaster, which Mancherge [leader of the tradition-alist party] guarantees to be the most authentic and exact to be found in Surat. I beg you to take care not to lose any of its pages, and to send it back to me as soon as possible.

A Pahlavi-Farsi glossary, rendering into modern Persian the vocabu-lary of the Zoroastrian text, arrived soon after from another quarter. Du Perron had what he needed to begin his task. Translation of the glossary was soon accomplished.

This work, the first of its kind ever undertaken by a European, seems to me an event in the history of literature. I mark the date as the 24th of March 1759 of J.-C., the day of Amerdad, sixth of the month of Meher, in the year 1128 of Iezdedjerd, year 1172 of the Hegira, and 1813 of the reign of Bekermadjit.

Abraham Hyacynthe now turned to translating the *Vendidad* itself, the sight of scraps of which had first stimulated his interest back in Paris five years previously. The traditionalists still refused to reveal any of their secret lore, so he took lessons in the *Vendidad*'s language from the leaders of the reformist sect, paying for tuition by the day, and constantly complaining that he was being purposely taught very slowly so as to maximise the fees that could be extracted from him.

The work would presumably have continued to its orderly conclusion had not another adventure intervened, and in a highly dramatic way. There was a real possibility that the entire enterprise of introducing of the works of Zarathustra to the West might end there and then on the streets of Surat.

Du Perron had offended a French ship's captain by the name of Biquant, who had accused the young scholar of being his native wife's lover and forbidden him to cross his threshold ever again. Biquant's wife now gave birth to a baby boy. Having been sternly reproved by the authorities for taking no steps to have the child baptised, Biquant reluctantly went to the priest's house to make arrangements. There he met Du Perron and asked him if he would hold the baby at the font during the ceremony.

"Monsieur," replied Du Perron quietly, "you have asked me not to come to your house on account of false rumours. What would people say if I held your child!"

Biquant bridled. "There's no need for such talk. Will you hold my child or not?"

"Monsieur Biquant, it is not done to threaten a gentleman."

"You refuse Monsieur? Then I shall go."

"The door is open," said Du Perron, pointing to it.

"Yes Monsieur, and I shall shake the dust from my feet outside it."

"Monsieur," retorted Du Perron, "you are a boor."

The priest tried to calm matters and sent the quarrellers home. Fearing the worst, he then wrote to both reminding them of the royal prohibition on fighting and duelling. Du Perron replied:

If Master Jean Biquant was in a position to measure up to me, your prohibition would stand; but having nothing but contempt for his conduct and his rank as a ship's captain, I would never come to blows except in self defence, and you know that you can never order me to allow myself to be dishonoured or killed.

The following week, Biquant turned up at Du Perron's house and was told that the scholar was visiting a M. Boucard. The captain sent his servant to fetch his weapons and made his way to the Boucard residence, where he chatted with Du Perron for about half an hour until the latter rose to leave. Biquant followed him to the door, grabbed his arm, and with sword in hand demanded:

"Give me satisfaction, Monsieur, or be dishonoured."

They began to fence and a large crowd gathered, eventually numbering some four hundred witnesses. Du Perron's sword broke. Biquant took the opportunity to thrust Du Perron through the chest, missing his heart by inches, and then inflicted another serious wound to his opponent's thigh. Du Perron dropped his sword-hilt and launched himself on to the captain, wrestling him to the ground and disarming him. He then got up and calmly walked away, carrying Biquant's sword under his arm and dripping blood in pools on to the street behind him.

Biquant got up, shouting "My sword! My sword!," grabbed his servant's sabre, ran after Du Perron and delivered three or four savage blows, inflicting further serious wounds. Du Perron, realising that he was lost if he did not finally respond, made a single thrust with the sword he had taken from Biquant and removed his adversary's sabre, receiving another wound to the elbow and cutting his hand on the sabre-blade in the process. Then he dropped the sword and walked off, carrying his own sword-hilt and Biquant's sabre and scabbard. Biquant picked up his sword and ran off, but had gone no more than a hundred paces before he dropped on to the paving—stone dead.

This was serious. Du Perron had by now fallen out with nearly everyone in the French colony, including even his brother, and could count on no support from that quarter. He was in real danger of being arrested by the local French authorities and charged with duelling and murder. His only recourse was to seek the protection of the English factory, where he was received with much hospitality, the head of the mission refusing to give him up to the French, citing "the universal practice of civilised nations." It took him all of another twelve months, with British help, to mend fences with his own, French, authorities. Meanwhile he continued spending what remained of his money on the purchase of further Zoroastrian texts, until he was offered a passage home to Europe on one of the British East India Company's ships.

Many of us know from personal experience how it feels to return home from brilliant tropical skies to cloudy dull English weather, bursting to tell of amazing sights seen, of fantastic adventures in faraway places, of extraordinary meetings with astonishing people, only to find that nobody is very interested and that hardly anybody has even noticed our absence. Anquetil's anticlimax was even greater. The British vessel on which he was sailing also carried French prisoners of war and when, after eight months, it docked at Portsmouth, the authorities took it for granted that the young Frenchman was one of them. He was straight away sent, in irons, to Winchester gaol. Luckily, in those days, a distinction was made between soldiers, who could be imprisoned, and mere nationals of an enemy country, who were allowed to travel freely between the belligerent sides. So, after negotiations, Anquetil was released and permitted to visit Oxford, where he was able to match his own documents against those whose copies he had seen in Paris eight years before and which had originally inspired his expedition to the East.

Anquetil Du Perron's translation of the *Avesta,* the collected works of the Zoroastrian canon, published in three volumes, finally appeared in 1771. If he was expecting universal acclaim, he was to be disappointed. The vested interests of too many established "experts" were threatened by this young, unknown upstart, who had arrived from who knows where, claiming, without a shred of evidence, to have translated works that had defeated the efforts of some of the greatest scholars of the age. The philosopher Voltaire and the *encyclopédiste* Diderot both spoke out against him.

What was worse, Du Perron had included, in passing, a number of typically incautious comments on the British in general and insults to the dons of Oxford in particular. This raised the patriotic ire of William Jones, a twenty-four-year-old student of Oriental languages, already fluent in Latin, Greek and Hebrew, whose first publication—a translation from Persian into French of a life of the Iranian king Nadir Shah—had been undertaken the previous year on behalf of the King of Denmark, in spite of misgivings about his ability, only "lest His Majesty should be obliged to send the manuscript into France." Perish the thought.

William, later Sir William, Jones was to become the foremost Orientalist of his day, and would make huge contributions to the study of Persian and Indian language and literature. Yet the man who would be famous for his tolerance and open mind, not to mention his opposition to slavery—"I pass with haste by the coast of Africa, whence my mind turns with indignation at the abominable traffic in the human species, from which a part of our countrymen dare to derive their most inauspicious wealth"—began his public life by publishing an extraordinary open letter "to M. A*** du P*** in which is contained an examination of his translation of the books attributed to Zoroaster" *(à M. A*** du P*** dans laquelle est compris l'examen de sa traduction des livres attribués à Zoroastre).* This squib, later described by another famous philologist as "a libel full of venom and gall and quite unworthy of its author's name," attacked Du Perron, the translation, and the authenticity of the entire enterprise. The letter began with sarcasm:

> Allow me to congratulate you on your fortunate discoveries. You have risked your precious life, you have crossed stormy oceans,

mountains infested by tigers, you have tarnished your complexion, which you inform us, with as much elegance as modesty, had been one of lilies and roses.

and ended with savagery:

> . . . we cannot believe that even the least skilful charlatan could have written the rubbish with which your volumes are filled . . . Either Zoroaster had no common sense, or he did not write the book you attribute to him. If he had no common sense, it were better to leave him in obscurity; if he did not write the book, it is an impertinence to publish it under his name. Thus, you have either insulted the public by presenting it with nonsense, or misled it by peddling falsehoods; in either case you deserve contempt . . .
>
> The result of all this, Monsieur, is that either you do not possess the knowledge of which you boast, or that your knowledge is vain, frivolous and unworthy of the mind of a forty year-old.

Jones's letter was partly prompted by plain English francophobia. He wrote to a friend with great self-satisfaction: *"conturbavi nationem gallicam"* (I have disconcerted the French nation). This was, however, irrelevant to the main charge against the Frenchman. In reality, Du Perron had fallen foul of the general assumption, held in the eighteenth century as earlier, that religious texts were truly and simply the work of the prophetic figures to whom they were attributed. Moses and no other was unquestionably the author of the Pentateuch, as was Muhammad of the Qu'ran. Thus the *Avesta* must bear the signature of Zoroaster alone. But the content of the Du Perron translation was unacceptable to those who had learned from the classics to honour and respect the Persian prophet as the greatest religious thinker of antiquity. If Zoroaster really was the author, the book should have been of the highest literary quality, full of penetrating insights and brilliant moral perceptions. Instead, what lay revealed seemed to its European readers a mish-mash of unoriginal ideas, absurd stories, ridiculous rules and weird gods and demons. They had no notion that the *Avesta* was actually, like most other sacred texts, a compilation of different materials, from different sources, collected at different times over a long period.

As for William Jones, he went on to take up the law, travel to India, learn Sanskrit—the ancient language of Indian religion—become the founder and first president of the Royal Asiatic Society and gain a knighthood. Anquetil du Perron, by contrast, though continuing to publish, did so from obscurity. His experiences in the East must have strongly affected him for he took a deep interest in Hinduism and chose to live out his days on a meagre few francs a day like a sort of Indian ascetic.

Years passed. One day Sir William was reading a Persian classic, thinking of making a translation. Trying to understand a particular word, he chanced to turn to the glossary of Du Perron's version of the *Avesta* and noticed something exceedingly odd among what he had once called the "misleading falsehoods peddled by Du Perron." He began to see words that he was sure could only be derived from Sanskrit. He was "inexpressibly surprised to find," he later wrote, "that six or seven words in ten were pure *Sanscrit*." Since Du Perron didn't know Sanskrit, this suggested that the word list might be authentic after all.

Rather than recant, Sir William put the blame on Du Perron's attitude:

> M. Anquetil had the merit of undertaking a voyage to India, in his earliest youth, with no other view than to recover the writings of Zer Atusht [his version of the name Zarathustra], and he would have acquired a brilliant reputation in France, if he had not sullied it by his immoderate vanity and virulence of temper, which alienated the goodwill of even his own countrymen.

Jones was wrong about the words in the *Avesta* being "pure *Sanscrit*." None the less, the notion of a link between the Persian and Indian tongues was a true and important one, leading Sir William to a striking conclusion about the development of the languages of Asia. As he put it in a famous address to the Royal Asiatic Society:

> The *Sanscrit* language, whatever be its antiquity, is of a wonderful structure; more perfect than the *Greek*, more copious than the *Latin*, and more exquisitely refined than either, yet bearing to both of them a stronger affinity, both in the roots of verbs and in the forms of grammar, than could possibly have been produced by accident; so strong indeed, that no philologer could examine them all three, without believing them to have sprung from some common source, which perhaps, no longer exists: there is a similar reason, though not quite so forcible, for supposing that both the

Gothick and the *Celtick,* though blended with a very different idiom, had the same origin with the *Sanscrit*; and the old *Persian* might be added to the same family.

With this speech Sir William Jones is remembered as having founded the study of comparative linguistics. Others would put the proposition on a firm scientific footing over the course of the next century, bringing ever more evidence to support Sir William's conjecture until nearly everyone came to accept that most of Europe's and Iran's languages, as well as a good half of India's, had evolved from a single original Indo-European variety of speech.

Central to this enterprise were the Zoroastrian texts brought to Europe by Du Perron, which were finally proven authentic by an eminent Danish philologist in the 1820s. Now everyone wanted to examine their contents. Sir Erskine Perry's 1857 publication mentions three translations— one French, one German, and one English—in preparation at the very time of his writing. Zarathustra and his sacred texts were a major topic of excited discussion in philological circles at the end of the 1850s and first half of the 1860s. And this was exactly the time when we left the young Friedrich Wilhelm Nietzsche freeze-framed in the doorway of the University of Bonn, about to begin his second year as a student of philology. Let us now reanimate him and watch him walk in.

ZARATHUSTRA PASSED ME BY

Nietzsche may well have heard of the Persian prophet at the very start of the semester, though the event is nowhere recorded. He would have learned that the newly translated Zoroastrian texts saw in the struggle between good and evil "the essential wheel in the working of things," and though it took a long time to come to the surface, the impact of that discovery was profound and disturbing. His sister Elisabeth would later write that the figure of Zarathustra frequently appeared to her brother in his dreams long before it emerged in his writing. But it is hard to say what Zarathustra can have meant to him at this stage. Other important influences and much personal suffering would intervene before Nietzsche's philosophical ideas were fully formed.

He would discover Schopenhauer by chance while browsing in a local bookshop, struck like thunder by the gloomy German philosopher's denial of any possible meaning to life and his suggestion that it was better not to be born, or at least to die quickly. "It seemed as if Schopenhauer were addressing me personally. I felt his enthusiasm, and seemed to see him before me. Every line cried aloud for renunciation, denial, resignation."

He would be mesmerised by Wagner—perhaps a substitute for his own long-dead father—and be inspired to write a book which brought him to public attention: *The Birth of Tragedy*. He would then exercise his talent for making a scene by walking out of the gala first-night opening of Wagner's Bayreuth opera house and violently and publicly throwing up, being the first to recognise the composer's fatal flaws of sentimentality and bombast (flaws which would make Wagner—serve him right, the old anti-Semite— an inspiration to generations of Jewish Hollywood film composers).

He would be called up for military service as a student and be attached to a regiment of field artillery near his home, where a serious accident while trying to leap on to a horse would lead to sick leave, discharge, and his speedy and ignominious return home. Later, after graduating and receiving his doctorate, he would take a sabbatical from his professorship at the University of Basel to serve in the Franco-Prussian War as an orderly in a military hospital, where he would contract diphtheria and dysentery and take months to recover.

He would become distinctly odd, writing defensively: "If we have our own *why* of life, we shall get along with almost any *how*. Man does not strive for pleasure; only the Englishman does." He would find himself always the outsider, always ill at ease in company, always somehow doing the wrong thing. Carl Jung had friends who had studied under Nietzsche:

In Basel it appealed to his fantasy to appear in society as an elegant Englishman. In those days Englishmen were considered the summit of everything marvellous, and they used to wear grey gloves and grey top hats; so Nietzsche went about in a grey *redingote*, a grey top hat, and grey gloves, and thought that he looked like an Englishman. And with that moustache!

After one lecture about Greece, a student came up to ask a question.

But before he could put in his very humble request, Nietzsche said: "Ah now, you are the man! That blue sky of Hellas! We are going together!"

And the young man thought: "How can I go with this famous professor and how have I the money to do it?"—and he retreated further and further, Nietzsche going at him and talking of the eternal smile of the skies of Hellas and God knows what, till the young man was backed up against the wall. Then suddenly Nietzsche realised that the fellow was frightened by his enthusiasm, and he turned away abruptly and never spoke to him again.

He would become a chronic invalid, probably with second-stage syphilis caught during his student days, so sick that he was forced to retire from his chair at Basel after only ten years. No drugs, neither chloral, nor strychnine, nor paregoric, nor paraldehyde, could help his desperate effort to sleep at night and work by day. "Every two or three weeks, I have to spend about 36 hours in bed. I am surprised at how difficult living is." Yet his health was a key to his developing vision. "My illness has been my greatest boon: it unblocked me, it gave me the courage to be myself."

He would find himself increasingly alone. Proposals of marriage ended in humiliation. He lost his students. His circle would become ever narrower, his friends ever fewer, his book sales ever smaller. Stateless—for he had never taken Swiss citizenship and never remained in any one place for any length of time—he would move with the seasons between Italy, Switzerland and Germany, always returning at intervals to his mother's house in Naumburg.

During all this time a response to Zarathustra's teaching had been taking shape in Nietzsche's mind. But he needed a very particular setting to bring it to birth. He eventually discovered the perfect place: the little Swiss mountain village of Sils-Maria in the upper Engadine valley, close to the Italian border and not far from Saint Moritz, where he took "cheap but agreeable" lodgings with the Durisch family. "I emerged into the morning air, I was greeted by the most beautiful day the Upper Engadine had ever disclosed to me—clear, glowing with colour, and including all the contrasts and all the intermediary gradations between ice and the south."

Here, in the summer months of 1881, "two thousand metres above good and evil," Nietzsche had at last found the right environment to deliver his philosophy.

Philosophy, as I have so far understood and lived it, means living willingly among ice and high mountains, seeking out everything strange and questionable in existence, everything so far placed under a ban by morality. The ice is near, the solitude tremendous, but how serenely all things lie, how freely one breathes, how much one feels lies beneath one's-self.

He walked daily in the lush green flower-strewn meadows, by the ice-blue lakes and along the deep and shady forest pathways between glittering snow-covered Alpine peaks. And finally he had the experience for which his whole life had been a preparation:

> *I sat there waiting—not for anything.*
> *Beyond good and evil, enjoying now the light*
> *Now the shade, now only play, now*
> *The lake, now the noon, wholly time without end.*
> *Then suddenly, friend, one became two—*
> *And Zarathustra passed me by.*

"One became two and Zarathustra passed me by" *(Da wurde eins zwei und Zarathustra ging an mir vorbei)*. The spirit of Zarathustra suddenly emerged and claimed an independent existence. To Nietzsche, it was a revelation. "One hears—one does not seek; one takes—one does not ask who gives; a thought suddenly flashes up like lightning, it comes with necessity, unhesitatingly—I have never had any choice in the matter."

Also Sprach Zarathustra (Thus spake Zarathustra) was to be his title, suggesting that Zarathustra, not Nietzsche, was the true author. Nietzsche did not write in the name of Zarathustra; Zarathustra wrote through the medium of Nietzsche. Three of the four parts of the masterpiece were composed and set down in an astonishing ten days each.

Nietzsche said that his task was to undo the damage caused to humanity by Zarathustra's original teachings. The Iranian sage, he said, was the source of the profoundest error in human history, namely the invention of morality. Therefore it was up to Zarathustra himself to reverse the mistake. It's a tall order—not to speak of presumptuous—to try summing up Zarathustra's new teachings in two paragraphs. But here goes:

God is dead. Religious belief is a comforting but debilitating self-delusion. A Christian God can no longer express the highest ideals of Western civilisation. Belief in God is now a burden on the individual and on society. A system of ethics and morality founded on faith is no longer valid; the time has come for a new set of values to take its place, beyond good and evil as religion has until now defined them.

Values are the creation of human beings. One person's good is another's evil. None the less, we are all responsible for creating values for ourselves and for then living up to them. And the highest of all values is the duty to transcend ourselves, to struggle for the next step in our personal evolution: to leave behind the animal-natured "blond beast" and strive for the "super-human," to become a "super-human." Though most will never achieve it, this self-overcoming, this "will to power," is the proper task of all human beings. Anything that supports this goal is good and anything that undermines it is evil:

> What is good? Everything that heightens the feeling of power in man, the will to power, power itself. What is bad? Everything that is born of weakness.

But nobody wanted to listen. The response to the book was total public indifference. The first parts sold sixty or seventy copies each, the last part reduced the author to the ignominy of having an edition of forty copies printed at his own expense. Yet by now Nietzsche was accustomed to his isolation. He was convinced that one day his truths would be recognised. Though his health continued its steep decline, he went on working furiously, publishing seven more books in the time that remained to him.

On a damp and gloomy morning, the 3rd of January 1889, Nietzsche was walking near his lodgings in the Via Carlo Alberto in Turin, "opposite the mighty Palazzo Carignano, in which Vittorio Emanuele was born," when he turned into the grand Piazza Carlo Alberto, within distant sight of his beloved Alpine mountains, snow-covered at this time of year. On the other side of the square, in front of the imposing National Library, a carter was savagely beating his horse. The horse fell to its knees. The austere philosopher, who had uncompromisingly condemned pity as a debilitating weakness, sped across the road and flung his arms about the horse's neck—a gesture of sympathy and solidarity with another living being. It was his last sane and human act. He would never return to his senses again. He had finally passed beyond good and evil.

> Alas, I have begun my loneliest walk. But whoever is of my kind cannot escape such an hour, the hour which says to him: only now are you going your way to greatness. Peak and abyss, they are now joined together, for all things are baptised in a well of eternity and lie beyond good and evil.

His greatness would come but he would not be aware of it. He would live on for another decade, looked after first by his mother and then by his sister, mute and apparently unaware of his surroundings. Once or twice a glimpse of his former self broke through, as when he suddenly turned to his sister and, in a voice of shattering normality, spoke. "Lisbeth, why are you crying? Aren't we happy?" And once, only once, hearing his visitors speak of books, he unexpectedly raised his head and said like a child: "I too have written some good books."

He died of a stroke with his century, in August 1900. He was only fifty-five years old.

Not long ago I was sitting on the train that runs between Vienna and Zurich, down the stretch of track that passes through the Austrian province of Vorarlberg, speeding along the bottom of a lush valley, while close by on every side rose mighty Alpine peaks. Outside the window was some of the most spectacularly beautiful scenery in the world. A young traveller in anorak and woolly ski hat was sitting opposite, his rucksack on the seat next to him. He too was staring out at the mountainscape, listening to something on his Walkman that obviously deeply moved and affected him. He saw my look and, in response to the unspoken question, pulled the phones from his ears and held them out to me. "Strauss," he said. "*Also Sprach Zarathustra*. Music for mountains." I thought it very striking that a hundred years after Nietzsche's death, the name of his greatest and most difficult work was still current among the young as we prepared to enter a new century.

The last century, the twentieth, was undoubtedly the century of Nietz-sche's *Zarathustra*. There was hardly a thinker, writer, artist, musician or psychologist who didn't owe him a debt. Not only Richard Strauss, but Gustav Mahler and Frederick Delius set him to music. Equally, his philos-ophy was claimed as the inspiration behind many of the darker forces at work in the world. During the First World War 150,000 copies of *Also Sprach Zarathustra* were printed by the German government and distrib-uted to young conscripts, along with the Bible, as inspirational reading. What irony, when Nietzsche had passionately denounced the Judaeo-Christian tradition: "After coming into contact with a religious man I always feel I must wash my hands." Nietzsche's sister Elisabeth worked untiringly to find material in her brother's writings to support the Nazi ideology, even though he had despised anti-Semitism and nationalism, and his last written note had read: "I am just out having all the anti-Semites shot, signed Dionysos." She personally welcomed Hitler to her house in Weimar, which she had turned into a museum. Nietzsche himself predicted as much when he wrote:

> I know my fate. One day there will be associated with my name the recollection of something frightful—of a crisis like no other before on earth, of the profoundest collision of conscience, of a decision evoked against everything that until then had been believed in, demanded, sanctified. I am not a man. I am dynamite.

Yet the roll-call of Nietzsche's followers and those influenced by him also reads like a list of the greatest positive personalities of the modern age. Sigmund Freud said that Nietzsche had a more penetrating understanding of himself than any man who ever lived or was ever likely to live. Carl Jung held regular weekly seminars on the meaning of Nietzsche's *Zarathustra* with a group from the Zurich Psychological Club from 1934 until 1939, when impending war brought them to an end. The Jewish mystical thinker Martin Buber counted Nietzsche among his most important influences and even translated part of *Zarathustra* into his native Polish. Existentialism, deconstructionism and a clutch of the other philosophical and critical "—isms" of our day were all built on foundations of Nietzsche's masterwork. Galsworthy's German officer's words turned out to be prophetic: "Nietzsche is the true philosopher, the only one."

In reversing Zarathustra's original teaching, in overthrowing traditional morality, had Nietzsche finally made the ancient Persian message a historical irrelevance? I hardly think so. We have only to look around us at the prevailing myths of the twentieth century—in books and films—to see how strongly Zarathustra's ethical dualism, the eternal battle between good and evil, continues as a constant theme in the human imagination.

While travelling on that Alpine train, my heart uplifted by the sight of the majestic peaks, the young man in front of me listening to Strauss's "music for mountains," I came to my own conclusion about what Nietzsche really stood for. He thought he was overturning Zarathustra's teaching. I think he was simply reinterpreting it for a post-religious age.

Two thousand years of Christian thought—combined with a strong dash of Plato—had taken the Persian prophet's message as implying a material world that was wholly evil, and a spiritual world that was entirely good. But Nietzsche was no longer a Christian, no longer a believer in God. His love of high mountains, snow and ice, was his atheist's way of rising above a corrupt earth and coming closer to heaven. No longer a believer in life after death, he knew that the drama must be played out within each individual—the struggle between what a person is and what he or she might become. No longer a believer in the liberation of the soul, he proposed striving to become superhuman in its place.

So, I concluded, Nietzsche was actually preaching a form of Zarathustra's philosophy after all. His genius was to wrap in modern packaging a belief that has run as a constant thread through European history, a heretical doctrine that orthodox Christianity spent centuries trying bloodily to extirpate. Humanity is flawed, said Nietzsche; rise above it. The world is evil, said the heretics; leave it behind. The Church called that the Great Heresy.

3

The Great Heresy

MARTIRS DEL PUR AMOR CRESTIAN

In the foothills of the Pyrenean mountains of southern France, not far from the border with Spain, the ruined fortress of Montségur grows like a stone nipple from the top of a giant rock that suddenly shoots up, in the shape of a pert breast, three and a half thousand precipitous feet above the village that the castle once protected. It was here that the last persecuted followers of the Great Heresy—a faith that once commanded the allegiance of a third of the population of southern France—retreated into the sky. And it was at the base of this rock, after ten months of siege had forced the submission of the stronghold's garrison, that some two hundred and twenty of the elders of the faith were flung, living, on to a huge blazing pyre that filled the entire valley with the acrid stench of burning flesh.

Though not the very last hold-out to fall to the forces of Catholic orthodoxy, the capture of Montségur in 1244 signalled the end of the Great Heresy in the West. It would take the Inquisition another hundred years to root it out completely, but the capture of this castle was the final act in what has become known as the Albigensian Crusade—after the town of Albi, a hotbed of the heresy. The fifty-year war of terror and horror initiated by Pope Innocent III not only utterly destroyed—by what would now be called "collateral damage"—the most glittering civilisation of Western Europe, but also made destitute those it left alive. The terrible vengeance wrought on the Cathars, one of the many names by which the heretics were known, was punishment for having incorporated into their Christianity a belief in dualism—that there are two ruling powers, one good, the other evil. Today we may recognise that belief as a legacy of Zarathustra's ancient teaching. The medieval Church saw it as plain devil-derived heresy.

I made my own pilgrimage to Montségur in January, the last month of the siege, when conditions in the castle must have been at their most desperate. Standing at the base of this mini-mountain, the citadel on the top seemed a very, very long way up—too difficult a climb, I thought, at this season of the year. Even the path from the road to the site of the pyre was heavily iced over and dangerously slippery underfoot. Surprisingly steep, too, so much so as to be quite taxing to those no longer in the first flush even of middle age. The website I consulted had warned as much: *"le visiteur, transformé pour l'occasion en montagnard, emprunte un chemin difficile, sinueux, étroit, traversant des bois sombres, pour accéder au château"* (the visitor, forced by conditions into mountaineering, must take a difficult, narrow and serpentine path, passing through gloomy woods, to reach the chateau). However, there was little point in coming all this way without at least going up the first stage, to the memorial that marks the traditional site where the martyrs of Montségur were consigned to the flames.

I had prepared myself for the visit to Cathar country with Zoé Oldenbourg's exhaustive and exhausting account of the war against heresy: *Massacre at Montségur. A History of the Albigensian Crusade.* Thus I was primed with knowledge of every sally, sortie, siege and slaughter, every battle, bombardment, bloodletting and burning at the stake, as well as every feint and parry, lunge and riposte in the political duel between Arnald Amalric, the Pope's representative, and Raymond VI, Count of Toulouse, who seem to have begun and prosecuted the conflict in a spirit of personal vendetta. Fittingly enough, they died within three years of each other, though the war they had let loose would continue on its savage course for a few more decades until all the independent territories of the French Midi were incorporated among the possessions of the Kingdom of France.

Such carnage demands an explanation. How could it be that a Christian Pope decreed a crusade against a Christian territory? The recent sack, in 1204, of Christian Constantinople by the knights of the fourth Crusade had been an embarrassing aberration, unplanned, unexpected and unwelcome, but this time the onslaught was both intended and pursued with a ruthless single-mindedness. The Great Heresy was a hated enemy that must at whatever cost be destroyed.

Remembering the abominations of the twentieth century, we are hardly in a position to feel superior to those who perpetrated the excesses of the thirteenth. Far from it—we should feel a kinship. For though all too many wars have brought chaos and destruction down on our continent during the intervening centuries, only in our own time and in theirs has the slaughter of civilian populations rather than soldiery been intentional, official, state policy. An age that witnessed the Nazi death camps ought to understand an age when, after the capture of the grand and wealthy city of Béziers, the Papal Legate Arnald Amalric was asked how to distinguish good Catholics from heretics among the seven thousand men, women, invalids, babies and priests crushed into the Church of the Madeleine, crying and praying and holding out crucifixes, chalices and bibles to demonstrate their orthodoxy, he could coldly reply: "Kill them all. God will recognise his own." And then, as the city burned, could write with pride to the Pope his master that "nearly twenty thousand of the citizens were put to the sword, regardless of age and sex."

Unlike many of the victims of our own day, the hundreds of thousands left dead by the Crusade were neither ethnically nor linguistically different from their murderers. They merely followed a form of Christianity other than that prescribed by the Catholic Church. Translated into twentieth-century terms, the crime of which they were guilty is a familiar one: ideological deviation.

The more one reads accounts like Oldenbourg's, or the many other descriptions of the conquest of the Midi by Catholic orthodoxy, the more one is reminded of the totalitarian tyrannies of our own time. In historian Le Roy Ladurie's best-selling account of medieval life in the Pyrenean village of Montaillou, not far from Montségur, taken directly from evidence recorded by the Inquisition, one brief anecdote jogged my memory. The bailiff of another mountain village was overheard consoling the mother of a dead son. "Do not weep," he told her, "God will give the soul of your dead son to the next child you conceive, male or female. Or else his soul will find a good home somewhere else." For making this tiny, kindly attempt at consolation, invoking the concept of transmigration of souls, apparently part of Cathar belief, the bailiff was sent to prison for eight years and was condemned to wear the yellow cross of heresy on his coat for the rest of his days—no minor punishment in an age when befriending, assisting, or even approaching a confirmed heretic could lead to being accused of heresy oneself. The story instantly brought to mind the father of an Austrian friend of mine, who disappeared into the Nazi labour and death camp at Mauthausen near Linz in 1939 because, an irrepressible wit, he had been overheard joking that with the onset of war, the name of the new *KDF-wagen*—the car that would became the VW beetle—should be interpreted, not as the official *Kraft Durch Freude,* Strength through Joy, but as *Kack Durch's Fenster,* Shit through the Window.

There is no moral equivalence between the medieval Catholic Church and the Nazis, even in their attitude to Jews. But like the Communist rulers of the USSR and the other tyrants of the twentieth century, they felt a pressing need to keep the people loyal to their version of the truth. No accident, then, that a ruler like Stalin took careful lessons from medieval Christendom. Like communism to the USSR, Christianity to medieval Europe was the doctrine that supported the state. The legitimacy of the ruler, the justness of the law, the acceptance of the social and economic system, all depended on belief in the Christian message as taught by the Catholic Church. Without that, it was feared, Europe would slide back into the centuries-long chaos from which the Church had rescued it. In an age when religious explanations of the condition of the world were all that were available, at a time when the Church of Rome saw itself as the fulfilment of Christ's promise of a second coming and as the Kingdom of God on Earth, the Pope summed it up simply: heresy was treason against God.

From the road at the base of the *pog,* the local name for the rock on which the citadel of Montségur stands, you can just make out the small memorial on the edge of the forest line, marking the spot where the heretics were consigned to the flames. Struggle up the icy track and you find that it is not an old construction; it dates only from 1960. Yet it is not without its own interest. At the top of the face of the four-foot-high round-topped tapering stele, mounted on a stone base, are inscribed a star, three crosses and an open book, and below them the words: ALS CATARS—ALS MARTIRS DEL PUR AMOR CRESTIAN—16 MARS 1244 (To the Cathars—to the martyrs of pure Christian love—16 March 1244). The language is Provençal, the *langue d'oc* (the language in which "yes" is *oc*) as opposed to the *langue d'oïl* (Old French, in which "yes" was *oïl*). It is a reminder that in early medieval times the Midi was neither politically, culturally nor linguistically French but a land of its own. Sometimes known as Occitania (where they say *oc*) or Septimania (after the Seventh Roman Legion which was once stationed or retired here), this was the wealthiest, most cultured and glamorous corner of Western Europe.

Here at Montségur, looking out today over exactly the same snow-capped highland vista as in that bitter January three-quarters of a millennium ago, it is easy to imagine the desperation of the fugitives crowded into this last bastion of Cathar belief. To discover themselves pushed to the very edge of civilisation, driven nearly four thousand feet above the sea, close to the deserted, frozen white peaks of the high Pyrenees just to the south. To feel themselves so far from the warm, rich valleys of the rivers Aude and Garonne, the fruitful wheatfields, the lush vineyards, the great palaces of Toulouse and Narbonne, the impregnable fortifications of Carcassonne, Béziers and Peyrepertuse.

These lands were the home of chivalry, of mounted knights in shining armour, of respect for—not to say adulation of—women, of courtly love, of poetry, music, dancing, of the troubadours. *"Kalenda maya. Ni fuelhs de faya, ni chanz d'auzelh, ni flors de glaya, de vostre belh cors qu'em retraya, e jaya em traya no vos domna veraya,"* sang Raimbault de Vaqueyras, in his best-known verse. "The first of May. Neither leaf of beech, nor song of bird, nor flower of sword lily, give me pleasure, noble and gay lady, until I receive news from your fair self." Occitania was the wellspring of Gothic architecture, of fairy-tale castles with pennanted arrow-slit round towers and conical pointed roofs, looking as if built to plans from a children's storybook, of gleaming jewels, sparkling polychrome enamels and filigree goldwork, of shiny silken banners and brightly coloured clothes, of extrovert heraldry and solemn court ritual. Here was the source of our popular images of King Arthur and the Round Table. The twelfth-century French poet Chrétien de Troyes, on whose epic *Perceval ou Le Conte du Graal* (Percival or The Story of the Grail) most subsequent Arthurian literature was based, said he had heard the story from Kyot the Provençal. The language of this fabulous realm, the *langue d'oc*, was the foremost European medium of literature from the eleventh to the fourteenth centuries, used by writers far and wide—Dante considered composing his *Divina Commedia* in Provençal before taking the commercially risky step of turning to his local Tuscan peasant dialect.

At the same time, here was the western heartland of the Great Heresy of the Middle Ages (as it was of Kabbalah, the Jewish mystical doctrine which shared so many of the tenets of Catharism that it must surely have been influenced by the same source). Somehow, Zarathustra's message that there were two powers on earth rather than a single God, had struck deeper roots in this corner of the Mediterranean than elsewhere. While professed all across Europe in the tenth, twelfth and thirteenth centuries by the variously named Albigensians, Bogomils, Cathars, Kudugers, Manichaeans, Patarenes, Paulicians, Phundaites, Poplicani, Publicans, Runkeler and more, their number was usually sufficiently small to require no more than swift police action. A mission of heretics who arrived in England soon after Thomas à Becket's consecration as Archbishop of Canterbury in 1162, were quickly denounced to a synod in Oxford, publicly flogged, branded, expelled from the city and left to die in the frozen winter countryside. The chronicler William of Newburgh called this a "pious severity." But here in the Languedoc, where about a third of the population were heretics, the combined efforts of kings, popes, princes, knights and a crusade of the utmost savagery were needed to stamp out the unacceptable faith.

This heresy threatened Christian orthodoxy like no other—from within. It wasn't a matter of nit-picking disagreements about whether Christ had one nature or more, or whether the Holy Spirit was subordinate or equal to the Father and the Son. Instead, by combining the faith in Jesus Christ the Saviour with a strangely altered version of Zarathustra's two equal powers, one good, the other evil, it stood the entire teaching of Jesus's Church on its head.

The Church accepted that there was a Devil, and that he was a dangerous force. But Satan was no equal to God. He was merely a fallen angel, whose might could be resisted with the help of God's grace. The Great Heresy reversed this order of power to create what must surely have been the most pessimistic philosophy in history. Its basic tenet was this: that the whole of human existence, birth, life and death, the kingly state, the Church, yea the great globe itself and the sky above it, were the creation of the Devil. It held that the God of the Old Testament, the God of Abraham, Isaac and Jacob, the Lord of Hosts of the Jews, was in reality none other than the Power of Evil, Old Nick himself, now sometimes called *Satanael*—Satan the God. And he was in charge down here. So don't expect anything from this world. Expect no peace, no mercy, no joy, no happiness, no kindness, no charity, no love. In short, the Cathar message was simple and despairing: however you live your time on earth, no good can ever come of it.

Of course, holding to such ideas made everyday life rather difficult—so difficult in fact, that it was given to only a few, the so-called Perfects or *Bonshommes* as the French peasants called them ("Goodmen," though many were women), to live in true accordance with their beliefs. They did no paid labour, for any effort in this world would only support the Prince of Darkness—though they were apparently never slow to roll up their sleeves to help out someone in need. They drank neither wine nor milk; they ate no meat, fish, eggs, butter or cheese. They were, in other words, teetotal Vegans, avoiding all animal products, for animals were produced by sex, which was the Devil's own way of restocking his creation. Nor did they marry or, supposedly, ever indulge in lovemaking. They owned no possessions, living only from alms donated by their followers, and gave their entire lives over to travelling, preaching, praying and carrying out good works.

Those who were not Perfects and had to make their living in this world were either Listeners or, after a rite called the Baptism, became Believers. These appear to have been bound by no ritual obligations other than to salute the Perfects in an act of veneration called the *Melioramentum* (Improvement). The ceremony involved bowing to the *Bonhomme* and repeating the prayer: "Pray God to make a good Christian of me and bring me to a good end."

This heretical system of belief was supported by an elaborate theology. As far as we know, the Cathars were quite unaware of the role of Zarathustra's teaching in their system of belief. Instead it was the Christian Gospels that they re-read and reinterpreted in a radically new way. The Great Heresy was a Gnostic faith: higher ranks would be initiated into secret knowledge and hidden interpretations not available to ordinary folk. The spiritual gap between Believers and Perfects seems to have been bridged by a popular belief in metempsychosis—the transmigration of souls. Three hundred years later, Shakespeare knew that this doctrine had been brought to Europe by Pythagoras. ("What is the opinion of Pythagoras concerning wild fowl?" "That the soul of our grandam might haply inhabit a bird.") The Cathars may have inherited the idea from the ancient Greek mathematician, or perhaps from even further east. Or they may have been forced to develop it for themselves, since it was not given to everybody to be able to live a Perfect's life. The best an ordinary Believer could hope for was to be reborn as a *Bonhomme* next time round. To improve their chances, Believers could choose a moment for conversion, usually just before death, when by a ceremony called the *Consolamentum* (meaning, perhaps, consolation) they would be raised to the status of Perfects themselves. Thereafter— it is said but also disputed—they would accept no food and drink until death took them, a fast known as the *Endura*.

To read the accounts of the churchmen who fought against Catharism in the West and its many relatives in other parts of Europe is to be reminded that almost everything we know about the followers of the Great Heresy is drawn from the attacks of their enemies. Nevertheless, the reports of the Inquisition, like those of Jacques Fournier, the Bishop of Pamiers, who later became Pope, and whose papers are the basis for Le Roy Ladurie's *Montaillou,* seem to be careful transcriptions of the testimony of both accusers and the accused. The clerics thundered extravagantly against the heretics, but it is usually possible to distinguish accurate reportage from propaganda.

The fullest description of what the Great Heresy stood for was written, not in the French Midi, but further east, in the Balkans. The Bogomils, as the heretics there called themselves, were active earlier than in the West, and they continued to flourish right up to the conquest of the area for Islam by the Ottoman Sultan at the end of the fourteenth century. Throughout the time that they coexisted, much religious traffic flowed between the different branches of the heretical faith: a stream of books, missionaries and organisers came from the East to assist the Western brethren, and in return, many who were forced to flee the domains of the Popes of Rome found refuge under the rule of the Patriarchs of Constantinople. We can therefore be reasonably safe in applying to the refugees at Montségur what was written about their co-believers in Bulgaria, Serbia, Croatia, Bosnia, and even holy Byzantium itself, by the tenth-century Bulgarian priest Cosmas, in his *Sermon against the Heretics*:

> Outwardly, the heretics seem like sheep; they are gentle, humble, and silent; they do not speak vain words or laugh or behave in such a way as to distinguish themselves from the true Christians. But inside they are ravenous wolves . . .
>
> They are worse than demons, for demons are afraid of the cross of Christ and the images of the Lord. The heretics do not venerate icons but call them idols. They mock the relics of the saints and make fun of us when we prostrate ourselves before them . . .
>
> They say that miracles do not happen by the will of God but by the Devil, who performs them to seduce mankind . . .
>
> They claim that it was not God but the Devil who was the creator of the visible world . . .
>
> Holy Communion was not instituted by the command of God, and the Eucharist is not the body of Christ but simple bread like any other . . .
>
> They oppose priests, churches, all prayers except for the Lord's Prayer, and reject the Law of Moses and the Books of the Prophets, nor do they honour the Virgin Mary . . .

Lest his account be found too persuasive and lead the innocent and ignorant into being seduced by such ideas, Cosmas constantly repeats his warning not to take the piety and self-denial of the Cathar elders at face value. The heretics claim, he tells us, that "it is the Devil who seduces men into taking wives, eating meat, and drinking wine. They refuse all the joys of life not from pious abstinence as we Orthodox monks do, but because they claim that these acts are impure."

It is not just that these traitors against God held false and wicked beliefs. In the many diatribes against the heretics we are offered more than a hint of a major, though unspoken, complaint: that the Cathar Perfects offered better models of sanctity than priests consecrated by the Church. The priests could only respond by blackguarding the false believers' motives and by calling their saintly appearance into question. Because Perfects usually travelled in pairs of the same sex—for they included both men and women among their number—they must be guilty of "unnatural practices." And because, from the Western perspective, the main source of the heresy seemed to be Bulgaria, the heretics were often called Bulgars—*bougres* in French, thus buggers in English.

Of course the Church's own monks and nuns were also supposed to be totally celibate. The fact that only the heretics and not the inhabitants of monasteries and convents were stereotyped as homosexuals strongly suggests that the monks and nuns were well known for preferring heterosexual fornication. As indeed they were. *Massacre at Montségur* gives us Abbot Radulph of Coggeshall's grim story about the Archbishop of Rheims, who was strolling one day with some of his clergy outside the city. One canon, Gervais Tilbury, seeing a young girl walking by herself through a nearby vineyard, went up and propositioned her. The girl, "with modest and solemn mien, scarce daring to look at him," refused, on the grounds that "if I were to lose my virginity, my body would be corrupted on the instant, and I should be damned irremediably for all eternity." The canon, recognising that this was heretical talk, promptly denounced her to the archbishop. After a summary trial, the girl and her Cathar mentor were burnt at the stake. No questions were asked about the canon's act of sexual harassment.

Sexual laxity was not the only failing of which the Christian establishment could be, and frequently was, accused. After centuries of successful self-aggrandisement and self-enrichment, the Churches, both Catholic in the West and Orthodox in the East, had famously become sinks of iniquity and immorality. Matters had surely come to a pretty pass when Pope John XII was brought to trial in the tenth century for perjury, sacrilege, simony, adultery, incest and murder—and for having turned the Church of St. John Lateran into a brothel.

I hadn't actually intended to climb up to the citadel at Montségur. I just wanted to see the setting and pay my respects to the long dead martyrs who had perished there so horribly. But having come so close it now seemed a shame not even to try. I stepped on to the trail that led straight up the forested flanks of the *pog*. The rocks underfoot were dangerously slippery. Even where wooden stair-treads had been nailed to the track to make the climb less perilous, these were now covered in a layer of ice so lethally slick that I often had to grab hold of a branch to stop myself sliding off the path and plunging down the slope. At one point I decided that I must be crazy—no sane person would attempt the climb at this season and in such weather. But I had quickly to remind myself of the laughable absurdity of that thought. During the siege many hundreds had made the ascent in just this season: aged Perfects of around eighty years old, women, children, the sick and the wounded, soldiers burdened with the parts of the giant rock-throwing *trebuchet* machine, specially designed by the Bishop of Albi, no less, to batter down Montségur's fortress walls. One party of attackers even made the climb by night though it was said that at dawn, when they saw the route up which they had come, they were near to fainting with fright.

The summit still looks out over an ageless mountain scene. In every direction, ranges of white peaks fade into the distance and dissolve into a low grey sky. The isolation is complete. Five hundred or so Cathars and men-at-arms had inhabited the top of the *pog*, both in the fortress itself and in shacks and houses built against its walls or dug into the rock, clinging to the edge of the precipice like swallows' nests. Once the attackers had established themselves on the summit, all now had to cram themselves into the castle keep, a living space no more than some hundred feet by sixty. With the stench of sweat, excrement and decomposition constantly in their noses, the thundering of the wall-breaking rocks flung day and night without respite from the bishop's artillery always in their ears, this should have been a place of utter desperation.

And yet it was not. The siege of the castle had lasted from May through to February. Now the besiegers had a foothold on the summit. On the morning of the 1st of March, the sound of a trumpet from the ramparts announced that the garrison was seeking a parley with the enemy. Negotiations began at once. An agreement was quickly made. Four of the clauses were generous enough: a pardon for all past crimes, fighters to keep their weapons (as long as they confessed their errors), others to go free (ditto), the castle to go to the French crown (naturally). One condition was savage though predictable: those who did not recant were to be burnt. But the first clause of all was the most unexpected: there was to be a peaceful stand-off for fifteen days, during which neither side would attack the other, nor change their positions. The fight was over but nothing was to happen for two more weeks. It was to be a sort of holiday.

That the Montségur refugees should want to perpetuate what must have been the most miserable of living conditions is singular enough. That many should have used the time, as they did, to receive the *Consolamentum*, to convert from Believers to Perfects, in spite of the horrible sentence of death by burning that was the inevitable result, is even more striking. It bears witness to the extraordinary power of the Great Heresy and the self-evident sanctity of its devotees. And though many of the Cathar Believers were simple folk, many of the Perfects were intelligent and educated. The Great Heresy must have appealed to the head as well as to the heart.

Why would such a hopeless, life-denying faith, one that could see no good at all in any aspect of creation, convince so many people, not just here in the Midi, but in so many parts of Europe? What problem could only be solved by believing in a world created by the Power of Evil? The answer must surely be found in the conditions under which most people had to live. Their ultra-pessimistic heresy only makes sense if they were desperate people clinging to a despairing belief. "Continual fear and danger of violent death; and the life of man solitary, poor, nasty, brutish and short," was Hobbes's familiar rendering. Fear of plague and sickness, fear of childbirth, fear of drought, fear of crop failure and famine, fear of arbitrary injustice, of torture and execution, fear of war and the devastation it left in its wake. And the Church must have failed, in its wealth, arrogance, corruption, sinfulness and decadence, to offer any consolation worth the name. A world of which one could expect no good demanded an explanation. A kind, merciful and loving God could not possibly have been the author of such a cruel and frightful place, as the Church insisted He was. Only Satan could have created such a miserable existence.

It's tempting to see the mentality of early medieval Europeans as rather childlike, marked, like infants, by innocence, ignorance, irrationality, fatalism, thoughtless cruelty, extraordinary credulity and unquestioning acceptance of authority and of "the rich man in his castle, the poor man at his gate." By and large, it was enough for the illiterate masses that something had been written down in a book, or even spoken by a priest or *Bonhomme*, to make it certainly true.

There were, of course, exceptions. In *Montaillou* Le Roy Ladurie quotes one "larger than life" peasant, Raymond de l'Aire, who believed in none of the teachings of the Church and publicly claimed that Jesus Christ had been brought into this world "through fucking . . . in other words through the coitus of a man and a woman, just like all the rest of us." But then he was well known in his village to be a former madman and witch.

In general, a wide and deep intellectual fault separates the medieval mind-set from our own. The difference is not merely that these people lived so long ago. Go yet further back into the past, to Roman times, and we find people much like ourselves, with beliefs, attitudes and perceptions not so very different from our own. So why the change? What could have brought Europe to such a low ebb?

I think that, even though half a millennium had passed, it was the decline and fall of Rome which led, albeit indirectly, to the early medieval culture of despair.

The long-drawn-out collapse of the Roman Empire in the West wasn't just a matter of geopolitical rearrangement, a mere change of masters. It was a complete break with the past. To its citizens, and even to its slaves, the Roman Empire had been an economic system, a communications network, an ideological structure, and a cultural reference. All this, which had grown over centuries, disappeared in only a few generations.

What was more, the people's ancient links to the land were suddenly broken, disrupting a pattern of settlement that went back as far as anyone could remember. If current scholarship is correct, the populations of the European subcontinent had mostly remained rooted in their ancestral territories since the very beginnings of agriculture during the New Stone Age thousands of years before. Now, from the fourth century onwards, the world seemed to be on the move. Nobody knows exactly why. Perhaps climate change was responsible; perhaps improvements in the conditions of life in some quarters led to an explosion of population. Whatever the cause, it was as if part of humanity had suddenly grown up and for the first time was ready and eager to leave home and begin a new life in a new place. Those who already lived in that place must make room or move on in their turn.

The collapse of Rome, the greatest Western political and social institution of earlier times, ruling a quarter of all humanity, was accomplished by the incoming peoples who first sought refuge in the empire and, in so doing, destroyed it. The incomers arrived as uncivilised barbarians—that is to say they were societies cast in heroic mould, with no city life, no intellectual tradition and no belief in the possibilities of the progressive accumulation of knowledge. Unable therefore to pick up the march of progress from where the Romans had left off, they had to start afresh and build up a new civilisation from scratch. But each time order was reimposed, each time that it seemed some kind of new stability could be achieved, each time a ruler like Charlemagne tried to create a functioning state, yet more new peoples would arrive to destroy the fragile borders. The turbulent times lasted for almost a thousand years, from the fifth century, when a Germanic general deposed the last Western emperor, to the fifteenth, when the migration of the Turks was more or less over and the new nations of Europe had settled into their present positions.

In all but two cases, the Vikings whose sails first appeared over the northern horizon and the Arabs who erupted on their camels from the south, the threat came from the east, always the East—a dim consciousness of which seems to have remained at the back of the Central European mind right into the present. "What we can never forgive," a Czech dissident musician protested to me soon after his country's Velvet Revolution, "is that the Soviets made us part of The East, instead of The West, to which we properly belong." Not an uncommon feeling in the area, judging by the long Polish hatred of the Russians, the fear and loathing with which the Nazi rulers of the Reich regarded the peoples to their east, the suspicion with which many West German *Wessis* still regard their East German *Ossi* compatriots, not to mention the simmering conflict between the secular West and the Islamic East, perceived by American analyst Samuel Huntingdon as a "Clash of Civilizations."

The danger came from the East, but so did solace. The Great Heresy, the religious solution to the high anxiety of medieval Westerners, arrived from the same point of the compass as the cause. Yuri Stoyanov's *The Hidden Tradition in Europe,* an authoritative and scholarly account of the spread of the dualist idea, starting with Zarathustra's mission to the Persians, gives chapter and verse for the claim that Catharism's source was Eastern Europe, the Balkans and Byzantium.

In about 1170, he tells us, a Cathar "Pope," Nicetas, arrived from Constantinople to preside over a Grand Cathar Council at St. Félix de Caraman near Toulouse, attended by a "great multitude." The records of that meeting, which still exist, record five primal churches of the Great Heresy in the Balkans. A century later, the Dominican inquisitor Rainerius Sacchoni, who had himself been a Cathar Perfect for seventeen years, wrote that the mother churches of all Cathar communities were the *Ecclesia Bulgariae* (the Church of Bulgaria) and *Ecclesia Drugunthiae* (the Church of Drugunthia, in Macedonia or Thrace). All chroniclers agreed that the Great Heresy had infiltrated western Christendom through its southeastern marches.

It is hard to understand why so many people with so very different a background and culture from that of the Balkans, let alone of the Iranian world, clung so passionately to the teachings of a long dead Persian prophet—and how his philosophy gained such a grip that only torture, fire and death in a sea of blood could prise it away. Yet such events have found an echo even in our own times. Let us turn from the ruined ramparts of Montségur to the wrecked remains of another siege and another religious minority—eight centuries and a thousand miles away.

SIEGES, MURDERS, MAYHEM

Some city names are so familiar from newspaper headlines and so resounding with historical associations that one is bound to be disappointed when landing at the airport, only to find the same dirty tarmac, peeling buildings, littered walkways and sullen immigration officers as everywhere else. Sarajevo is like that. It's hard to know what to expect from the city that not only saw the First World War sparked off by the assassination of Archduke Franz Ferdinand, but which also, three-quarters of a century later, was subjected to the longest siege of modern European history, when, starting in 1992, a rebel Serbian army surrounded, shelled, mortared and bombed it for 1,395 days. Here was a modern parallel to the siege of Montségur. Landing in Bosnia not very long after the 1996 cease-fire, I learned what the reality of siege warfare looks and smells like. I also learned something unexpected about the Bosnian faith.

I hadn't come to explore the city. I wasn't one of the disaster tourists then flocking in to the Bosnian capital to view the destruction and to buy the "siege maps" on sale at every street kiosk, with their tasteful illustrations of artillery positions and exploding mortar bombs. I was there as a filmmaker in the entourage of Yusuf Islam, a Muslim convert who had once been a world-famous popular singer-songwriter. The Irish band U2 had given an international concert here soon after the end of the siege, to mark the city's return to the normal world. This time the excitement was even greater, for Yusuf's aim was to help reaffirm Bosnia's Islamic identity. The whole town was buzzing with pious expectation. We could see posters for the concert decorating nearly every lamp-post and traffic sign on the way to our hotel. Television cameras were everywhere, recording the great man's arrival in town. Recognition as Muslims was obviously very important for the Sarajevans.

But, in the event, they seemed a little taken aback by Yusuf. They weren't at all sure what to make of his performance. Yusuf believes that Islam frowns on instrumental music and secular lyrics. So he sang devotional songs *a cappella*—accompanied only by a group of drummers in *Mevlevi Sufi*, Whirling Dervish, costume, all tall conical hats and long white robes. The audience was rather mystified. I think they were expecting rock-and-roll. It seemed that the Bosnian idea of being a Muslim was different from Yusuf's—their religion is no purist faith. Indeed, Sarajevo's Muslims are inclusive, tolerant and relaxed. Not that this made their Orthodox Christian Serb attackers hate them any the less.

Sarajevo is such a pretty city, its architecture a mixture of Ottoman, Hapsburg baroque and sixties Titoist, spiked with minarets, its red-roofed houses clambering up the steep wooded slopes on either side of the Miljacka river. Its very prettiness, ordinariness and innocence made the destruction visited on it by modern weaponry even more horrific.

We were faced with it right away as we drove in from the airport. On the housing estates that had been behind rebel lines, every fourth home was now a pile of smashed masonry, pavements were blocked by incinerated cars. Everywhere sinister black-and-yellow wasp-striped plastic ribbon snaked around front yards and street edges, screaming "DANGER!—MINES!" in three languages.

Further into town, every building within sight was pocked with bullet- and shell-holes and ulcerated by shrapnel. Sometimes the entire corner of a construction had been torn off, leaving broken steel reinforcement rods sticking into the air and asbestos insulation weeping from the wound, like some frightful compound fracture. Sometimes a front wall had been stripped away, exposing the private interior to the public gaze like a Victorian doll's house. It was especially moving to see how, immediately beside the devastation, people still made every effort to live as if nothing had happened next door. The two great slab-sided town-centre tower blocks nicknamed "Momo and Uzeir," characters from popular Sarajevan jokes, had been punched right through as if by a giant fist. Above, below and on either side of the shell-holes and burned-out levels, flowered curtains dressed the windows of still-occupied apartments.

This was no scene of random destruction. The enemy had been carefully discriminating, though precisely what had sparked their aggression was often difficult to understand. That the Holiday Inn Hotel should have remained relatively unscathed was understandable in its cynicism: this was where the foreign journalists camped. On the other hand, the Oslobodjenje newspaper building, now reduced to a single cracked concrete finger pointing skyward out of a great mound of shattered masonry, was an obvious target. But why smash and ruin the multicoloured modernist old people's home that locals used to call Disneyland? Because the old are repositories of the national past? What was the offence of the children's music school which had been systematically trashed, the pupils' paintings torn up and scattered in the playground, the instruments savagely broken, the walls smeared with excrement? Because the young are the national future? And what of the little Jewish synagogue on the hillside, its interior burned and piled with burst sandbags, piss in the corners, the stone filigreed windows knocked out for sniper rifles to poke through?

On the giant city-centre entertainment and sports complex called the Skenderia, its elegantly curved walls now scarred and pitted, and surrounded, when I saw it, by parked SFOR (UN Stabilisation Force) armoured personnel carriers, high up above the entrance, flanked by shell-holes, someone had managed to inscribe in English the graffito: WHY?

I put the question to the teacher who was taking me round the music school. A short woman with greying hair, dressed in a green skirt, brown cardigan and "sensible" flat shoes—very ordinary-looking, nothing about her to betray the fact that she had been one of the heroines of the siege, who had taken displaced children into her home so that they could continue their lessons while enemy shells and mortars rained down all around.

"They have always hated us because we chose to be different," she said, simply.

"But surely, ethnically speaking, you are all of the same Slav stock?"

"Not at all. We Bosnians are a mixture of many peoples, most of whom were here before the Slavs arrived: Illyrians, Dalmatians, Huns, Avars, Alans. The Slavs—the Croats and Serbs—came later. And the Turks, too, of course. So in Bosnia it was always important for us to keep our own identity. We were never prepared to bow our heads to any foreign power. In the Middle Ages, when Serbs lay down under the feet of the emperor in Constantinople and became Orthodox Christians, and Croats sank to their knees before the Pope in Rome and became Catholics, we made our own Bosnian Bogomil Church. We were proud to be Bogomil."

I asked her what kind of church the Bogomils had made, but she wasn't sure. "Bogomil means lovers of God," was all she could tell me.

"Was it a Christian Church?"

"Not exactly."

Perhaps I was looking sceptical, for she immediately suggested that I go off to see for myself the remaining traces of the Bogomil period—the monuments sometimes known as "Bogomil gravestones." Thousands of them stand on Bosnian hillsides, particularly in the neighbourhood of Sarajevo. They come in different sizes, some quite huge. Many have no inscription or decoration. Those which do are utterly enigmatic, sometimes written in the antique Glagolitic (the original Cyrillic) alphabet, and often bearing symbols of different kinds: rosettes, swastikas, sunbursts, as well as scenes of hunting, feasting and dancing. One, in the Zemaljski Museum garden, has a distinctly Iranian look, carved with what seems to be the figure of a hunter or a warrior, wearing an unlikely short skirt over big boots, like a caricature of a 1960s fashion idol, and holding up a bow in one hand with the other raised towards a circle in the sky, perhaps representing the sun or the moon. There is nothing Christian about the stone, either Catholic or Orthodox. But neither does it tell the onlooker anything about the beliefs of whoever lies underneath.

It seemed odd to me that the Bosnians, once proud to be Bogomil, were now just as proud to be Muslim. I phrased the question as politely as I could.

"But during Ottoman times, you adopted the conqueror's religion—Islam."

The teacher shrugged her shoulders.

"After the Ottoman conquest, we still wanted to be distinct from the Croats and the Serbs. And now we had the possibility of Islam. You know, to be Bogomil must have been very lonely; there were no other Bogomil nations in the entire world. To become Muslim meant for us to connect with, to become part of, another great civilisation."

"But not a Christian one."

"Christian civilisation?" she asked with an ironic edge to her voice, and led me outside to where the school's own memorial to the siege of Sarajevo stood in a little triangular patch of grass in front of the building. Set in a glass case was the school's grand piano as the rebel Serbs had left it: smashed and burned, keys prised up, bent and twisted, great raw gashes in the lid, as if someone had tried to play it with an axe. On the front it bore a plaque with the caption in Bosnian: CIVILIZACIJA '92–'96 (Civilisation '92–'96).

Remembering my Sarajevo brush with the Bogomils sent me scurrying to the history books to discover what the Bosnian faith might have really been and how it came about that, of all the nations of Europe, only Bosnia had resisted the overwhelming forces of mainstream Christianity.

What I discovered is a story of centuries of grotesque black, Grand Guignol, history: a saga of battles, sieges, murders, mayhem, sudden death and toasts drunk by barbarian chieftains from the skulls of slain emperors and generals.

In the year 680, a nomadic pagan people of Hunnish and Iranian descent who called themselves Bulgars (probably meaning "mixed") were led by their Khan Asparuch to the borders of Byzantium and imposed such a humiliating defeat on the Roman Emperor Constantine IV—"The Bearded"—that they were officially allotted all of the formerly Byzantine lands north of the Balkan mountain range. So began the First Bulgarian Empire, that was to challenge and confront the Eastern Roman Empire, and all that it represented, for more than three hundred years.

Chroniclers and annalists are big on actions and events but very sparing of detail and description. Yet it is sometimes possible to read between the lines of their bare accounts and imagine how it must have been, say, on the day in 814 when the fearsome Khan Krum, after a whole year of preparation, led a huge army south from his territory in Thrace to besiege Constantinople. The battering-rams alone needed five thousand carts drawn by ten thousand oxen.

Defenders would have been rushing to their positions on the walls with their weapons and ammunition. In the innumerable churches, every available priest and monk would have been drafted into the prayer commando, begging God in loud voices to spare the sacred city from the pagans. Outside, beyond arrow range, Krum's army has flowed like a great black stain over the fields as far as the eye can see. Its technology doesn't run to siege engines or giant stone-throwers that can breach walls, nor to tunnelling under the defences. But Krum has defeated three Roman emperors in succession on the battlefield, and drunk wine from the silver-lined skull of Nicephorus, the last of them. If he succeeds in taking the city, nobody will be spared. It only takes a single traitor, perhaps a disaffected slave, a politician with a grievance, a heretic, or a Jew, to unlock a gate or put down a ladder, for all to be irretrievably lost.

Krum himself comes forward, recognisable from the standards carried by the guards at his side, followed by a group of priests dragging an animal—maybe a sheep. The Khan intends to sacrifice before the walls. He takes off his helmet and slips a priest's robe over his armour. For a moment he stands still, his arm raised high in the air. The watchers on the city walls see a sudden glint from his hand—the sun reflected on a polished metal knife-blade. Nothing moves except the sheep. And then suddenly, shockingly, unaccountably, the Khan collapses to the ground. Krum fell, it says in Leo Grammaticus's *Chronographia*, "as if slain by an invisible hand." Divine intervention had saved the sacred city from pagan conquest.

But what was the Bulgars' pagan faith? Was it they who brought the teachings of Zarathustra to south-east Europe? They were a religious nation, built many shrines and temples, and their "Sublime Khans" adopted the title "divine ruler chosen by God." One Khan's inscription reads: "The Bulgars rendered many favours to the Christians and the Christians forgot. But God sees all." It is not clear who this God was. Arabic authors described the Bulgars as "Magians" (i.e., Zoroastrians). Yuri Stoyanov writes that the closest parallel to the square-shaped, flat-topped Bulgar temples are the fire temples of Zoroastrian Persia.

Even if the Bulgars had indeed originally followed Zarathustra's teachings, by the ninth century the growing Bulgar state's religion had begun to seem out of date. What had once been the Roman Empire had now transformed itself into Christendom, with faith in Jesus and all that it implies as its unifying ideology. If the Bulgarian Empire was really to challenge Byzantium and become a true part of the European world, the Bulgars would have to abandon their ancestral religion and convert. But to which flavour of Christianity: Roman or Orthodox? Though the Church had not yet officially split in two, the gap between East and West had already by then become unbridgeable. The question of the age was from which side the Bulgar Khan should accept the new religion. Khan Boris had been negotiating with Louis the German, grandson of Charlemagne, over the exact line of demarcation between their realms—a border that now ran through Central Europe. The obvious next step was to accept Christianity from the Frankish ruler, making the Bulgarians vassals of the West. In Constantinople, the Emperor Michael III was horrified. The Bulgars had been enough of a threat to eastern Rome on their own. Allied with the

Franks they might be unstoppable. The crisis was urgent. Something had to be done.

At great risk, Michael pulled the East Roman army out of its engagement against the Arabs and dedicated it to a massive attack on the Bulgarian borders in the north. Earthquakes and a devastating plague of locusts, popularly ascribed to the intervention of the Lord, accompanied the assault. The combined efforts of God, nature and the emperor proved enough to change Boris's mind. In 864, he accepted baptism from Michael's Orthodox rather than Louis's Catholic missionaries—taking the Christian title Prince Michael, after his new godparent, and reneging on his agreement with the Frankish king. Bulgaria was from now on to be part of the Eastern Orthodox Christian world. The move did not go down well with the Prince Khan's own aristocracy. Only a vicious bloodletting, and the decimation of many a noble Bulgar family, secured the throne for the new disciple of the God of love and forgiveness.

How deep the conversion went is as difficult a question to answer as how Zoroastrian the Bulgars' original beliefs had been. We can only infer from occasional hints that their new Christianity was shallowly rooted and that underneath they still kept faith with Zarathustra's doctrine of the Two Powers. And if the court at Constantinople thought that the Bulgars had been brought to heel, they were to be disappointed. The Bulgars never abandoned their ambition of creating a single Balkan superstate. At the end of the ninth century, the Bulgarian ruler Symeon absorbed Serbia into his domains and declared himself "Emperor (Tsar) and Autocrat of the Romans and the Bulgars"—a title that was ratified by the Pope. Thirty years of unrelenting aggression brought him close to victory over the emperor in Constantinople.

By now it was becoming obvious to all that Bulgarian Christianity was not as orthodox, or even Orthodox, as might have been expected more than fifty years after accepting Holy Baptism. Thus in 922, when the Emperor Romanus Lecapenus urged his army on against Symeon's forces, they responded by vowing to die "on behalf of the Christians," suggesting that, at least in their eyes, the Bulgarian religion was something else. Not that Byzantine Christianity had rid itself entirely of pagan beliefs. Romanus Lecapenus finally achieved victory over Symeon in a distinctly unconventional way. According to a Byzantine chronicle known as *Theophanes Continuatus,* the emperor was approached by a soothsayer, who informed him that a certain statue in the city was Symeon's double. Lecapenus ordered that the statue's head be struck off, whereupon, four hundred miles away, Symeon promptly dropped dead.

It was to take another hundred years of bitter and bloody struggle between the two rival Balkan empires to settle the issue of which state would survive. In the end it was to be a Roman rather than a Bulgar victory. At the beginning of the eleventh century, a more than usually ruthless and savage emperor, Basil II, came to the throne in Constantinople and set out to end the conflict once and for all. He won his victory at Balathista on their common border, in what is now Macedonia, when a Byzantine force "yomped" over the mountains and took the Bulgarian army by surprise. To make his future intentions absolutely clear, he ordered that all fourteen thousand Bulgar prisoners be blinded—except for one in every hundred, who was left one eye to act as guide—and sent home. When Tsar Samuel saw his soldiers return defeated and mutilated, he collapsed and died within a few days. In 1018, the First Bulgarian Empire was no more. After three hundred and thirty-eight years, the Byzantine Empire once again controlled the entire Balkan Peninsula and Basil was called "The Bulgar Slayer."

But by incorporating the Bulgarians into his empire, the emperor had imported a headache for the Orthodox Church. At the time of the conquest, the Bulgarian state had been following its heterodox religion for over a hundred years. It was fifty years since Presbyter Cosmas had written his *Sermon against the Heretics,* damning their dualist beliefs, and claiming that the inventor of the cult had been a renegade pastor called Bogomil (lover of God)—the Slavic translation of the common Greek name Theophilus or Latin Amadeus—though this was more likely an invented explanation than a historic fact. But, however the heresy had begun, successive emperors and patriarchs of Constantinople would from now on have to make huge efforts if the venomous viper of spiritual error was to be suppressed.

At the turn of the twelfth century, the Emperor Alexius I Comnenus thought he had cut the head off the snake. Indeed, one of the best-known chroniclers of his reign, his own daughter Anna, wrote that the heresy was like "a serpent hidden in a crevice" that her father had "lured and brought out into the light by chanting mysterious incantations."

Alexius had heard that the heretics' most prominent preacher was a monk called Basil: Basil the Bogomil. If this man could be brought down it would grievously wound the heretics' cause. The emperor invited Basil to the palace in Constantinople, claiming personal interest in the Bogomil faith and requesting instruction in its doctrines. The emperor and his brother sent everyone out of the room and sat down to listen as the preacher explained at length what their conversion would involve and what they would be required to believe. At the end of the interview Alexius got up and, in a theatrical gesture fully worthy of his distant successor Stalin, drew back a curtain, behind which a secretary had taken down in writing every word of the heresiarch's self-incriminating speech.

Basil was burned to death in the year IIII. "The flames," Anna wrote, "as if deeply enraged against him, ate the impious man up, without any odour arising or even a fresh appearance of smoke, only one thin smoky line could be seen in the middle of the flames." This was "the crowning act of the Emperor's long labours and successes."

But in actual fact the Bogomils were not, and could never be, fully suppressed. The most that could be achieved was to squeeze them slowly and successively out of Greece, Macedonia, Serbia and Croatia, with all the bloody brute force which medieval religious warfare involved. Thousands, perhaps hundreds of thousands, perished in the process. But in spite of the best efforts of Christian kings and emperors, mountainous Bosnia and Herzegovina still managed to resist both Byzantium and the Pope and long remained a heretics' haven. Condemned all over Europe as the very heartland of the Great Heresy the territory continued for centuries to supply the rest of the subcontinent with heretical teachers and preachers, organisers and legislators.

It was the Ottoman conquest in the second half of the fifteenth century that finally brought an end to the rôle of the Balkans as Western Europe's principal source of dualist subversion. When the Turks took over, Bogomilism seems to have just slowly faded away. It is not known exactly how long the proscribed faith took to disappear, or even why it did so. The Ottomans were no religious bigots and though Islam was the state religion, they were happy to include Catholics, Eastern Orthodox, Jews, Zoroastrians and even pagans in their empire. Perhaps the Sarajevo teacher's explanation is as good as any other. In fact it is possible that the Great Heresy survived in the Balkans for much longer than is commonly thought. In *The Hidden Tradition in Europe*, Yuri Stoyanov quotes one source which claims that the last remaining Bogomil clan in Herzegovina converted to Islam in 1867, the very time when, far off in Germany, Nietzsche was discovering Zarathustra at university and preparing to transform his message for the modern age. The Great Heresy had managed to survive in the teeth of all the furious attempts to eradicate it.

"ASIA BEGINS AT THE LANDSTRASSE"

There still remains the mystery of what the Balkans and the French Midi had in common that made them so susceptible to the Great Heresy, Zarathustra's legacy. I was pondering this question as I walked around the outside of the *cité,* the old town, of Carcassonne, perched on an isolated bluff overlooking the River Aude, not so very far from Montségur.

Here are the finest early medieval fortifications in Europe, the innermost ring begun in the fifth century by King Euric of the Visigoths in the sort of "story-book" architectural style that inspired children's illustrations in Victorian times and Walt Disney's cartoons in our own day. As I battled against the freezing January wind trying to find the entrance through the magnificently crenellated ancient double walls, with their towers and turrets, their arches and arrow-slits, their bastions and barbican, I was strongly reminded of another castle built at a similar time but in a very different place and in a very different climate, far away in Dagestan by the Caucasus Mountains, which I had explored and filmed, years ago, for the same television series as had taken me to Samarkand.

Derbent castle on the Caspian shore was built in the fifth or sixth century by the Sassanid rulers of Persia to protect its lands against nomad raiders from the north. Its name comes from the Persian for "closed gate." But like Singapore's famous guns, it turned out to have been facing the wrong way for its last stand. It fell to the Arab conquerors of Persia, who attacked from the south in the eighth century. The newcomers left it be, except for carving an Islamic inscription over the main gateway in place of the original Sassanian dedication. The fortress still stands high above the city market-place, looking as impregnable today as it was fifteen hundred years ago.

Its likeness to this French medieval town had brought the memory rushing back. But I set the thought aside. The similarity of appearance between Carcassonne's and Derbent's fortifications must surely have been dictated by similarity of function. After all, how many ways can there be to erect a defensive wall around a town? And how could the Germanic Visigoths' building style have been influenced by a nation so far away in spirit as well as geography as Persia?

A light freezing rain started to fall. Having eventually found my way in through the city walls, I located a café in which to warm myself and sat down with a cup of coffee, pulling out my copy of *Massacre at Montségur* to pass the time. The book happened to fall open at a page describing the reception given by Pierre-Roger de Mirepoix, one of the knight-defenders of the citadel and a supporter of the heretic cause, to a group of assassins who had been sent out to murder a party of Papal inquisitors. According to the written testimony Pierre-Roger asked:

"Ah, traitor, where is Arnald's cup?"

"It is broken," Acermat replied. The "cup" was brother Arnald's skull.

"Why did you not bring me the pieces?" Pierre-Roger thundered. "I would have bound them together with a circlet of gold and drunk wine from this cup all the days of my life."

Drunk wine from the skull of his enemy? Wasn't that how the Bulgar Khan Krum had treated the Byzantine Emperor Nicephorus? This was no European Christian custom, but a pagan barbarian tradition from Central Asia. Could there really be some link after all between the heretical rulers of south-western France and the distant pagan, Zoroastrian, East? It was the Visigoths who had founded the first Germanic kingdoms in what had been Roman Septimania and who had built Carcassonne's first walls. I needed to explore more about who they were and where they had come from.

Prince Metternich, the nineteenth-century Austrian chancellor, once noted that "Asia begins at the Landstrasse," the main road east out of Vienna. Stand even today in any of the towns or cities of the lower Danube valley, north of the Balkan and south of the Carpathian mountain ranges—Bucharest perhaps—and you will often catch a glimpse of a different world. Something in the cast of a woman's face, something in a young boy's swagger, something about the shape of a pot, the cut of a peasant costume, the pattern on a rug, sometimes even a scent in the air, reminds you that this is where the East really begins, that the flatlands on which you stand extend ever onwards all the way to China.

The Eurasian Steppe stretches out some 2,500 miles from the Hungarian puszta, squeezing through the Iron Gate gorge of the Danube to the plains of Romania and Bulgaria, sweeping around the northern shores of the Black Sea, extending across southern Ukraine and Russia, narrowing between the Ural Mountains and the Caspian Sea and expanding again through Central Asia until it loses itself among the passes of the Altai Mountains of Chinese Turkestan. Beyond, through the Dzungarian Gap, the Eastern Steppe, higher, drier, bleaker and colder, extends all the way to Manchuria. The full length of the steppelands reaches from close to the

Mediterranean coast almost as far as the Pacific rim. It is one vast sea of grass, between 200 and 600 miles wide—though some of it today has been ploughed up and planted, particularly after Nikita Khrushchev's disastrous Virgin Lands programme of the 1950s.

Travel across the central portion of the steppe on the Trans-Siberian railway, as I once did long ago, and you journey for days on end seeing nothing but grass: a vista as uniform and flat as in the great plains of the American Midwest. Just sometimes the land gently rolls, rising and falling over anciently eroded bedrock; here a river crosses, trees sprouting from the water's edge, there a hill rears up in a landmark visible for tens of miles. In one place, a patch of swamp, in another a swathe of desert, in yet another, the tomb-mounds of long-dead nomads are the only feature visible to the horizon. Thus though marked, like the sea, by occasional ripples in the topography, the steppe appears, in the main, as limitless and featureless as the open ocean. Hardly anywhere does one see a human figure. Occasionally, perhaps twice a day, you might glimpse a single lonely figure driving a cart—whither and whence always a mystery. At the rare stops in small steppe towns, there is just time—maybe three and a half minutes—to jump off the train, run out of the station and look down the single main street beyond which the vista of grass extends to infinity before the carriage concierge, the fat lady, blows her whistle.

Even in the 1960s, parts of the steppe were still largely uninhabited, and untransformed by human interference. On my Trans-Siberian journey I was given a sleeping compartment, shared—surely not by chance—with an English-speaking schoolmaster. He was a small wiry man in a tweed jacket two sizes too large, of such exquisite discretion that he wore his Communist Party badge on the back, rather than the front, of his lapel. We didn't talk politics, but once while comparing the Soviet communist and British capitalist lifestyles, I asked him if he owned a car. He looked genuinely puzzled. "What use would it be? The next town to where I live is six hundred miles away."

I remember being rather saddened by the realisation that the Communists seemed to have succeeded in crushing an immemorial style of living. From more than a thousand years before the Romans until the twentieth century, this vast Eurasian steppe had supported wandering peoples, who lived in the portable tent dwellings we now call yurts, travelling huge distances on horseback, guiding their herds of sheep, goats, oxen, camels or horses from pasture to pasture in larger or smaller family or clan groups. Their animals supplied most of the nomads' needs: milk, meat, skins and wool for clothing and shelter—though they also raided and traded for what they could not produce themselves. Pasture was always limited, so no more than a few families would travel together, but in the winter, entire tribes might gather in one place in huge tent-cities.

In the thirteenth century, when Friar Willem van Ruysbroeck was sent on an intelligence mission to report on the Tatars who then ruled the steppe, he found that "They have divided among themselves Scythia, which stretches from the Danube as far as the rising of the sun. Each captain, according to whether he has more or fewer men under him, knows the limits of his pasturage and where to feed his flocks in winter, summer, spring and autumn, for in winter they come down to the warmer districts in the south, in summer they go up to the cooler places in the north." He found the experience unnerving: "When I came among them it seemed indeed to me as if I were entering into some other world . . . "

Ruysbroeck's Mongols were late eastern arrivals to the western steppe. From the very beginning it was part of the Iranian world, peopled by nomads speaking Iranian languages, following Iranian culture and influenced by Iranian religious ideas. In classical times it was the Iranian Scythians who sailed the steppe ocean, sometimes casting themselves ashore, as when unfavourable conditions in the interior sent them on plundering raids into village lands. Anyone born, as I was, under the sign of Sagittarius, will recognise how they appeared to their terrified ancient Greek neighbours: horse archers so born and bred to the saddle that it was impossible to tell where man ended and steed began. But in the main, relations between Scythians and Greeks were collaborative rather than combative. Scythians grew wheat for the Greek cities and thousands of Greek craft-workers made a living by creating gaudy trinkets for the barbarian trade.

Looking for similarities with the Visigothic region, I turned to the Greek historian Herodotus who, in the fifth century BC, gave us our first, highly coloured, picture of the Scythians. Many details entertained me, like the funeral rites at which mourners gathered to inhale the smoke of burning hemp seeds. Whereupon "the Scythians in their delight . . . howl loudly." Herodotus wrote about the Amazons, the women warriors who were believed to cut off one breast (*a-mazon* means "without a breast" in Greek) the better to bend the bow. His Greek readers, who had created a society in which women were given no public place at all, must have been outraged by the speech Herodotus put into the mouth of an Amazon woman: "We cannot live with your women. For we and they have not the same customs. We shoot the bow and the javelin and ride horses, but, for women's tasks, we know them not. Your women do none of these things we have spoken of. They stay in their wagons and do women's work and never go hunting or anywhere else. We cannot get on with women like these." In the nineteenth century, when burial sites of the steppe nomads were first scientifically excavated, many of those interred with full military honours, their bows and swords and shields laid around them, were found to have been women.

Herodotus ascribed the Scythians' military invincibility to their way of life, explaining "how no invader who comes against them can ever escape and how none can catch them if they do not wish to be caught. For this people has no cities or settled forts: they carry their houses with them and shoot with bows from horseback; they live off herds of cattle, not from tillage, and their dwellings are on their wagons."

There was one kind of invader, however, that the Scythians couldn't resist: another nomad nation. For, from about Herodotus's own time onwards, another, related, Iranian people, speaking a related Iranian language, began to take over rule of the steppe. By the end of the first century, they had largely displaced and absorbed the Scythians. We give their many tribes, clans and septs the collective name Sarmatians.

The Sarmatians also lived and fought on horseback, men and women together, but they had new, more powerful weapons: long spears and the Sarmatian long sword, with gold-laced wooden hilt and pommel of semi-precious stone. They wore armour: iron helmets and chainmail. They used—and perhaps invented—both the spur and the stirrup, which allow a mounted warrior to charge and then remain in the saddle after the clash with his opponent. They bred heavier horses, able to carry a greater weight than the light Scythian ponies. Culturally they seem closer to their settled Iranian kinfolk in Persia than to their Scythian predecessors on the steppe, like provincials who look to the big city for their ideas. Like the Persians, they used fire in their religious rituals. It is not recorded how Zoroastrian their beliefs were, but their territory did include areas where Zarathustra's teachings were much heard, particularly in the form espoused by the Manichaean followers of the third-century preacher Mani.

To learn more about the Sarmatians, I turned to Neal Ascherson's inspiring book *The Black Sea*. And there I found the connection that I was searching for between Occitania and the Orient—an even stronger link than I had expected.

For Ascherson explains that much of what we think of as typical of the Middle Ages originated with the Sarmatians—"a taste for heavy, ornate forms and for metalwork encrusted with coloured enamel and semi-precious stones—the style that in the nineteenth century was misleadingly called 'Gothic' " as well as "the class of mailed horsemen who hold land and whose manner of living is called 'chivalrous.' "

We know it as Gothic rather than Sarmatian because the Sarmatians didn't have the grasslands to themselves for long. Early in the second century of our era, a Scandinavian people who called themselves Goths launched themselves on to the grass sea from the north-east after making their first landfall on the Baltic coast. Expanding eastward, by the fourth century they controlled a huge swathe of territory, and its residents, all the way from the Baltic to the Black Sea.

The Sarmatians presented a more refractory foe. The Goths soon found that they could only hold their own against the rulers of the steppes by giving up their settled ways and adopting the same horseback lifestyle and the same heavy weaponry as their competitors. In the process they adopted much of the Sarmatian decorative style. Over time the two peoples became intermingled, particularly at the edges of their respective territories, where they all went by the name Goth irrespective of their actual stem. Thus the familiar "Gothic" style and the medieval knight on horseback are the results of that mix of Germanic power with Iranian tradition. The name "Gothic" stuck, because it was through these Goths that the Iranian culture of the steppe was transmitted to the nations of the West.

A tempest in the far east of the grass ocean had sent waves of Huns, a Turkic-speaking people from the eastern steppe, whose harsher conditions had bred a leaner and meaner nomadic nation, rushing westward, sweeping every opposition aside. In the fourth century, they came face to face with the Goths and Sarmatians at the western end of the steppe, crushing their resistance and sending them fleeing into Roman territory. At first the German-Iranians were granted sanctuary within the Roman border on the Rhine, but soon the overbearing actions of the emperor drove them to revolt and they set off on a rampage across the weakened Mediterranean superstate. It was the beginning of the end for western Rome. As the Empire declined and fell, the mix of Iranian and Germanic peoples travelled the subcontinent, winning and losing territory together in great tribal groups which, by the sixth century, had brought the steppe culture right into the heart of Western Europe.

In *The Black Sea* Ascherson notes the path of one Sarmatian tribe called the Alans through today's Austria and the Rhineland, then, joined by allies, through what is now France, Spain and Portugal, into Spanish

Galicia. Others travelled across the north of France, "in some cases putting down roots and forming small Alan kingdoms of their own. Over thirty French place-names, including that of the town of Alançon, allude to their presence, and there is some evidence of a long-lasting Sarmatian settlement near Orléans."

There was little resistance. Europe had lost about a third of its population since the Roman heyday. Huge tracts supported fewer than twenty people per square mile, about the same as the Amazon rain forest today. Much of the land had become wilderness and was available for settlement. The nations on the move were small. When a combined Sarmatian-Vandal confederation crossed the Straits of Gibraltar on their way to set up a kingdom in North Africa, their King Gaiseric had them counted, to requisition the necessary shipping. The total of men, women and children and slaves in this "nation" came to 80,000.

The Visigoths and Ostrogoths (western and eastern divisions of the original Gothic nation), as well as the Alans, now controlled extensive territories in Europe through their steppe-bred knights in armour, their steppe-developed military technology, and their steppe-inspired realisation that it was just a short jump from herding livestock to herding peasants. In fact peasants are easier—they stay put and don't have to be moved constantly on to pastures new. The new style of political control became what we now recognise as feudalism—a mounted and heavily armed nobility managing a sedentary peasant flock. The Visigoths took Spain for a kingdom, the Ostrogoths northern Italy, and the Alans ruled islands in between.

If Iranian influence helps account for the growth of Gothic civilisation and feudal politics in Western Europe—as well as a tendency to dualist, Zarathustrian, theology—so it does in the East too, among not only the Bulgars, thought to be of mixed Hun and Sarmatian descent, but also of the Slavic peoples who appear on the pages of history from the sixth century onwards. At their first appearance in the annals of the chroniclers, the names Serb and Croat belonged to Sarmatian war bands emerging from the western end of the steppe. The Polish nobility, the *szlachta*, once prided itself on its Sarmatian ancestry—as opposed to the reviled Slav peasantry. Even after the nobility was abolished in the new Polish Republic of 1921, the *szlachta* maintained its self-consciously separate identity. In his *Europe: A History*, Norman Davies relates that as late as the 1950s "sociologists found collective farmers in Mazovia who shunned their 'peasant' neighbours, dressed differently, spoke differently and observed complex betrothal customs to prevent intermarriage. In 1990, when Poland's Communist regime collapsed, there were still young Poles who would wear a signet ring with a coat of arms, just to show who they were." Neal Ascherson even proposes (tongue in cheek, I presume) that anti-communist leader Lech Wałęsa's political popularity may have had something to do with the "Sarmatism" of his moustachios.

Wherever the new masters settled, in today's France, Spain, Eastern Europe and the Balkans, the new "Gothic" way of life took over, with its heavy cavalry and mounted aristocracy, its social division between rulers and ruled, its music, poetry, art and craftsmanship, as well as its special status for women. In Iberia, southern France and the Slav lands, unlike almost everywhere else, wife and family were not subordinate to the husband, and women kept their maiden names after marriage.

Of course many ethnic nationalists, particularly among the south Slavs—Croats and Serbs—dispute the Iranian connection. And even if a cultural inheritance from the East could be definitively demonstrated, that wouldn't necessarily prove that the Great Heresy entered Europe with the Sarmatians. However, there is one indisputable fact that does suggest a connection. In all Slav languages much of the religious vocabulary—even the word for God Himself: *Bog,* and for paradise: *Raj*—is borrowed from the Iranian. And the twelfth-century chronicler Hetmold of Lübeck wrote that the Slavs of what is now north Germany believed in a good God and a bad God—clear evidence for the mark of Zoroaster.

This suggests it was no accident that the Occitanian region of southern France had been both a centre of the Great Heresy as well as the showpiece of Gothic civilisation, for both had derived from the same source. No accident that the heresy was concentrated in the Slavic Balkans and the Gothic Mediterranean, for here the influence of the steppe remained closest to the surface. No accident that aristocrats had been among the foremost proponents of heresy, that women as often as men were among the teachers and the preachers of dualism, and that noble ladies had played as prominent a rôle as their menfolk, for that was the Sarmatian way.

Looking out across the mountains from the Cathars' final isolated redoubt at Montségur, I wonder what the legacy of this period of history might be. The Franks, a sterner and soberer Germanic people, had come in from the north-east to create a new French kingdom. Their crusade against the Cathars that brought the Great Heresy to an end in Western Europe was as much a matter of power politics as of religion. By adding the heretic south to its national territory, France made itself the most strategically powerful state in Europe, connecting the Mediterranean, the Atlantic and the North Sea. For perhaps another hundred years, individual villages, particularly those high in the mountains, far from prying priests, still sheltered numbers of heretical believers, while occasional brave Perfects still travelled the high passes bringing consolation to their flocks. The very last known Cathar Perfect, Bélibaste, was burned at Villerouge-Termenès in 1321.

Occitan culture, however, did not disappear. The heresy may have vanished, but the culture that supported it was too strong, spreading throughout the newly enlarged kingdom to become part of the French way of life. I like to think that many of the familiar features of French culture have roots in the Iranian nomad inheritance of the Midi: French elegance and style, French poetry and literature, even French gallantry towards women. But what of Zarathustra's teachings? Though the doctrine of the two powers may have become obscured behind other, newer, interpretations of the world, I think it still possible to see it reflected even today in the French philosophical tradition, still so influential, which began with the dualist philosopher René Descartes.

Of course, finding a solution to the mystery of Cathar origins simply pushes back further in time the obvious follow-up: how did Zarathustra's belief in two powers battling for control of this world become transformed into the life-denying, other-worldly faith of the Albigensians? One hint to a possible answer lies in the fact that many of the Church writings both against the Cathars and the Bogomils accuse them not just of heresy but of Manichaeism, which seems the worst possible insult the writer can think of. Modern scholars dismiss the accusation as empty invective since the Middle Eastern Manichaeans weren't Christians at all. Yet on close examination there seems more similarity between the two faiths than can be ascribed to chance, even though the Cathars prayed to Jesus Christ the Son of God and the Manichaeans followed Mani, the Prophet of Light.

4

The Religion of Light

Not far off the road that runs south across the high desert of Iran from the oasis city of Yazd to the perfumed gardens of Shiraz—famous as the home of the great medieval poets Hafez and Sa'adi, whose verse claiming the unity of all humankind is inscribed on the wall of the United Nations Center in New York—there straggles a rugged high wall of fawn limestone cliffs, liberally decorated with carvings. Modern Iranians call it Naqsh-e-Rustam, the Picture of Rustam, a legendary popular Iranian hero who was reputedly so strong that no feat was beyond him. It is a misnomer, the result of the great amnesia about their ancient past that settled over the Iranians after being conquered by the Arab forces of Islam. In fact this place was the dynastic burial site, from 550 BC or so onwards, of the first, and arguably the greatest, dynasty of Iranian kings, the Achaemenids. Here, overlooking the long-gone city of Istakhr, where once their ancestors held the priesthood of the water goddess Anahita, the tombs of four of the Shahs of ancient Persia, Darius, Xerxes, Artaxerxes and Darius II, were cut out of the living rock high up on the cliff-face. Their remains were laid behind bas-relief renderings of the façades of their palaces, so carefully executed that we can still see exactly how the great kings' residences must have looked before time reduced them to noble ruins. On the roofs we see the kings themselves praying.

In front of the tombs stands a mysterious short tower, built of limestone blocks, square in ground plan, blind windows in the sides, a ruined staircase leading up to a door at the front, and a totally empty interior. Though much debate and dissension about its purpose has heated the academic air over the years, most scholars now believe it to be an Achaemenid

Zoroastrian temple, the only one in such a perfect state of preservation. Modern Iranians call it the Ka'abah-ye-Zardosht (Zoroaster's *Ka'abah* or cube) after the Ka'abah in Mecca, Islam's sacred focal point. That it stands here, so close to the tombs of the great Kings of Kings suggests that Naqsh-e-Rustam was no mere burial site, unvisited except at times of mourning, but a living ceremonial centre, where great crowds would gather on festive days to watch the Shahanshah perform his devotions to Ahura Mazda, Zarathustra's one and indivisible God.

This spot still wove such a spell on the psyche of later wearers of the Iranian imperial mantle—the Sassanians, who ruled here from the third century—that, like children running to tell their parents all about their latest exploits, they felt compelled to add their own more coarsely sculptured panels below the ancient tombs, detailing their glories and victories. More than seventeen hundred years later, these stone billboards of spin still proclaim the Sassanian Shahanshahs' famous victories. Propaganda was intended to last in those days.

The panel that I had come all this way to see was carefully situated below and between the tombs of Xerxes and Darius the Great. It is a celebration of one of the high points of Persian history, the subjection of two Roman emperors by the second Sassanian Shah, Shapur by name, who died in 272. The Persian monarch sits on his horse, wearing the absurd headgear that the Greeks called the *Korymbos* (inflorescence), seemingly a mark of Sassanian royalty—long hair wrapped in a large silk-gauze globe, looking like a party balloon balanced on top of the head. The thin material of his trousers ripples in the breeze, the toes of his visible foot are curiously turned down like a ballerina on point—this was before the invention of the stirrup. His left hand grasps the hilt of his sheathed sword, his right stretches out to grip the arm of one of the two men in Roman military dress before him—in skirts, actually. The Shah is pulling on the man's sleeve and the Roman's hand has disappeared up it, like that of a small child being dragged along by an impatient parent. This, the guidebook says, is how the Sassanians symbolised submission.

More obviously defeated is the second Roman character who is pictured kneeling in front of the King of Kings' horse, his arms stretched out in supplication. Behind the Shah is a long inscription in an old form of the Persian language, detailing Shapur's royal ancestry and his tremendous victory over the superpower, the Great Satan, in the third-century equivalent of the 1979 Iran hostage crisis. The standing figure is Valerian, Emperor of Rome, defeated in the year 260 by Shapur at the Battle of Edessa (today's

Urfa, near Turkey's Syrian border), who died in Iranian chains. The kneeling Roman is the Emperor Philip the Arabian, who came to sue for peace and to ransom the captured legionaries for the sum of half a million drachmas in gold. They were worth it because, technically more skilled than the Iranians, they had been put to work, like the Hebrews by Pharaoh, on a new city named after the king himself, Bi-Shapur, and on the great dam that is still today called Band-e-Qaysar (Caesar's dam).

Shapur's stunning victory was worthy of its rocky immortality. But that is not all there is to the relief. Someone else intrudes into the scene, a figure added some way behind the mounted king almost like an afterthought, only his top half visible, as if looking out of a nearby window. It really does look like a later addition. What we see is the image of a beardless man, a Zoroastrian priest's hat fitted over his head, the hair that falls below it done up in ringlets, a rope of beads around his neck, his right hand held up, the index finger—his "praying finger," the guidebook says—crooked in a gesture of religious admonition. This is Kartir or Kerder, Zoroastrian chief priest, *Mobed-e-mobedan* (Priest of Priests) of three Sassanian rulers.

He is the only non-royal whose personal image and personal boasts appear on the rock reliefs of the Sassanian Shahs, suggesting the key rôle that he and the religion he served played in manipulating the identity and image of the reborn Persian state. He claims to have restored—we might guess reinvented—the ancestral Persian religion after a six-hundred-year eclipse under the Macedonian successors of Alexander the Great and the dynasty of barbarian Parthians who followed them. Zoroastrian tradition has it that Alexander killed all the priests and burned the sacred books. Though another priest, Tansar or Tosar, is credited with having collected and edited together what remained, it was Kartir's ambition and ruthlessness that were largely responsible for putting the faith of Zarathustra back centre-stage in Iran and, in the process, turning it, apparently for the first time, into an intolerant orthodoxy. And it was he who, in the year 276 or 277, plotted the downfall and finally achieved the death of the last great prophet of antiquity, Mani or Manes, the figure who came closest to turning Zarathustra's vision into a true world-faith.

Kartir probably wasn't actually present to witness Shapur's great victory over Rome, while Mani very likely was, for a later Arab historian claimed that he was in Shapur's train at the time of the battle. Though he is neither pictured nor mentioned by name, the story of Mani begins on this panel at Naqsh-e-Rustam, with the monarch who welcomed his mission,

Shapur, and ends, just round the corner, in another frame, with the one who had him destroyed, Bahram. The priest Kartir appears in both.

There can hardly be a greater contrast between this hot and dusty roadside rock-face on the margin of the Iranian plateau and the high snowy mountains of the south of France, yet this is where any attempt to trace the Cathar legacy of Europe back to its inspiration must inevitably lead. Time and again, as you read the Church's denunciations of the Cathar heretics, you see them condemned as Manichaeans, followers of Mani. Any theology which included Zarathustra's message, that the universe was torn between the powers of good and of evil, was labelled Manichaeism (just as the name Manichaean is still applied today to any highly polarised view). In fact, almost all the dualist sects and cults that sprouted so prolifically from European soil at the start of the last millennium were vilified under that name. Less than a hundred years ago, in 1913, an article about medieval heresy in the *Journal of the Royal Asiatic Society* claimed that all of Southern Europe was "parcelled out into Manichaean dioceses whose bishops paid allegiance to a Manichaean pope seated in Bulgaria." Sir Steven Runciman, arguably the greatest twentieth-century British historian of the period, explored the link between the religion of Mani and European heresy in his *The Medieval Manichee.* "In the end it was stamped out," he wrote of Manichaeism. "But the alarm that it caused was proved by the horror with which the word 'Manichaean' came to be regarded. In future the average orthodox Christian, when faced with any sign of dualism, would cry out 'Manichaean,' and everyone would know that here was rank heresy, and the authorities be seriously disquieted and take action."

For the medievals themselves this was really no more than a convenient shorthand, a *façon de parler.* The Bogomils, Cathars, Albigensians and others believed themselves to be true Christians, the only ones. Nothing they said or wrote suggests that they honoured Manichaeism or had even heard of anyone called Mani. Yet it's impossible to believe that there was really no connection at all between the medieval heresy and Mani's version of Zarathustra's message. In spite of the Christian heretics' dedication to Jesus of Nazareth, so many particulars of Cathar belief and organisation were similar, even identical, to those of the Manichaeans. But by what process could Mani's religious beliefs have reached Europe? Where and how could the transmission have taken place? Much spiritual traffic was recorded—and condemned by the Church—between the Balkans and the West but neither from Mani's time nor later do we know of any protest by the religious establishment against dualist preachers from Iran or the Middle East contaminating the European religious scene. It is easy enough to write vaguely of Iranian influence in Bosnia and the French Midi, much harder to specify the point of contact.

To me, Mani first became more than just a name when I came across the Lebanese novelist Amin Maalouf's beautiful book *The Gardens of Light*, which turned out to be an account, in the style of a fiction, of what is known about Mani's life: "He is said to have been born in the year 527, as calculated by the astronomers of Babel, on the eighth day of the month of Nisan—the year 216 of the Christian era, 14th April, a Sunday. In Ctesiphon, Artabanus, the last of the Parthian sovereigns, sat enthroned, and Rome was suffering under the barbarous emperor Caracalla."

Maalouf immediately plunges us back into the strange world of the third century, a world hesitating, in the West between the classical age of Rome and the Christianity of the Dark and Middle ages, in the East between the bright Hellenism of Alexander's successors and the sudden reimposition and long-drawn-out decay of a revised Zoroastrianism—an interregnum that would last until Muslim conquest gave the exhausted East a brilliant fresh start in the seventh century.

With Maalouf's book in my pocket, I was pondering what it must have been like to inhabit this historical no man's land, as I and my travelling companions drove down the shoulders of the Zagros Mountains from the high Iranian plateau, with its great monuments like Naqsh-e-Rustam, towards the wide, hot and marshy Mesopotamian plain. It happened by chance that we were making the last part of the journey by night. This is oil country and our descent was turned into an awesome *son et lumière* by the gigantic gas flares whose flickering tongues sprang roaring from the ground on all sides and licked the sky, painting the entire vault above us a quivering and diabolical red. The road seemed to quiver and squirm in front of our eyes. At times the driver was so distracted and misled by the shifting flames as to be unsure in which direction to steer.

This anxious disorientation provided a perfect accompaniment to the historical change which is the setting for Maalouf's book, from the high certainties of the ancient Persian world to the low confusions of a new age of religious indecision—from assured heaven to possible hell. Living in times that have lost their cultural momentum is not easy. The force of tradition withers and now any individual's conception of truth is accounted as valid as any other's. Received wisdom explodes into a myriad of atomised beliefs. "When people stop believing in Christ," said G. K. Chesterton, "they don't believe in nothing. They'll believe in anything."

Like the nightscape around us now, sprouting random bursts of illumination on all sides, the world into which Mani was born, the world of Maalouf's *Gardens of Light,* is one of a kaleidoscope of cults, sects and schisms, each man his own prophet—for here in the East they are almost always men—and each with his own personal divine revelation. In his Book of Heresies, Philastrius, Bishop of Brixia in the fourth century, listed twenty-eight Jewish, and one hundred and eighty Christian heresies, from the Antitactes, the Basilides, Cainites, Docetists and Ebionites, through the Marcionites, the Naassenes, the Ophites, Peratae and Sethians, all the way to the Valentinians. And these were merely the groups who professed eccentric versions of already established faiths, which is why we know their names. Those who constructed their spiritual fantasies out of whole new cloth were beyond the orthodox believers' attacks and are mostly forgotten by history.

Third-century Mesopotamians inhabited a very strange time indeed, one in which a grasp on reality seems to have totally slipped. They looked out on the world and where we see reality, they—like the Hindu and Buddhist sages of India—saw only illusion and confusion. To their way of thinking, the mass of ignorant humanity is utterly deceived in accepting the logic of rationality and the evidence of its senses. A glimpse of the underlying true nature of things is granted to only a select few by the divine powers. This glimpse was the Gnosis, the Knowledge, and those to whom it had been granted were Gnostics.

Being divinely revealed, the Gnosis didn't have to make sense, or even be consistent. At times it seems as if all that was necessary for spiritual salvation in this looking-glass world was to be able, like Alice's Red Queen, to believe six impossible things before breakfast. The great St. Augustine, who had toyed with Manichaeism in his youth, ultimately rejected its doctrines at least partly because they were, of all things, too unscientific. " . . . I was commanded to believe; and yet it corresponded not with reasonings obtained by calculations, and by my own observations, but was quite contrary."

Exploring the world of the Gnostics is a bewildering exercise. A kind of intellectual vertigo is a real occupational hazard. All those names, all those preposterous claims. One is quickly overpowered by a desire to find some kind of objective reality, some concrete fact that one can hang on to. This is what had brought me to Naqsh-e-Rustam in the first place, to the rock-reliefs that celebrated the success of Kartir, Zoroastrian priest-in-chief of the Sassanids, in stamping out all rival religions. Here I could find the image of someone real, someone who had actually met Mani and his disciples and disputed with them, and somebody who had left a permanent record of his actions, self-serving though his account certainly was. In one of the incised inscriptions on the site, in which Kartir rather than the King boasts of his achievements, he claims to have defeated Ahriman, Zarathustra's force of evil, turned the abodes of evil demons "into thrones and seats of God," and chastised Jews, Christians, Manichaeans, Mandeans, Buddhists and Brahmins.

Kartir may have been exaggerating his impact on other religions, for Arian Christianity kept its place in Sassanian Iran, and the Babylonian Talmud, the compendium of Jewish law and lore compiled during Sassanian times, records little conflict between Jews and the Persian ruling powers. Just about the only bone of contention between the two monotheisms was the use of fire, since both give flames special status. For Zoroastrians, fire symbolises divinity. Jews light candles on many religious occasions, to mark the onset of Sabbath and Holy Days—as many as eight candles are lit at once during *Chanukkah*, the Festival of Lights. That this use of fire was a cause of dispute is revealed by the Talmud's discussion of whether one is permitted "to move a *Chanukkah* lamp on the Sabbath on account of the *Habbars*." (*Habbars*, here meaning Zoroastrian priests and close to the derogatory modern *gabr* used by Iranian Muslims, is Aramaic for "unbeliever" and related to the modern Arabic *kafir*.) A medieval rabbi wrote that "during the reign of the Persians, the *Habbars* would make the rounds of all Jewish households, where they would extinguish the lamps and gather the embers . . . " confirming a Talmudic anecdote in which a Babylonian rabbi was lying sick in bed, when a *Habbar* broke in to confiscate his bedside lamp. "Merciful God," the rabbi protested, "would it not be better to live under Your shadow or even in the shadow of the Children of Esau [the Romans]?"

Deviant Zoroastrians were, however, a more vulnerable target. They were forbidden to spread their beliefs: "Heretics and apostates who were within the Magian community were spared for the religion of the worshippers of Mazda and the rites of God," Kartir claims, "but not for propaganda. I chastised and upbraided them and improved them."

As I was trying to photograph this text, a shadow suddenly and annoyingly fell across it. Mani would have interpreted it as a sign of the eternal cosmic battle—evil darkness conquering sacred light. In fact it was only an indication that the hours were slipping by and yet another group of Iranian visitors had arrived at the site.

The best time to see the monuments is early in the morning, when the sun's rays glance sideways off the cliff-face and bring out the variations in depth of the bas-reliefs to their best advantage. But though it was not yet ten o'clock, large families of Iranian tourists were already gathering in great parties with their unruly children—the men in holiday clothes, white shirts and grey trousers, the women of course in *chadors*—gazing up at the tombs of their ancestral monarchs and having their picture taken while standing smirking and embarrassed in front of the rock carvings. In any other country, local tourists would be nothing out of the ordinary. In the Iran of the Islamic Revolution, however, it surprised me to find how keen today's Iranians are to relate to their ancient pre-Muslim past, their time of *jahiliyya*, religious ignorance.

Comparing the sculptured Sassanid nobility with the look of their descendants of today, conveniently posed as they were for the camera, made me look more closely at the faces portrayed on the rock: Kartir's particularly, since I don't much like the sound of him from what I have read. I don't know whether the third-century sculptors of these triumphal scenes were aiming for true likenesses of their subjects—the stylised treatment of the profiles suggests perhaps not. But there is something about Kartir's sour mouth with its downturned corners that seems truthful enough. Here is the image of a man with no observable sense of humour whatsoever.

This priest-in-chief belonged to a period when a new synthesis of politics and religion was being assembled, when emperors and kings were discovering that insistence on religious conformity was a powerful tool of statecraft. Looking at his grim visage, it occurred to me that what is being celebrated here is the invention of the thought police. This is the time when—in most of the world west of India—the power of orthodoxy begins its Thousand-year Reich, with its insistence that those who refuse to believe or act in accordance with what the ruling powers demand, must be compelled to do so.

It would have been a novel idea in the third century. Oriental paganism had always been an eclectic, pick-and-mix affair. The Romans of classical times cared little about correct doctrine either—citizens might think what they liked, as long as they made sacrifice to the emperor. And though the Jewish prophets, for example, had insisted that the troubles of the Hebrew nation were the result of disobedience to God, it was again actions rather than thoughts which were being judged. The Mosaic religion had never been greatly concerned with what went on in people's minds. What Jewish orthodoxy demanded—and still demands—was correct behaviour, rather than correct thoughts: circumcise male children, keep the dietary laws, attend the Synagogue and do no work on the Saturday Sabbath. This is orthopraxy rather than orthodoxy. But in the third century, times were changing both in the West and in the East; everybody was now suddenly supposed not only to behave but also to think in the same way. Kartir, the orthodox Zoroastrian priest of Sassanid Iran and his supporting Magi, the Persian hereditary priestly tribe, were among the beneficiaries. Mani and his Religion of Light were among the first victims.

What was it then that Mani taught, that was so abhorrent to the Magian clergy? We won't find any evidence of it here on the rocky cliffside. But though Manichaeism was soon wiped out in its homeland and further west, it did not finally disappear completely in its distant diaspora until over fourteen hundred years later. As a result, we know much more about Mani's message than most other extinct faiths.

The contemporary but now long-vanished religions of Marduk and Asshur, of Baal and Ashtorath, violently execrated in the Old Testament, remain largely mysterious, but visit any scholarly library and you will find row upon row of books about Mani and Manichaeism. Mani's teaching is well attested, both by its enemies and its followers, as well as by later Arab historians. A library of textual fragments representing the philosophy and history of the Religion of Light has come down to us in many languages, from the Coptic of Egypt, the Aramaic, the Parthian and middle Persian of the Sassanian Empire, the Tocharian of eastern Turkestan to the Chinese of the Middle Kingdom. We even have writings credited to Mani's own hand. And though some of the most precious documents, including letters by the Prophet of Light himself, disappeared in the turmoil of the Second World War, never alas to be seen again—for it was largely German archaeologists and palaeographers who had devoted the greatest effort to collecting and studying the Manichaean relics, and Berlin still has one of the greatest collections of Manichaean art and literature—it remains possible to sketch his story and his teachings in reasonable detail.

IN AN ALIEN FLOCK

"When I was twenty-four years old, in the year in which Ardashir, King of Persia, subjected the city of Hatra, and in which Shapur his son assumed the mighty diadem . . . the most blessed Lord had compassion on me and called me to his grace and sent my Divine Twin down to me." These words—so reminiscent of Nietzsche's "one became two, and Zarathustra passed me by"—come from a tiny Greek codex in the papyrus collection of the University of Cologne, known to the initiated as the *Codex Manichaicus Coloniensis,* which outlines the beginnings of Manichaean history as told by the Manichaeans themselves.

They may be Mani's very own words, though they may possibly have been put into his mouth by a later follower. No mention here that, as hinted in other texts, he was probably born with one short and twisted leg, a deformity which may have made him feel an outsider from his earliest years. In any case, according to his legend, this was not the first twinly visit. As a twelve-year-old, it seems, Mani had already received his first intimation that he was not as others—though back then, the heavenly messenger had only told him to prepare himself for the time when he would be old enough to take an important message to the world. Even at that time, he was already living in an ascetic monastic religious community, to which he had been taken by his father as a young child.

The identity of this cult settlement has long posed a historical conundrum. Scholars have thought it important to know who these people were, as Mani's upbringing doubtless contributed greatly to his later view of the world. At the end of the tenth century an Arab bookseller, the Tim Waterstone of his day, with the not inconsiderable name of Abu'l Faraj Muhammad ben Ishak al-Warrak Ibn Abi Ja'kub an-Nadim, compiled an amazing "Catalogue of Knowledge," *Fihrist al 'Ulum,* from all the literature known to him. In this extraordinary work, he first sketches the biography of each author, then outlines the author's major works. In book nine, he provides a dispassionate and even-handed account of Mani's life and a résumé of Manichaean beliefs, history and sacred canon, in which he states that Mani was taken by his father at the age of four to live with the *Mughtasilah.* The word means "baptisers" in Arabic.

There does exist one Gnostic community which has survived into modern times and whose main sacrament is the rite of baptism. These are the Mandeans (Aramaic for *Those Who Know*), Jewish-Christian sectarians of a kind, a tiny remnant of whom are still to be found—or at least were before their region was devastated by Saddam Hussein's wars and they were dispersed—in southern Iraq and, living very quietly, in Iran. They may well be descended from followers of John the Baptist for they say, with Jesus in St. Matthew's Gospel, "Among them that are born of women, there hath not risen a greater than John the Baptist."

For a long time it was believed that it was among the Mandeans that Mani had been raised, and great efforts were made to trace links between his beliefs and theirs. But the decipherment of the Cologne codex in 1970 finally put the record straight. No, they were not Mandeans, though their ideas were very close. They were the mysterious Elchasaites, a sect of Jewish-Christians, who venerated a text revealed to their founder Elchasai (hidden power) in or around the year 100 by two gigantic angels, twenty miles high, one male—the Son of God—and one female—the Holy Spirit.

Elchasai taught that the Jewish use of fire for sacrifice was leading to error. The Zoroastrian veneration of fire as a symbol of the divine was ill-judged as well. In fact, he claimed to know, fire was abhorrent to God, whereas He did approve of water. So the Elchasaites became vegetarian, teetotal, celibate baptists. They forbade all laughter, joy, music, painting and other arts. Preoccupied with ritual cleanliness and hatred for the hellish world they found themselves in, they lived according to strict Jewish law, loved Christ, detested the apostle Paul, and occupied themselves with tilling the fields around their settlements close to the head of the Persian Gulf, near Al Basrah.

One can easily imagine their confusion when the young Mani, brought up as one of their own after all, began to criticise their ways in general and to attack their wilful cruelty to the plant world in particular. According to the story in the Cologne codex, it began when he refused to collect vegetables from the fields. Then one day, when a fellow baptist took him to help pick dates, the palm cried out that if he did not at once desist from inflicting pain on its babies, he would die a murderer. Other vegetables soon joined the protest, human-like cries resounding as the harvesters' blows fell and blood oozing from the places where the sickle had cut them.

Mani drifted through his days with the cult as if in a trance. "He was like a lamb dwelling in an alien flock or a bird living with other birds who do not speak the same language," wrote one of his later disciples. But while meaningful communication with his fellow Elchasaites became ever more difficult, the revelations of his Divine Twin opened up entirely new vistas of truth. "He revealed to me the mystery of light and of darkness, the mystery of destruction . . . the mystery of the creation of Adam, the first man. He also taught me the mystery of the tree of knowledge from which Adam ate and his eyes were opened."

To those who believed that Mani was truly divinely inspired, the communion with his Divine Twin revealed supremely important knowledge about the hidden meaning and purpose of the world. To those of us who don't, he seems to have been seriously disturbed, perhaps even autistic, for—uniquely among religious prophets—he had a genius for drawing and painting. Traumatically separated from his mother at an early age, he was self-obsessed, isolated, unable to build healthy relationships with his fellows, and had a pathological disgust for the human body and its natural functions. His arguments against baptism focused on the inability of water to overcome the revolting realities of life. "Consider how, when someone purifies his food and then eats it, it is apparent that, even after it has been ritually washed, from it come blood, bile, wind, shameful excrement and the foulness of the body."

The horror which he felt for the human vessel clearly made no distinction between physical dirt and spiritual evil. "Why do you ritually wash yourself every day?" he asked one of his baptist peers. "From this it is evident that you become loathsome to yourself every day, and because of that foulness you ritually wash yourself before you can be purified. It is clear and very plain that all defilement is from the body. Behold, you yourself are clothed in it."

When taken to task for his deviant pronouncements by the other sectarians, he would defend himself by suddenly producing revisionist versions of Elchasaite history. When their founder was going to bathe one day, he told them, a vision had appeared from the pool in protest at Elchasai's defilement of the water. When he took a plough to the fields, the earth complained. When his disciples were putting bread into the oven, a loaf spoke up and forbade them ever to bake again. "Consider these famous men of your rule," Mani declared, "who saw these visions, were moved by them and preached them to others. All I have achieved was learned from them."

And on top of his argumentative assaults on their convictions he outraged their horror of idolatry and art by insisting on making paintings, even perhaps going to decorate houses in a nearby village.

The sectarians' answer was apparently to set upon the renegade and beat him up—he might have been severely injured had his father not intervened. Now Mani fell into a slough of despond, despairing of his future within the sect. But his Twin soon appeared and—in words uncannily reminiscent of the epigraph to those old Dent's Everyman Edition books: "Everyman, I will go with thee, and be thy guide. In thy most need to go by thy side"—explained that he should set his sights upon the wider world: "You were not only sent to this [monastic] rule, but to every people and school of learning and to every city and region . . . Go from here and travel about. For I will be with you as your helper and protector at every place where you will preach everything that I have revealed to you. Therefore do not grieve and be distressed."

So Mani packed up and left the Elchasaite settlement and travelled north to Ctesiphon on the River Tigris, the winter capital of the Persian Empire. There he was joined by two acolytes from among the baptists and, a little later, by his father, who had followed in fear that something bad had happened to his son, but quickly became one of his most devoted disciples.

The four now set out on an extended series of missionary journeys, taking them east from Babylonia into today's Iran, Afghanistan, India, even maybe as far as China. The familiar adage that travel broadens the mind can never have been truer than in Mani's case, for it was in the course of these expeditions that he discovered himself to be the Paraclete (intercessor), foretold by Jesus in the Gospel of John, called himself also the Apostle of Christ, and elaborated the full details of his novel theology. From his background among the baptists, he already had an understanding of the basic tenets of Judaism and Christianity, even if he disputed their interpretation. From his father, who came from Ecbatana (today's Hamadan) in Iran, he had absorbed the dualist teachings of Zarathustra. Now, by travelling east, he was moving out of the Judaeo-Christian-Zoroastrian milieu into a new realm and confronting, presumably for the first time, the very different world of the Buddha.

At just this historical moment, Afghanistan was being reattached to the Persian Empire after centuries of control by Kushans from Central Asia. Perhaps this new frontier was what inspired Mani and his companions to take the north-east trail. The texts don't tell us exactly where they travelled, nor by what route. But, if you look at a map of the area, you will see that their trek along what was called the Khorasan Road would have taken them across Iran and through the highlands of Afghanistan.

In the 1960s, when I travelled it, this was still a difficult dirt road over a spur of the Hindu Kush Mountains, suited only to packhorses and mules, snaking up through dizzying passes, clinging to the sides of precipitous ravines, squeezing between the narrowest of clefts in mile-high mountain walls, splashing through forded hillside torrents and leaping over chasms on rickety wooden bridges that seemed as perilous as the one, "as thin as a hair and as sharp as a sword," over which Zoroastrians as well as Muslims pass after death to be judged.

Such a road can lead only to paradise. Suddenly you look down from the heights over a wide fertile valley, with wheat and barley fields, orchards and fishponds. In the distance, beside a sparkling stream, runs a tree-lined road past little houses in their high-walled compounds and a tiny mosque. This is the valley of Bamian.

In the beetling cliffsides which wall the valley, a myriad of frescoed caves and crevices brightly painted with religious illustrations housed relics of the bygone age when more than eight thousand monks lived in what was one of the holiest Buddhist sanctuaries of all. This was the showplace of the Kushan Empire and of its mightiest ruler, Kanishka, a world centre of Buddhist art in the second century. Two giant statues of the Buddha, well over a hundred feet high, were carved in niches from the solid rock. Their faces were smashed off centuries ago by outraged idol-breakers.

On my first visit to the valley, I drove down to the mosque and spoke to the Imam, a very small man of about fifty years old, dressed in black, with hands that fluttered like birds as he spoke, and a skin disease that had left bald patches in his beard. What could he tell me about the history of the Buddhas? Who had carved them from the rock? He seemed embarrassed. It was a long time ago, he said. They were idolaters from India. He didn't know why they had chosen this valley to settle.

But surely, I suggested, all of the Afghan people had been idolaters back then. The little Imam was outraged. Of course not, he snorted. We believed in God and the Devil—he used the Arabic *Allah* and *Shaitan*—even before the Prophet came to teach us the way.

Had it been a Muslim army that had shattered the Buddhas' faces? Not Muslims but pagan Mongols or Turks, he claimed, defensively. Muslims don't do such things.

Muslims don't do such things? Even back then I didn't think he was right. Smashing graven images is the work of religious iconoclasts, not rampaging warlords. More recent events confirmed my doubt, when the Islamist Afghan Taliban regime went back to finish what its predecessors had begun, blew up the Buddhas in their entirety and eradicated what remained of the frescoes.

Many pagan armies, the Imam went on, had rampaged through the valley, destroying everybody and everything in their path. And that much at least was clearly true. The signs were all around us. On Bamian's surrounding crags, ancient broken watchtowers and ruined forts still stand in silent witness to the fearful morning in the year 1220 or 1221 when the valley's inhabitants must have woken in terror to shouts and screams, a hail of arrows, a clashing of arms and a beating of horses' hoofs, as Genghis Khan's horde surged through the settlement, killing, burning, looting and destroying everything it encountered. The entire landscape appears untouched from that day to this, as if forever frozen in a snapshot of that awful moment.

For the Iranian world has had to suffer foreign conquest on all too many occasions: Alexander, Genghis, the armies of Islam, Tamerlaine, Babur. One after another they came, they saw, they conquered and they destroyed. Everywhere throughout the country, the ruins left by successive invasions still dot hillsides and valley floors: castles whose entire garrisons were put to the sword; townships abandoned and never resettled; walled villages of sun-dried brick, forever bereft of population and slowly crumbling back to the dust from which they were built. And each time Iranian civilisation and culture discovered a way of surviving, of rising again from the flames like a phoenix, of clothing its old ways in new clothes. Until, some time in the eighteenth century, finally exhausted by millennia of struggle and bloodshed, the Central Asian hinterland gave up the effort and allowed itself to sink back into ignorance, lethargy and underdevelopment.

But in Mani's day this was a flourishing, teeming centre of civilisation. Under its Kushan rulers, the greatest of whom was Kanishka, who held sway from the eastern deserts of Iran to the Yamuna river in India, Afghanistan was a crossroad of world religions. At Bamian, Buddhist monks scurried about the rock-cut temples which warren the sandstone cliffs; at Pul-i-Khumri, Magian priests tended the Zoroastrian sacred fire and sang the praises of Ahura Mazda in Kanishka's stupendous fire temple; at Herat, Maimana and Ghazni orthodox Jews chanted their morning, noon and evening services in synagogues already ancient of days, while Jewish-Christian sectarian communes walled themselves in against the corruptions of urban life.

"Wisdom and deeds have always from time to time been brought to mankind by the messengers of God," Mani later wrote. "So in one age they have been brought by the messenger called Buddha to India, in another by Zarathustra to Persia, in another by Jesus to the West. Thereupon this revelation has come down and this prophecy has appeared in the form of myself, Mani, the envoy of the true God in the Land of Babylon."

What was the revelation and what the prophesy? In *Manichaeism*, his useful survey and summary of the Mani phenomenon both West and East, Samuel Lieu of the University of Warwick quotes a Chinese Manichaean handbook:

> Everyone who wishes to join the sect must know that Light and Darkness are principles, each in their own right and that their natures are completely distinct . . . Next he must be enlightened on the Three Moments: the Former Time, the Present Time, the Future Time.
>
> In the Former Time, there are yet no heavens or earths, there exists only Light and Darkness. The nature of Light is wisdom, that of Darkness is folly . . .
>
> In the Present Time, Darkness invades Light and gives rein to its passion to chase the Light away. Light in turn enters Darkness and is deputed with pledges to push back this Great Calamity. It detests its departure from its original body and pleads to leave the Fiery Abode. One must therefore wear out the physical body in order to save its [luminous] nature . . .
>
> In the Future Time . . . Light once more belongs to the Great Light and Darkness returns to the ultimate Darkness. The Two Principles return to their normal state and give up and return to each other what they have received from each other.

"This drama," says Dr. Lieu, "is central to Mani's teaching as it explains how the enlightened souls of men which are of divine origin came to be clothed in the body of matter which is evil."

Good and evil, lightness and darkness, soul and body, such is the dualist division in the Manichaean universe.

Zoroastrians and others before Mani—for instance the Jewish Hellenist philosopher Philo Judaeus, or the authors of one of the Dead Sea Scrolls, the library of Jewish texts secreted in a cave in the Holy Land around the start of the first millennium—had seen light and darkness as useful metaphors for, or realisations of, Zarathustra's good and evil powers. But Mani went further. His light was no analogy but was intended to be understood as literally and materially true. It was one of the complaints of later critics that Manichaeans insisted on the reality of their fantastical interpretation of physical phenomena. A sixth-century philosopher, Simplicius, loudly complained about their excessive literalism. Their explanation of eclipses particularly offended him.

"They say that when the Evil ones chained in creation cause upheaval and disorder by their own movements, the light particles inside them throw up a kind of veil so as not to be affected by the excitement. Eclipses are therefore caused by the interposition of this veil."

Simplicius shakes his head in despair: "They fabricate certain marvels which are not even worthy to be called myths. But they do not use them as myths, nor do they think that they have any other meaning, but believe that all the things which they say are true."

For Mani, it was real, visible light and actual, literal darkness which made the world their battleground. This was what made his inspiration unique.

Pondering how much of his theology was developed here in Afghanistan, I turned to the *Encyclopædia Britannica* to check the valley's physical location. It struck me that, as it lies more than 8,000 feet above sea level, the clarity of its air and the dualism of its blazing summers and crackling winters might have made some contribution to the prophet's thought.

"The Buddhist art of central Afghanistan is admirably represented at Bamian," I read, "where Mani, the Iranian founder of the Manichaean religion, probably lived and encouraged the growth of a religious pictorial art in the 3rd century A.D."

And then I realised it: Mani was a painter. Manichaeism's battle between the light and the darkness is a painter's vision. Caravaggio, who said "Painting is light," would have understood, so would de La Tour, Cézanne and every other artist who ever strove to create a world by the interplay of *chiaroscuro*, brightness and shadow. So would Germany's greatest poet Goethe, who had wanted to be a painter in his youth and who opposed Newton's mechanistic theory of light with his own explanation, because of his passionate conviction that light is indivisible and cannot be reduced to a procession of particles. Manichaeism was fine art raised to the status of revealed religion—unique in spiritual history.

The texts give no idea of how long Mani remained in Afghanistan. He certainly travelled on to India, and maybe China, at some time in these early years of his mission, founding communities of followers that long outlived him. The texts tell us only tall tales. Somewhere in Turan, in Central Asia, he was directed by the king to debate his metaphysics with a local holy man. To impress the king with his powers of levitation, he lifted his opponent into mid-air. The king was so overcome by the profundity of the argument, let alone the ability to make a holy man hover above the floor, that he converted with all his court.

One aspect of the tale does ring true, however. Mani had very acute strategic instincts. Unlike the Jesus of the Gospels who addressed himself to the poor and to the powerless, Mani always directed his attentions first to the ruling class, starting with the local Shah and working his way up. His aim from the start was plain: to target the greatest ruler of the region and of the age, Shapur I, Shahanshah of Iran and Non-Iran (the non-Persian lands of his empire), who had taken the throne when the Prophet of Light was twenty-eight years old.

He aimed first for a lesser power. Mehr-Shah, the ruler of Mesene, at the junction of the Tigris and Euphrates, was one of Shapur's brothers. Mani was brought in to find him sitting relaxing in his palace garden. Imagine this refuge of cool tranquillity and peace, sheltering from the burning Mesopotamian sun under its lush greenery, with its flower-scented aroma, bird song ornamenting the delicate music of its water fountains. Recall that paradise is the Persian word for garden. After hearing the prophet out, the Shah asks: "In the paradise which you praise, is there such a garden as this garden of mine?" Mani responds by presenting the Shah with a vision. "By his miraculous power he showed the Paradise of Light with all the gods, deities and the immortal spirit of life, and gardens of every kind and other beautiful sights." Mehr-Shah was immediately won over.

Having succeeded with one of Shapur's brothers, Mani then trekked across Iran to Khorasan in the north-east, where Firuz, another, more senior brother, was governor. The meeting was as great a success as the encounter with Mehr-Shah—in fact even more so, for after his conversion to the Religion of Light, Firuz agreed to introduce the prophet to Shapur himself.

Sadly, no full Manichaean account of the crucial interview with the great Sassanian Shahanshah survives. Only a tiny fragment of autobiography describes what were probably the opening exchanges of the audience:

"I have come before the king. Peace be upon you from the gods."

The king said: "Where have you come from?"

I said: "I am a doctor from Babylon."

According to an-Nadim, the Shahanshah first intended to have this irritating missionary taken off and executed, but when he looked up at him—Mani was, of course, standing in the Shah's presence—Shapur seemed to see two bright lights like candles radiating from his shoulders, whereupon he immediately became more conciliatory and asked Mani what he wanted. The prophet requested permission that he and his acolytes might travel freely about Shapur's realm preaching the new revelation. The boon was granted and Mani was given letters of accreditation.

All the sources agree that Shapur and Mani struck it off particularly well from the first, and what we know of the next decades of the apostle's life suggests that they were telling the truth. The prophet soon found himself frequently summoned to the royal presence to converse with the king. He travelled about with the court. According to a later Greek polemicist, Alexander Lycopolitanus, he even went on campaign with Shapur against the Romans. He may have witnessed the Emperor Valerian's capture. And yet there was never any suggestion that Shapur might become a convert. His inscriptions at Naqsh-e-Rustam confirm his deep commitment to the Zoroastrian faith; and he maintained the fanatical Kartir as high priest. Some scholars have speculated that the Shahanshah saw Mani's claim—to be next in line to the Jewish prophets, Christ, Zarathustra and the Buddha—as a possible way of unifying the religious diversity of his huge empire. But historical records show that it was Zarathustra's cause that the Sassanians energetically promoted, not Mani's. It is more likely that what attracted Shapur to the Paraclete of Jesus was simply the sheer power of his extraordinary personality, adding a valuable embellishment to an already glamorous court.

Mani must, after all, have been remarkably charismatic. He seemed to make converts with no difficulty. His legendary exploits suggest that he could easily convince sceptics that he had, say, raised a holy man into the air, or revealed a vision of paradise, or made his shoulders glow like candles in the dark. And he was an artist, too. I can't help wondering whether he made drawings or paintings of what he saw while on the road with his monarch. And if he did, what became of them.

The next years were prodigiously productive for the Apostle of God. He taught and evangelised all over Iran and Non-Iran. He wrote numerous books, among them *The Living Gospel, The Treasure of Life, The Pragmateia, The Book of Mysteries, The Book of Giants, The Epistles,* and a book of Psalms and Prayers. Especially for his patron Shapur, he wrote the *Shaburagan*, a summary of his life and teachings. He also drew and painted.

He elaborated the basic Zarathustrian principle of a war between light and darkness into a grand narrative with a dramatis personae as huge as the whole of the Complete Works of Dickens and Shakespeare and a plot-line as convoluted as all of Greek mythology put together. Reminiscent of Buddhism was the way in which the main players in the struggle for power—the Father of Greatness of the Kingdom of Light and the Prince of Darkness—spun off multiple avatars, manifestations, or embodiments of aspects of themselves, sometimes numbering in the hundreds, each in some way different from the others. A Jewish-Christian-Greek spirit manifested itself in the concept of the Great *Nous*, Cosmic Intelligence or Logos, embodied on earth in a line of perfect men, from Seth, Shem, Noah and Abraham to the Buddha, Zarathustra and Jesus the Messiah, who transmit to humanity knowledge of the light particles within and so make redemption possible.

A Manichaean's duty was to help liberate light particles by avoiding blasphemy, animal killing, meat eating, wine drinking, soil tilling, fruit picking, plant harvesting, bathing and sex. Work was of course out of the question.

Strict adherence to these rules would naturally result in speedy starvation and death of the community. So, just as with the Cathars and the Bogomils, believers were to be divided between a minority of the Elect, who followed the full ascetic path, and the majority of Hearers, who were permitted to fall short in their observance as long as they helped feed, sustain and maintain the Elect, who prayed during ritual meals to absolve themselves from responsibility for having procured the food. At death, the Elect were transported straight to the Kingdom of Light, while the Hearers were reincarnated, apparently first as vegetables and "luminous fruits" but ultimately as members of the Elect. Those whom the *Nous* had not awakened were forever prisoners of darkness and were destined for eternal damnation.

What strikes me as noteworthy about this baroque theology is that, unlike other mythical systems, elaborated over the centuries by successive generations of believers, the Manichaean story of creation seems to have been developed by Mani, by himself, in a few short decades. It was a truly astonishing feat of the imagination, even if the prophet himself believed it was all revealed to him by his Divine Twin.

At the same time, Mani was busy with his art. Among the most tantalising hints in the texts are references to a "Book of Drawings," *Ardahang,* which he made to express his visions of the divine in concrete images. According to Ephraim of Nisibis, a fourth-century Christian opponent, "Mani painted in colours on a scroll . . . placing on hideous pictures the names of the Sons of Darkness . . . and on beautiful things the names of the Sons of Light." He quotes from what was probably Mani's own introduction to his work: "I have written them in books and pictured them in colours. Let him who hears them in words also see them in images, and he who is unable to learn them from writing, let him learn them from pictures." In the references to missions sent out to distant lands, "book painters" are occasionally included among the scribes and teachers listed—one guesses that these would have been engaged in copying Mani's artwork. In later centuries, at the annual Bimah (throne) festival, a chair was left vacant for the Paraclete himself. There are suggestions that a copy of the Book of Drawings was placed on this chair. It's just possible that one day, a copy of this work may be found somewhere, perhaps under the sands of Egypt or Mongolia, or in a ruined building in the wilderness of Afghanistan. A version of the *Ardahang* still apparently existed in eleventh-century China, but no description of its contents has survived.

Ultimately all good things come to an end, even for prophets of light. In or about the year 272 Shapur died, to be succeeded by his son Hormizd (a contraction of Ahura Mazda). Mani must have worried that, with their patron gone, he and his flock would be left without high-level support. He hurried to meet the new ruler and asked for his most-favoured-prophet status to be reconfirmed. It is recorded that he was received warmly by the Shahanshah and reassured that his Religion of Light would continue to receive imperial approval. But, of all people, prophets should know that the future is never certain. If Mani allowed himself to relax it was a mistake.

Hormizd was himself dead within the year, perhaps poisoned, maybe—on the instigation of conservative Magi—by his own brother. And it was this brother, Bahram, who now took the Sassanian throne. His was a very different character from his father's. Shapur had been a wise ruler as well as a great military leader, thoughtful and serious-minded, a devout Zoroastrian but also tolerant to other faiths and other ways. Bahram was small-minded, intolerant, self-indulgent and venal. A later Arab author described him as "trifling with his slaves" and "foolishly and excessively fond of music." He wanted an easy life with no problems. He was clearly under the thumb of Kartir, the humourless chief priest, who was ever ready to take advantage of his new master's weaknesses. As a first move he persuaded Bahram to ban Mani from the country. The Manichaean case had altered, and considerably for the worse.

Mani knew it. His first thought was to seek help from his early supporters in the ruling house of Mesene. When he arrived there, however, he was shocked to find the palace destroyed, the famous garden a wilderness, and Mehr-Shah's family nowhere to be found. The discovery seems to have hit the prophet hard. He could perhaps have journeyed back east to Kushan and Afghanistan where he had powerful allies, but the new Shahanshah had specifically forbidden him to enter or to cross Iran. It must have been now that he realised his days were numbered. Travelling among his numerous flock on the sun-scorched plains of Babylonia, he warned them that he was moving towards his crucifixion and that they would soon have to make do without him. The only option now for him was to beard the Lion of Iran in his den, to go to the royal court in the city of Gundeshapur in defiance of the ban, and to confront Bahram in person.

MANI LIVES!

Speeding along the spanking new highway through the oil country of Khuzestan, western Iran, towards the wealthy modern provincial capital of Ahwaz, I am trying in vain to use Maalouf's *Gardens of Light* as a guidebook. Somewhere here was the ancient Aramaic settlement of Beth Lapat, Mani's own village. Somewhere here was the royal city of Gundeshapur, built in the Great King's name to magnify his glory.

The land is flat, dissected by streams and rivers, mottled today with greenery under a hot and leaden sky. Apart from the basic topography, nothing at all remains which I can recognise from Maalouf's account, or which might be recognised by its third-century inhabitants. Unrestricted development has changed rural landscape into industrial cityscape. It is not an improvement. The great grey, green, greasy Karun river flows sluggishly through the city, all set about with sweating concrete embankments. Incongruously, pleasure boats dot the oily surface. Here is the commercial heartland of twentieth-century Iran. As we pass under yet another triumphal arch celebrating the Islamic Revolution, just past yet another statue of a heroic Mullah-Martyr, I look aside and see a sign.

"Wait. Stop the car."

"What is it? Have we hit something?" My Iranian friend always thinks the worst has happened.

"Look." I point to the sign. "Jondishapur University."

Once Gundeshapur was the foremost centre of learning in the world west of India, staffed by Greek exiles after the academy in Athens was closed down by the Christian Emperor Justinian in 529 and its teachers expelled. It was here that the Latin and Greek classics were preserved for later Arab scholars to transmit back to renaissance Christendom.

My companions laugh. "It's just Ahwaz University, not even a pale reflection."

"At least I know that I am in the right place."

"No you're not. Gundeshapur was kilometres away. It's called Gotwand now."

Mani, nearly sixty years old, came to Gundeshapur accompanied by a handful of followers. He was dressed in a blue gown over multicoloured trousers, an ebony stick in his right hand, a "Babylonian" book under his left arm, his face as noble as an artist or as a general—at least, so says a fragment of biography preserved in a later document. Of the difficult interview with the sovereign himself, we have two reports, including most of an account by Nuhzadeh, the interpreter Mani took with him to translate between his own Aramaic and the Shahanshah's Persian. Putting it all together, we can recreate the scene in some detail and, probably, accuracy.

The king is sitting at the dinner table in his sumptuous private apartments with the "Queen of the Sakas" (Scythians) who is actually his mistress, some forty years his junior and conveniently married off to his grandson, the future Bahram III. With him sit Kerder, son of Ardawan, a high religious official—maybe the same person as Kartir the chief priest, but maybe not. He has not yet finished eating when guards fling open the heavy cedarwood doors and a liveried attendant bows himself in, to fall at the king's feet. The king pauses, the morsel of meat on the point of his knife halfway to his mouth, and silently raises an eyebrow.

"Great King, Mani has come and is outside the door."

"Tell him to wait. I shall see him when I am good and ready."

Mani sits down outside the king's door beside the guards and waits for the king to finish his meal and prepare to go off hunting.

Eventually the king rises from the table and, putting one arm around the Queen of the Sakas and the other around Kerder, son of Ardawan, he comes through the door. Mani stands, then kneels and touches the floor

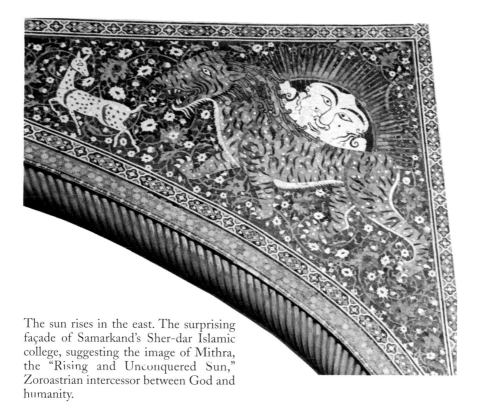

The sun rises in the east. The surprising façade of Samarkand's Sher-dar Islamic college, suggesting the image of Mithra, the "Rising and Unconquered Sun," Zoroastrian intercessor between God and humanity.

Friedrich Wilhelm Nietzsche. He brought Zarathustra to life again for the modern age.

Sils Maria. The Swiss village in the Upper Engadine valley, "two thousand metres above good and evil," where Zarathustra appeared to Nietzsche and inspired him to compose his masterpiece.

The "pog" of Montségur. Here the last followers of the Great Heresy—which once commanded the allegiance of a third of the population of southern France—retreated into the sky.

The citadel of Montségur. In 1244, five hundred heretics crammed themselves into this final redoubt after ten months of siege ended the last attempt to establish Zarathustra's dualist teachings in western Europe.

Carcassonne city wall. The fortifications were begun by the fifth-century King of the Visigoths in a style which inspired a thousand Victorian fairy-tale illustrators, but reminded me of Zoroastrian Iran.

Momo and Uzeir. Two Sarajevo tower blocks, named after popular joke characters, stand amid the devastation of the latest crusade against the descendants of the Bogomils, late followers of Zarathustra's dualist beliefs.

The humbling of Rome. Sassanian emperor Shapur receives the submission of Roman emperors Valerian and Philip the Arabian, while the ruthless Zoroastrian chief priest Kartir looks on from behind. Near Shiraz, Iran.

Brocolita Mithraeum. The ruins of the Temple of Mithras near Carrawburgh on Hadrian's Wall, twice rebuilt to accommodate a growing congregation but abandoned towards the end of Roman rule in Britain.

"Mithras, God of the Midnight, here where the great bull dies." The Carrawburgh Mithraic Temple as reconstructed by the Newcastle Museum of Antiquities, with altars dedicated "To the Invincible God Mithras."

Gifts for Darius. This relief shows delegates to the New Year Festival at Persepolis bringing presents for the Shah. The guidebook calls them Assyrians or Phoenicians, but they could be Hebrews from Babylon.

At the shrine of the Israelite Prophet. The tomb of Daniel near ancient Susa in western Iran. In this biblical figure were united the apocalyptic traditions of Mesopotamian Jews and Iranian Zoroastrians.

"Everything was built by the grace of Ahura Mazda." The remains of Darius's royal city of Persepolis, once the most magnificent city in Asia, but destroyed in 331 BC by Alexander the Great.

"Grudge me not this little earth that covers my body." The tomb at Pasagardae (not far from Persepolis) of Cyrus the Great, founder of the Achaemenian empire, who released the Jews from Babylonian captivity.

"The most important historical document in Asia." Darius's own story, carved into the rock above the road at Behistun, giving his version of the events which gained him the throne.

History hidden by engineering. Darius's great rock relief as I found it, totally obscured by scaffolding, after travelling two and a half thousand miles to see it. (Two tiny human figures at the base of the scaffolding indicate the scale.)

"Darius the King says." Detail of King Darius from his self-justifying Behistun monument.

The Immortals. Archers of the Achaemenian palace guard, who helped Cyrus carve out the first Persian empire, but whose later descendants lost it again to Alexander the Great's Macedonians. They now stand in a Berlin museum.

The Ishtar Gate. Far from its original homeland, the glorious gateway at the end of the Babylonian Ceremonial Way, through which Nebuchadnezzar once walked, now rests in Berlin's Pergamon Museum.

Seven things beginning with 's.' The *haft sin* table in a Tehran hotel. In spite of thirteen centuries of Islam, the pre-Islamic Noruz festival still keeps its special place in Iranian culture.

Shir-e-sangi, the Stone Lion. The sculpture of a sad lion in Hamadan, reputedly commissioned by Alexander the Great in memory of his friend, and perhaps lover, Hephaistion.

Esther and Mordecai's tomb in Hamadan. Claimed as the burial site of the protagonists of the biblical Book of Esther, it more probably holds the bones of a Jewish queen of Sassanian Iran.

Darius the Great with his courtiers, Tehran Museum. After suppressing a veritable army of false pretenders to the Achaemenid throne, Darius oversaw the establishment of Zoroastrianism as Iran's official state religion.

Ateshkadeh. The Zoroastrian fire temple in Yazd, central Iran, whose sacred flames have supposedly been burning since the year 470—a major tourist site for Iranian Muslims during their New Year celebrations.

"Those great strong walls now called Ecbatana." Herodotus wrote that this first capital of the Medes and Persians, now a dusty mound in Hamadan, once had six concentric rings of walls, each of a different colour.

Bamian. The idyllic Afghan valley, 8,000 feet above sea level, seventeen centuries after Mani founded its tradition of religious art. In the year 2000, the Taliban regime would destroy the spectacular remains.

The Wedding Tree. At this ancient way-station called Gissar, on the Silk Road in Tajikistan, wedding parties still come to tie cloth strips—representing wishes—to the sacred tree, before moving on to a fire ceremony.

A holy place high in the hills. An ancient Zoroastrian shrine, still in use, nestles among the rocks in central Iran. The cypresses and myrtles have special meanings to Zarathustra's followers.

with his forehead in the approved manner. But the king's first words are "You are not welcome here."

Mani finds himself immediately wrong-footed. "Why? What wrong have I done?"

"I have sworn not to permit you to enter this land."

Then, perhaps stressed by the constant nagging from his principal priest Kartir, the king flies into a sudden rage, like a small child working itself up into a temper all by itself. "What are you good for, anyway? You don't go fighting or hunting. Do you imagine we need you for your so-called doctoring and healing? And you don't even do that."

"I have never done you any wrong," Mani protests. "I have always done well by you and your family. I have freed countless servants of yours from demons and witches. I have cured all kinds of sicknesses. Many were even at the point of death and I brought them back to life."

Maybe because he has no answer to that, or because he is acting as Kartir's mouthpiece, Bahram takes another tack. "And what is this religion that you have taught King Baat? I hear he has given up our religion and taken up yours. Where did you get such an idea?" King Baat is a minor ruler who has come to Gundeshapur as part of Mani's entourage.

Mani is on firmer ground with this question. "I have no master and no teacher except God. If I have received wisdom it is from God's angel, who has instructed me to preach the truth in your majesty's realm."

"And what truth is that supposed to be?"

"The world has been led astray by lies. My preaching is only aimed at saving many souls."

Bahram suspects that there may be an insult hidden somewhere in the prophet's words, but can't quite put his finger on what it is. "And how do you know that yours is the truth and the rest lies?"

"There is nothing new in my teaching. Everything I preach has been known to previous generations. But it is usual that the path of truth sometimes remains hidden and sometimes reveals itself."

Now the king realises what irks him: "Why does God reveal himself to you, a complete nonentity, and not to me? I am lord of this whole land."

Mani gives a pious answer: "Only God has the power to decide that." But he recognises that this is not what Bahram wants to hear and hurriedly pleads: "Your father the divine Shapur and your much-mourned brother Hormizd had no problems with my teaching. They treated me kindly and gave me leave to spread my word throughout the kingdom. They even gave me written testimonials." Seeing the thunder in the king's eyes, he adds more humbly, "But you yourself will do with me as you wish."

Bahram looks long and hard at Mani without a word. Then he turns to the guards standing on either side of the prophet. "Arrest this man and put him in chains."

They locked a heavy chain about Mani's neck, three around his chest, three on each arm and on each leg. That was all. Even the King of Kings did not dare order the prophet's summary execution. He was given food and water. His disciples were allowed to visit him and receive instruction. The chains took twenty-six days to do their fatal work.

"Thus the Apostle of Light laid aside the warlike dress of the body and took his place in a ship of light . . . And in great happiness, with the gods of light on his right and his left and accompanied by the music of harps and songs of happiness, he flew up to the assembly place of the gods. And he remained there with the Father, the god Ohrmizd," says a Manichaean hymn. Maalouf's version ends, as it began, with the date: "It was the year 584 according to the astronomers of Babel, the fourth day of the month of Adar; 2 March 274, a Monday, in the Christian era."

Bahram, desperate to show that Mani had been a mere mortal, had the corpse flayed, the skin stuffed with straw and the head set up on a pole by the city gate. Centuries later, a Muslim Arab historian recorded that the gate was still known in his day as Mani's Gate.

But the Prophet of Light's followers refused to believe that their teacher was dead. Or, if they did believe it, refused to accept that it changed anything. All over Iran and Non-Iran the Aramaic cry "Mani Khai!," Mani Lives!, was raised. It became the watchword of the movement, the signal by which one devotee could recognise another. So much so that Christian Greek critics began referring to them dismissively as the "Mani Khai-s," or, as we now spell it, the Manichees or Manichaeans.

At Naqsh-e-Rustam, the sun is rising towards its noonday zenith over the mere hundred or so paces which represent Mani's thirty-five-year-long journey from obscurity to martyrdom—the distance from Shapur's victory panel to Bahram's memorial rock-relief. Shapur is now brightly toplit, Bahram is in shadow. Chief priest Kartir appears in both. In the former, he seems an afterthought; in the latter, he dominates the scene. The other figures look to the king, but the king looks to the priest.

I wonder whether any of the local tourists know what spiritual drama is here memorialised in stone. The answer is probably not. Many of the visitors are studying the scattered Farsi signs that briefly describe the carvings, looking backwards and forwards between the cliffside and the writing that describes it, their heads bobbing up and down like spectators at a trampolining competition, but they will find no account here of the ruthless priest-in-chief. I don't find the lack surprising—religious fundamentalists are not noted for their sense of irony. And today's clergy are no more benignly disposed towards Muslim revisionists like the Baha'is than was their predecessor towards a Zoroastrian revisionist like Mani.

History records that the long-lived Kartir achieved his aims. In the next reign—Bahram survived Mani by only two years—Kartir lived to be awarded the title created especially for him: "Soul Saviour" of the Shahanshah. The programme of oppression, repression and suppression of all unorthodox belief which he set in motion in the Iranian lands would outlive him by many centuries.

Propagation of Mani's teaching was forbidden throughout Sassanian Iran. Mani's successor as leader of the sect was crucified—literally. But the new faith couldn't simply be crushed, it had too great an appeal. Instead it managed for centuries to spread, and even to flourish, throughout the Iranian cultural area and beyond, in spite of orthodox Zoroastrian opposition. Eventually, however, pressure on Manichaeans became so constant and so severe that, though a remnant hung on in Babylonia into the tenth century, most were eventually forced to leave. As the Latin and Byzantine empires in their turn became ever more fervently Christian, open Manichaean survival in civilised Europe and North Africa was made impossible too. The Religion of Light seemed to have no long-term future in Iran, Byzantium or the West. The only alternative route of escape was to the north-east, to the open steppe, which acknowledged no single master and where there was no single faith to impose uniform orthodoxy.

It is here that we at last find the connection with the Bogomils and the Albigensians, who would appear as such a threat to European Christianity over the following millennium. For in Mani's day, and a century after, the steppe was still the stamping ground of the Sarmatians. Did Mani's followers convert at least some of these horseback warriors to Zarathustra's vision before they set off on their rampage across the West, to lay—together with their Gothic allies—the foundations for medieval civilisation and the dualist heresy that accompanied it? There is, alas, no proof of that. No record of relations between Iranian nomads and Manichaean refugees. Yet one piece of circumstantial evidence that Mani's message was well known to the steppe-dwellers is so persuasive as to be impossible to ignore.

The Sarmatians were driven west from the grasslands by incoming Turkic tribes. Mani's message survived the change of population, and it was these Turkic peoples of the steppes who took it up, giving Manichaeism its greatest historic triumph. In the eighth century, the Khagan—the ruler—of the Uighur Turks was converted to the faith and founded the first, the last, and the only officially Manichaean state in the world. From there, later Mongol conquerors brought Mani's teaching into China, where the Apostle of Christ became known as the Buddha of Light and an incarnation of Lao Tzu, the founder of Taoism. Marco Polo met Manichaeans in southern China in 1292. It is even possible that the dynasty which kicked out the Mongols in 1368, the Ming, borrowed its name from the Religion of Light, for that is what Ming means—light. Not until the seventeenth century does Manichaeism finally fade from the Chinese record.

A fourteenth-century Manichaean temple still stands on Hua-piaou Hill, in the Fujian province of south-eastern China. Renovated in 1922, it became an annexe to a Buddhist shrine dedicated to the "ancestral teachers of India and China." Rediscovered in the fervently communist 1950s, it is now preserved as the ancient monument of an extinct belief.

Mani's story raises so many questions. Why, I wonder, unlike so many other faiths that appeared from nowhere and vanished again into darkness, did the Religion of Light spread so far, survive so long, so nearly succeed in establishing itself as one of the canonical religions—and then finally fail? And why, at the same time, did it provoke a hostility quite out of proportion to any possible harm it might have done to anyone? "Mani, the Maniac, was driven by the Devil himself," wrote Eusebius, Bishop of Caesarea. Perhaps this was simply a recognition that Mani was a supremely charismatic prophet, skilled painter and writer, who had successfully taken Zarathustra's vision of the universe out into the wider world, to those who spoke no Persian or Aramaic and who lived beyond the Iranian domains.

May the peace of the invisible God and the knowledge of Truth
be with our holy and dearest brothers,
who believe in the precepts of heaven and fully keep them.
May the right hand of Light guard and save you
from every evil assault and from the snares of the world.

The Religion of Light

May the pity of the Holy Spirit open your heart,
and let you look into your soul with your own eyes.

(FROM THE FUNDAMENTAL EPISTLE OF MANI)

What a seductive idea it was, this painter's vision of a universe built of actual light and darkness. That made Manichaeism not just a religion but also a science, claiming to offer a rational explanation of the physical reality around us. Yet for exactly that reason it faced the insuperable opposition of the Greek philosophic tradition and of the gradual but inexorable development of true scientific understanding. In the face of knowledge gained by observation and experiment, the explanation of the world revealed by Mani's Twin proved to be an untenable hypothesis. Though, as Napoleon said to Laplace, after the scientist denied the need for the hypothesis of a God: "Ah, but what a beautiful hypothesis."

Or perhaps there was another crucial factor: competition. At the very time when Manichaeism was trying to smuggle itself into Europe, it had to vie with another version of the Iranian religion that had already found a congenial home in the Roman Empire. Among the profusion of imported cults and sects which flourished across Europe in the first centuries of our era—Jews, devotees of Isis, of Bacchus, early disciples of Jesus Christ—this one faith seems to have had the greatest success and to have gained the largest following. Yet in spite of its popularity, we know less about it than almost any other second-century belief. It is well called the Mystery of Mithras.

5

The Mystery of Mithras

AND THE BULL DOZES

On the night of 10 May 1941, London suffered its severest air raid yet by Hitler's Luftwaffe. London County Council records show that the attack killed nearly fifteen hundred people, seriously injured some eighteen hundred more and left eight thousand streets impassable. The London Fire Brigade attended over two thousand fires, of which nine were classified as full "conflagrations," the severest category.

The sun rose over the smoking ruins shortly after five o'clock the following morning, the air still thick with billowing ash and masonry dust and carrying the unmistakable stench of charred brick and burned flesh across the city, to reveal that nearly a tenth of the City of London had been converted to rubble. While St. Paul's Cathedral had—famously—survived, a great swathe of buildings from the Thames riverside in the south to the Cripplegate area in the north was now no more. In the entire, large, roughly triangular, block between the ancient thoroughfares named Walbrook, Bucklersbury and Budge Row, as well as nineteenth-century Queen Victoria Street, only four properties and one single basement remained habitable. To make the area safe, the shells of the remaining buildings were knocked down and the site rendered flat by bulldozing the rubble into the exposed basements and cellars. A large static ARP (Air Raid Protection) water tank was constructed on the Queen Victoria Street side of the block, a little late in the day, one might think. These details, I hasten to add, come not from my own memory—though I was in London that night, I was only three and a half years old—but from the fascinatingly full account by John Shepherd of the Museum of London.

The area remained a derelict bomb-site for eleven years until, in 1952, it was bought by a property development company, and the Roman and Mediaeval London Excavation Council was alerted by the company architect to the imminent disappearance of a site that lay over the very heart of the earliest Roman settlement of the capital, astride a vanished waterway once named the Walbrook (*Weala broc*—the brook of the *Wealas* or Welsh) by later Anglo-Saxon settlers. Since the stream had been banked, revetted, channelled, bridged, filled in, and finally built over during the two millennia of London's evolution, the Council's archaeologists and historians were keen to establish its exact course and profile before the deep foundations of the proposed fourteen-storey office block obliterated all evidence for good.

Excavation took place over the next two years, the work constantly bedevilled by water flowing into the trenches; the long-gone Walbrook was taking the opportunity to establish itself again. It was a year before the Corporation of London provided a mechanical pump and granted permission to discharge the water into one of the remaining unblocked drains. Severely limited funds also meant that the hire of compressors and pneumatic drills was out of the question and the concrete basement slabs had to be broken up by hand, using club hammers and cold chisels, technology that has not changed since the first Roman builders developed the area almost two thousand years before.

In spite of the difficulties, however, discoveries were made almost at once. To nobody's great surprise, the excavators uncovered substantial Roman remains under the bombed-out buildings and, by the spring of 1954, the archaeologists were sure that they had found pieces of a temple of some kind, though not to which god it was dedicated. The discovery of "relics of a number of eastern cults" was reported by the press but raised little public interest. The dig ended on Saturday 18 September, 1954. Shortly before the excavators put away their tools for the last time, the final discovery, a beautiful sculptured head, was unearthed and identified as that of Mithras, a deity associated with Persian Zoroastrianism, and well known from other Roman religious sites. Professor W. F. Grimes, in charge of the excavation and satisfied that all discoveries had been fully and properly recorded, packed up his things at lunch-time and left for the country; the other workers also dispersed. The site was left vacant for the developers to move in on the Monday.

But on Sunday all hell broke loose.

The *Sunday Times* published a photograph of the Mithras head, identified the excavated building as the remains of a Mithraic temple or Mith-raeum, the only one known in the London area, and pointed out that it was due for immediate obliteration. Crowds of visitors soon began to gather and clamber all over the site, at no small danger to themselves. On the Monday the London *Times,* still then known as "The Thunderer," printed an editorial, which, among other things, thundered that:

> Within a matter of hours from the writing of these words the whole structure, with anything else that may be hidden under adjoining parts of the site, is apparently due to be bulldozed out of existence to make way for the foundations of a new (and, no doubt, much-needed) building. There is something grievously wrong with our planning if an important antiquity of this sort can be destroyed almost before it has been seen. What other civilised nations may think of the matter is a point upon which one can only speculate apprehensively.

So began what became known as the Temple of Mithras Affair, represented by the newspapers of the day as a fight between Mithras and Mammon, between preservers and developers, between the backward- and the forward-looking, a battle which involved many of the great and the good of British historical scholarship and eventually extended all the way to Winston Churchill's Cabinet, where it was discussed in between such other weighty matters of state as France's rejection of a European Defence Community Treaty, the signing of the Pacific Charter and a forthcoming Commonwealth Prime Ministers' Meeting. The politicians concluded that delaying the development of the area and forcing the developers to change their plans would cost the government too much in compensation payments to the company; the nation had still not fully recovered from the economic consequences of the war. An unhelpful precedent would seriously damage the prospects of rebuilding the capital after its wartime devastation, since there were likely to be Roman relics under the foundations of nearly every City building. Even a decade later it was still being said that "if you wish to see building contractors cower and property developers turn pale, you need only whisper the words 'Temple of Mithras.'" However, the onslaught of the bulldozers was delayed for a fortnight, to give the archaeologists more time to find whatever there was to be found. *The New Statesman & Nation* ran a competition for a commemorative verse, from which I like a contribution by Robert Murray the best:

The Mystery of Mithras

Here, where the legionary slept at church parade,
Dreaming of Heaven and Lalage, all roses,
Big Business buries all that Mithras made,
And the bull dozes.

While the politicians clashed with the archaeologists and historians, the discovery of a Mithraeum in London and the delay in beginning the development work was particularly welcome to us boys in the Latin class at school, as it offered us a rare chance of a day out of the classroom. The prospect was greeted with great excitement, even though we were to be accompanied by our Latin master, an ancient (at least so it seemed to us then), craggy teacher of pre-war vintage, one of the few of whom we were actually for some reason afraid, not because he ever beat us, but simply because of the power of his personality, his mannerism of sucking air in between his teeth between sentences, so as to sibilate like a snake, and his teacher's tic of immediately demanding instant repetition by one or other pupil of any statement he made:

"... Thus the cult of Mithras was a Romanised version of the Persian religion of Zoroaster ... *hisss* ... What was it, Kriwaczek?"

"A Romanised version of the Persian religion of Zoroaster, sir!"

We all trooped down to the City of London to see the temple remains. I remember it as a mild and pleasant autumn day as we joined the huge queue that stretched around the site, along Walbrook and all the way out to the blind Bank of England building in Threadneedle Street. It took an hour of shuffling slowly forward—with us sixteen-year-olds only barely restrained from running riot among the waiting crowd—until we found ourselves overlooking the great hole in the ground. That it was a disappointment almost goes without saying. It takes a trained eye to see a building where the lay person sees only random piles of stones, and even the experts haven't always agreed on exactly what this Mithraeum may have looked like while still in use.

The Temple of Mithras, London—John Shepherd's Museum of London report—illustrates a long low building, some sixty feet by twenty, with a rounded apse at one end and double-doors at the other. The floor was below the ground level of the time, approached by two steps leading down from the entrance. At the far end would have stood one or more stone pedestal altars, each inscribed with a votive dedication—DEO INVICTAE SOLI MITHRAE, To Mithras, the unconquered sun—and up two more steps behind them, on a dais in the hollow of the apse, would have been displayed a panel sculpted with the principal icon of Mithraism, the god himself sacrificing a bull surrounded by astrological symbols. There would have been other statues as well, at least two representing the torch-bearers called—for no known reason—Cautes and Cautopates, who were always shown accompanying the god and were dressed just like him, one holding an upturned, the other a downturned flaming torch. Like Mithraic temples elsewhere, the interior was divided lengthwise into three, with two rows of pillars separating a narrow central aisle from the side aisles. In a Mithraeum, these side partitions were devoted to dining couches *(lecti)* rather than seats *(selli)* and, in London as elsewhere, were raised some two and a half feet higher than the central aisle. The whole would have been roofed over to simulate the interior of a dark cave, illuminated only by oil lamps or tapers, with little or no light entering from outside.

Naturally, none of this was obvious to the crowds peering down on to the excavations. Not that Mithraism was entirely unknown to us school-boys. Most of us had an idea of what the "Romanised version of the Persian religion of Zoroaster" stood for from Rudyard Kipling's stirring tale about "A Centurion of the Thirtieth" in *Puck of Pook's Hill,* a book then still avidly read by youngsters. Those were the days before the views of the old arch-imperialist and literary genius made him unacceptable reading for impres-sionable minds. According to Kipling, Mithraism was a religion of honour, bravery, faith and trust, exemplified in the noble, self-sacrificing figure of Parnesius, the Isle of Wight–born Roman centurion and sometime "Cap-tain of the Wall"—Hadrian's Wall, that is. Supported by honest and loyal local Pictish tribespeople, he leads the fight against the attacks of the "Winged Hats," Germanic raiders who come across the sea to pillage the settlements of peace-loving Britons. The centurion is a supporter of the ill-fated general Magnus Maximus who launched his bid for the imperial throne from the province of Britain in the 380s, only to be defeated by Theodosius the Great and executed at Aquileia on the Adriatic. Patriotic faith and exemplary courage enable Parnesius to escape retribution and to retire honourably. From Kipling's story "On the Great Wall" comes "A Song to Mithras," that poem which hardly any description of the cult seems able to avoid quoting; even English Heritage's sober archaeological report delivers it in full. It's the poem which ends:

Mithras, God of the Midnight, here where the great bull dies,
Look on thy children in darkness. Oh, take our sacrifice!

The Mystery of Mithras

Many roads thou hast fashioned: all of them lead to the Light!
Mithras, also a soldier, teach us to die aright!

Grand and noble sentiments. But how odd that even highly respectable academic publications should include this flight of poetic fancy, based on nothing more than a romantic, and rather muscular Christian, imagination. It was not until I began to look more closely into what is actually known about Mithraism that I understood why the poem is so often quoted. The simple fact is that we don't know anything at all about the liturgy of the Mithraic rites, and not much more about the ritual. *Faute de mieux,* the Kipling poem is all we have to suggest what may have gone on in temples of Mithras right across the late Roman world, from the Middle East to North Africa to the Spanish Peninsula, through Gaul and Italy right round to the Balkans, and even including disputed border areas like the island of Britain, the Rhineland and the Danube valley.

Relics there are aplenty: more than a hundred Mithraic temples, more than four hundred inscriptions, more than five hundred items of sculpture and visual art, and a half-dozen texts by contemporary outside observers. But in spite of the efforts of so many scholars and even more charlatans, the meaning of the symbolism escapes us. Mithraism was a "mystery religion" and remains a mystery today; its initiates were sworn to strictest secrecy.

Though, ironically enough, our very ignorance does provide information of a kind. For, after all, it must say something for the respect and honour in which the Mithraic godhead was held, or at least for seriously heavy threats from the Brethren, that nobody in its four-hundred-year history seems to have broken the Mithraic *omertà,* its code of silence.

Because we know next to nothing about the Roman Mithras, any attempt to shed light on the meaning and significance of his cult must start with Mithra, the Persian deity whose name is so pervasively memorialised in the vocabulary and place-names of today's Iran. Why, I wondered, was the name Mithra, Mehr, a lesser divinity, so common, while the name Ahura Mazda, Zarathustra's one true God, never seemed to appear?

I first turned to my Farsi dictionary. What meanings does the word *mehr* and those compounded with it carry today? Apart from in phrases openly invoking the god, like the seventh month of the Persian solar year, the Persian Autumn Festival and the Mandrake plant ("Mithra's weed"), I found that modern *mehr* means love, affection, friendship, light, and the sun. Next, I consulted the work of one of the most distinguished historians of Iranian religion: R. C. Zaehner's *The Dawn and Twilight of Zoroastrianism.*

Mithra, I read, was one of the principal gods of the Aryan (Indo-Iranian) tribes even before they parted company and went their separate ways into India and Iran. Mithra's first appearance in the historical record is in an inscription found at Boghazköy in eastern Anatolia, dating from the fourteenth century BC and commemorating a treaty between two Indo-European peoples: the Hittites and the Mittani. Here are celebrated five divinities: Mitra, Varuna, Indra and the two Nasatyas, identical to those who reappear slightly later in the Rig Veda, the oldest book of the Hindu sacred canon. In the Rig Veda, Mitra and Varuna are Ashuras (lords) and are always mentioned together, often as the double or twin god Mitra-Varuna. R. C. Zaehner suggests that in Zarathustra's reform of traditional Indo-Iranian belief, Ashura Varuna (Lord Varuna) was raised and spiritualised to the status of the one true God under the title Ahura Mazda (Lord Wisdom), the others were demoted and denounced as *daevas* (demons), while Mitra, Varuna's inseparable twin, became an aspect of God, the Holy Spirit, through which Ahura Mazda performs his acts of creation. Over the following centuries, as the religion evolved beyond Zarathustra's inspiration, Mithra came to be seen as the Son of God—the three aspects of divinity unexpectedly prefiguring Christianity's God the Father, God the Son and God the Holy Spirit. By the fifth century BC, Iranians would sing, in their great hymn to Mithra:

> *I confess myself a worshipper of Mazda, a follower of Zarathushtra,*
> *who hates the Daevas and obeys the laws of Ahura;*
> *For sacrifice, prayer, propitiation, and glorification . . .*
> *to Mithra, the lord of wide pastures, who has a thousand ears,*
> *ten thousand eyes . . .*

> *Ahura Mazda spoke unto Zarathushtra Spitama, saying:*
> *"Truly, Spitama, when I created Mithra, the lord of wide pastures,*
> *I created him as worthy of sacrifice, as worthy of prayer, as myself*
> *Ahura Mazda."*

The word *mithra* was Old Persian for contract.

The wrongdoer who lies to Mithra brings death to the whole country, injuring the faithful world as much as a hundred evildoers. Do not break the contract, Spitama. Neither one you have entered into with one of the unfaithful, nor one you have entered into with one who is of your own faith. Mithra stands for both the faithful and the unfaithful.

Though frightful in his punishment of those who lie—"You bring terror to the bodies of men who lie to you; you take away the strength of their arms, angry and all-powerful; you take the swiftness from their feet, the eyesight from their eyes, the hearing from their ears"—Mithra brings salvation to those who are true to him.

> Who takes out of distress the man who has not lied to him, who takes him out of death. Take us out of distress, Mithra, for we have not lied to you . . .
> Not the wound of the well-sharpened spear nor of the flying arrow reaches the man whom Mithra comes to help with all the strength of his soul, he, of the ten thousand spies, the powerful, all-seeing, undeceivable Mithra.

Mithra stood for the contract, therefore for fairness, therefore for justice, therefore for honesty, therefore for truth, therefore for light, therefore for the sun. In Christendom, it is Jesus with whom believers have a personal relationship, rather than the austere, if unimaginably glorious, figure of God the Father. In Iran it was Mithra rather than Ahura Mazda. He became, like Christ, the mediator between God and humanity. The sacred rite in a Zoroastrian temple is performed in a consecrated area known as Mithra's gateway (Dar-e-Mehr). Upholder of truth and justice, it is he who bestows kingship. Hence the Mithra-sun on the *Sher-dar* madraseh in Samarkand.

If Mithra is the visible and much-loved sign of what its adherents called the "Good Religion of Ahura Mazda" one can understand the received wisdom, so obediently regurgitated by me to my Latin teacher, that the cult of Mithras was "a Romanised version of the Persian religion of Zoroaster, sir." At the end of the nineteenth century a single scholar, the distinguished Belgian historian of religion Franz Cumont, devoted much of his life to assembling everything that was known about Mithraic religion. His magisterial publication *Textes et monuments figurés relatifs aux mystères de Mithra* (Texts and symbolic monuments relating to the mysteries of Mithras) set it all out in detail. His conclusions became for most students of the late Roman Empire the established reality of the secret religion.

Cumont's story begins with a passage from the Roman historian Plutarch, who wrote that the teachings of Zarathustra had been first introduced to the Romans by the Cilician pirates of the south coast of Anatolia, whom the Roman general Pompey was sent to subdue in 69 BC. There was nothing improbable about this, as Cumont points out, since it is known, for example, that the first community of Jews "across the Tiber" was transplanted after being captured during the conquest of Jerusalem in 63 BC. In the process, the figure of Mithra the Mediator, the much-loved intermediary between this earth and God's spiritual world, guarantor of friendship, contracts, probity and honest dealing, was transformed into Mithras the Unconquered Sun, whose cult eventually became so popular right across the Roman world that the French historian and philosopher Ernest Renan could once famously claim, in a fit of excessive enthusiasm: "If Christianity had been stopped at its birth by some mortal illness, the world would have become Mithraic." As we know, the Persian Sun God was finally eclipsed by the Jewish Son of God and faded away around the turn of the fourth century, as would Rome itself soon after.

There was only one difficulty with this thesis, and not a minor one. Nothing that we know about the Roman Mithras matches the Persian Mithra, neither cult nor iconography. Taking the premise of Mithraism's origin in Iranian religion as a given, Cumont had to labour very hard indeed to interpret its symbols as illustrating a Roman development of the theology of Zarathustra. The result is a rather convoluted, one might almost say far-fetched, explanation of the remains, in which symbols are said to symbolise other symbols, which in turn symbolise yet others. One cannot lay too much blame on Professor Cumont for this, however. The sources with which he was working tended, themselves, towards the impenetrable. Here is the third-century neoplatonist philosopher Porphyry, writing about the use of honey in Mithraic ritual: "The ancients used to call the priestesses of the Earth-Mother Bees—in that they were initiates of the Earth Goddess—and called the Virgin herself Bee-like. They also called the moon the Bee, as the Lady of Generation; and especially because the exalted Moon is the Bull, and Bees are Ox-born—that is, souls about to be born are Ox-born."

Professor Cumont had to explain away major changes of dramatis personae in Mithraic mythology as of no consequence. His greatest difficulty was with what seems to have been a core Mithraic myth: the sacrifice of a bull by the divine Mithras himself. In no known version of Iranian Zoroastrianism is such an act performed by Mithra, who is in any case not the supreme God, but an intermediary between humanity and the divine. Zoroastrians do, however, attribute a bull-killing to Ahriman, the personification of evil, leading Cumont to surmise that somehow this primal act was transferred from Ahriman to Mithras, though it is difficult to imagine how and on what grounds this fundamental substitution can have come about.

The iconography of the Mithraic cult, the set of symbols displayed in the temples, is extraordinarily and consistently narrow. We are so used to a wide diversity of representations of the message of the Christian Gospel, there are so many stories to illustrate—the slaughter of the innocents, the Virgin with the Holy Child in the manger, the Crucifixion, the Pietà (the Virgin with the dead Christ in her arms)—that it is hard to come to terms with the poverty of subject-matter in the Mithraic images. Very occasionally, small panels surrounding the main tableau show enigmatic scenes from Mithras's life—Mithras being born out of a rock, Mithras dragging a bull into a cave, Mithras feasting with the sun god. But the faith's main, central belief is almost exclusively represented by one single, universal image. Turn the pages of Cumont's works and the same scene is illustrated again and again, sometimes with greater but more often with lesser artistry.

It is called the Tauroctony—the bull-slaying. This was the image placed at the sacred end of every Mithraeum, sometimes sculpted, sometimes painted, and probably usually both, in that shockingly garish way that must have made Greek and Roman religious sites look more like the Hindu temples of south India than the dignified, restrained and refined white marble edifices of our Victorianised imagination. Mithras, wearing his Persian outfit of Phrygian cap and loose trousers (to Romans, trousers were a sign of irredeemable barbarism), is perched with his left knee on the back of a great bull, whose nostrils he grasps with his left hand, pulling the creature's head back, while with his right he plunges a sacrificial knife into the animal's shoulder. He is almost always shown looking back and away from his bloody deed, with an expression of pathos and regret on his face. From the bull's wound flows either blood or, less commonly, ears of grain. A dog and a snake leap up towards the wound as if to lap the blood, while a scorpion attacks the bull's testicles. Usually a bird, a crow or raven, and a goblet are represented too, and sometimes also a small lion. Either side of Mithras stand the two torch-bearers, Cautes with his upturned brand and Cautopates with his downturned one, shown always—presumably for reasons of astrology rather than physiology—with crossed legs. Above Mithras's head are symbols of the sun god Sol and the moon god Luna. Around the god, and sometimes on his clothes too, are symbols of the night sky—stars, planets, a crescent moon—all the commonplaces of the Roman era's Hellenistic astrology.

Every known example of this universal *mis-en-scène* seems to be derived from a single original, sculpted in the style of a master-craftsman from the school of Pergamon, near the Aegean Coast of what is now Turkey, one of the great cities of the Hellenistic age. In turn, this original seems to have been modelled on an earlier, well-known image of the Greek goddess of victory (Nike) sacrificing a bull, which adorned the balustrade of the temple of Athena Nike on the Acropolis in Athens. Some have even recognised in Mithras's turned-away face the idealised likeness of Alexander the Great.

But what does it all mean? That there is a story attached to the scene seems clear: an instant in time is being pictured, the snapshot of one crucial moment during a sacrifice of some sort. Yet it can be no coincidence that every one of the characters portrayed, with the sole exception of Mithras himself, represents a heavenly constellation, the bull standing for Taurus, the dog for Canis Major or Minor, the snake for Hydra, the crow for Corvus, the goblet for Crater, the lion for Leo, the wheat for the star Spica. And what of Cautes and Cautopates, always represented in the scene as miniatures of Mithras himself, with their upturned and downturned torches and their crossed legs? Could they represent the equinoxes, vernal and autumnal, the crossing points of the celestial equator with the ecliptic, the apparent path of the sun among the stars? Are they images of the seasons themselves? Do they symbolise the passage of the soul after death: up to heaven or down to hell?

There is another icon found in Mithraic sites, though much less commonly: the extraordinary and mysterious image of the lion-headed god. He (though it could be a she, the gender is never made obvious) has a human body, the head of a roaring lion, four eagle's wings with a snake winding itself around the whole figure. This is very strange, for no matter how exotic the origins of their gods—and there were many popular deities, Isis, Cybele, Attis and Dionysus among them, who were well known to have come from other lands—they were always represented by Greek and Roman sculptors in human form. The classical world had no tradition of animal-headed gods as was commonplace in Egypt, for instance, or further east. Several dedications have been unearthed to a Deus Arimanius— including one on a headless statue discovered in York that is thought to have represented the lion-headed god—suggesting that here was a Roman-ised version of Zarathustra's Ahriman, the force of all evil in the world. Classical writers like Plutarch occasionally referred to a cult of Aremanius, in which the power of evil was celebrated or propitiated—and wolves were sacrificed.

The second half of the twentieth century saw numerous attempts to solve the mystery of Mithras by expunging the Zarathustrian link and suggesting that here was an entirely new religion whose only connection with the Persian divinity of the same name was just that—the same name. A similar suggestion has been made to account for the occasional ritual use of words which can only have an Iranian origin. On dedications, Mithras is sometimes referred to as Nabarze (unconquered); new initiates and some divinities are greeted with the word Nama (all hail!). These terms are, some propose, no more than attempts to give the cult an exotic frisson, rather as medieval conjurors employed fake Latin phrases like *hocus pocus, hax pax, vax Deus adimax* to give their performances an air of authentic secret knowledge. As part of their fatal drive to de-Islamise modern Iran and link it back to its pre-Muslim past, the Iranian royal family, particularly Queen Farah, the Shahbanu (the Mrs. Shah) of Iran, sponsored and supported a number of international congresses dedicated to the discussion and investigation of the Roman Mithras phenomenon. Perhaps she hoped to affirm the historic linkage between Iran and Europe. Ironically, the end result of her efforts was to cast doubt on the Persian connection altogether.

If the true nature of the Roman cult of Mithras, the beliefs its adherents held to and the meaning of the ceremonies they conducted, are a mystery, so is another aspect of this enigmatic religion. In a few decades, Mithraism swept through the Roman army from east to west, from Syria to Britain, like the sort of virulent virus infection to which the fundamentalist biologist Richard Dawkins likens all religions. Why should the Roman army choose to adopt a deity, or at the very least to borrow its name, from their sworn enemies in Persia? It is rather as if the British Army, facing the German Wehrmacht in the 1940s, should have enthusiastically taken up the worship of the Nordic gods favoured by Hitler. The early Roman Empire was contemporary with the Parthian dynasty of Iran, and in later centuries with the Sassanians (who conquered the Parthians in the year 224). The Romans waged almost continual, and largely unsuccessful, war against both. Indeed, in the middle of the third century, when Mithraism was at its most popular, the Romans came up against one of their most dangerous adversaries, the second Sassanian King, Shapur I, Mani's protector, who forced the Roman Emperor Philip the Arabian into submission, and captured the Emperor Valerian, keeping him in irons until he died, the event memorialised in the celebrated rock sculptures at Bishapur and Naqsh-e-Rustam in Iran. It certainly seems odd that the soldiers of the empire should have so honoured the best-loved heavenly figure of their most dangerous opponents—unless, perhaps, one can see in the cult an attempt by anxious warriors to ingratiate themselves with a divine power that may at the time have seemed more powerful than their own, home-grown, supernatural supporters.

LONDINIUM AUGUSTA TO PONS AELIUS

If scholars can't agree on the meaning of Mithraism, it is most unlikely that an untutored layman could come up with a convincing explanation. Nevertheless, in an attempt to find my own personal response to the cult of the perhaps Persian god, I set off to see some of the remains left to us in Britain by his second- and third-century devotees. My first port of call was the nearest: the Temple of Mithras, London, the site which I had visited as a teenager when it was first uncovered in the 1950s.

It is now much changed, of course. As part of the deal struck between the developers and the archaeologists, the stones of the ruin had been removed and stored at the back of a disused churchyard in the City. Eight years later, when the spanking new Bucklersbury House office complex was at last finished, the Mithraic jigsaw puzzle had been reassembled on a raised terrace fronting Victoria Street, approximately where the ARP fire tank once sat. Archaeologists have not been greatly impressed either by the site—neither positioned nor aligned as per the original—or by the way the remains had been reassembled into "a structure vaguely resembling a Mithraeum." The original excavator, Professor Grimes, particularly despised the suburban patio-style crazy-paving, decried the mistreatment of the varying floor levels, and judged that "the result is virtually meaningless."

Meaningless or not, there the reconstructed ruin still lies, well sign-posted and accessible, opposite a giant new pink-and-white-striped office complex designed in the recently fashionable neo-caravanserai style, close to the heart of London's financial district, with tourist coaches, red double-decker buses, black taxicabs and multicoloured delivery vans constantly speeding by, office workers in suits and trainers carrying sandwich-packs and carefully folded copies of the *Financial Times* streaming past from the nearby bus stop and Bank and Mansion House underground stations. This is the modern City of London at work. It is hard to shut all that out of one's consciousness as one stands at the entrance to the outlined Mithraeum and tries to assemble in one's mind's eye the scene as it must have appeared to Roman Londoners gathering at the doorway to attend a secret celebration or initiation, some time around the end of the second century.

The River Thames is on our left. Behind us, rather dilapidated now, rise the walls of the formerly magnificent palace of the provincial governor with its statue-mounted gables and its pilastered central portico overlooking a once fountain-filled but now rubbish-strewn pool. Beyond the Mithraeum: the bank of the Walbrook stream, which used to flow sluggishly through a muddy, marshy depression between higher gravel terraces on either side. By the time this spot was chosen for our temple in the 240s, the watercourse had been built up and revetted to form a narrow channel. The stream's opposite bank is lined with wood-framed, whitewashed, red-tiled two-storeyed storehouses, among which longshoremen in dirty tunics and leather aprons shout to each other or yell bawdy ditties as they heave on the ropes of wooden derricks, lug sacks, roll barrels and load amphoras on to carts. The smoke of burning rubbish mixes with the exotic aroma of spices and the stinging tang of old fish sauce from a smashed storage jar. All the sights, sounds and smells of Londinium Augusta, the great capital and port city of Britannia Superior, strike our eyes, beat on our eardrums and fill our noses.

If the people of the European Middle Ages seem distant and strange to us, the people of the Roman Empire are much easier to identify with. Here was a society in many respects very similar to our own—without the technology, of course. Only a few aspects of their lives would strike us as incomprehensible today, most notably the institution of slavery and the perverse enjoyment of savage death in the arena as popular entertainment. Otherwise Roman life has a very familiar feel. They too had their estate agents and property developers, their lawyers and accountants, their pampered performers and famous sports stars, their urban poor, small traders, craftsmen, *petite bourgeoisie,* their pompous professionals and wealthy landed gentry, their petty criminals and corrupt politicians. Even the Roman attitude to its official religion was not so very different from the traditional conservative British view of the Church of England: a unifying force to which lip-service ought to be paid but which should not be taken over-seriously. The deification of an emperor like Claudius was treated by many as little more than a joke. His predecessor, the mad Gaius (Caligula), was outraged that in spite of being proclaimed a god, people refused to worship him. He asked a delegation of Alexandrian Jews, "Are you the god-haters who do not believe me to be a god, a god acknowledged by all other nations but not to be named by you?" Most Romans would probably have agreed with Lord Melbourne that "things have come to a pretty pass when religion is allowed to invade the sphere of private life."

Just like in our own time, as the traditional religion of the Romans declined, new exotic faiths slipped in to satisfy popular spiritual needs. All sorts of what we would today call "new age" beliefs were eagerly imported from the East and followed with the same kind of insouciant naïveté that furnishes our city streets with chanting, drum-beating, saffron-clad devotees of Krishna from India—though in those days it was the followers of Dionysus from Asia Minor, of Isis from Egypt, or of Christ from Palestine. And the cultists of Mithras from Iran too, perhaps?

Our band of soldiers, lower-middle-class traders and freedmen—with maybe even an educated slave or two among them—waiting for admission to the temple, would not have been from the top drawer of Roman society. Though emperors and aristocrats, too, flirted with belief in the Zarathustrian god, "the capped one" as they also called him, their devotions were secretly performed in private temples attached to their palazzi. Lesser breeds must attend more public places of worship. We know that the lower orders were Mithras's principal devotees because of the dedications carved on plaques and altars, naming those whose donations had set them up: military officers as well as other ranks, small traders, petty bureaucrats, all in all the section of society that today's advertisers would group under social classes C1, C2 and D. The ceremonies in which they came to participate are, however, much less clear to us. Our small congregation may have assembled to witness an initiation, which Roman observers tell us played an important rôle in Mithraic observance. For worshippers were divided into seven ascending grades, and to move from one degree to the next demanded an elaborate, and perhaps painful, ritual.

St. Jerome, the Church Father, listed rank, name and serial number:

The lowest was the *Corax* or Raven, under the sign of the planet Mercury and symbolised by a cup. According to St. Augustine, during the ceremonies Ravens wore a black bird-head-dress and wings. Next higher was the *Nymphos,* the Male Bride (all Mithras worshippers were male; women were not admitted to the cult), under the sign of the planet Venus and symbolised by a lamp which was carried during rituals. Above the Male Bride was the *Miles,* the Soldier, protected by the planet Mars, symbolised by spear and helmet. The Latin author Tertullian recounts that during the initiation of a *Miles,* he must kneel, naked and blindfolded, while being offered a crown on the point of a sword. He rejects it and places it on his shoulder with the words: "Mithras is my divine crown."

The four higher grades were *Leo* (Lion), *Perses* (Persian), *Heliodromus* (Sun-runner) and *Pater* (Father).

Lions, under the sign of Jupiter, were symbolised by a fire-shovel and a sistrum—even then an antique musical instrument usually associated with ancient Egypt. St. Augustine refers to *Leos* crawling on all fours and growling, like big cats. Porphyry, another Roman writer, relates that during initiation, a *Leo* has his hands washed and his tongue anointed with honey. Associated with fire, a *Leo* might not touch water during the ceremony. The Persian was under the protection of the moon. His symbols were an ear of corn and a sickle. The Sun-runner was protected by the sun, wore a crown of sunbeams, and carried a torch and a whip. The Father, seniormost of the grades and under the sign of Saturn, was an important figure in the leadership and management of the Mithraic community. He wore a Phrygian cap like the god himself, and carried a staff, symbol of worldly authority.

What little else we know can be summarised in a few short lines. One author, the Pseudo-Ambrosius, reports that during initiation, a *Miles*'s hands were tied with chicken gut and that he was made to jump blindfold across a water channel. He was then set free by slicing the chicken-gut through with a sword-stroke. Others say that a resurrection was symbolically enacted, that there were ritual feasts of bread and water and even a form of baptism. Yet others, like St. Gregory of Nazianzus, claim that fearful ordeals had to be suffered: tortures, brandings and burials alive—though this may have just been the usual black propaganda fired by Christian enthusiasts against members of a competing faith.

But any attempt to imagine such scenes playing themselves out in the temple space before me has now been finally sabotaged by a newspaper seller on the street below the Mithraic terrace bellowing a headline about some Cabinet disagreement or other. It is a lost cause to carry on trying to bring back the London of two millennia past. In any case, the stones of the temple, reset in their new place by insensitive architectural site planners, kept constantly tidy by municipal street cleaners, and washed spotless by decades of London rain, have been long cleansed of whatever holy magic and sacred numinous vibrations they may have once possessed. To properly savour the supernatural flavour of a Mithraic temple, it would be necessary to find a location far away from the City, from the urgent bustle of this very model of a modern major metropolis.

One could of course travel to Rome, where, particularly around its port, Ostia, the remains of great numbers of Mithraic temples have been found—not surprising in the town which was for centuries the epicentre of Roman paganism. Towards the end, even the Roman nobility and imperial household were succumbing to the seductions of Mithras, perhaps receiving the good word from their own slaves, servants and guards. But in today's Italian capital one would find no less pandemonium than in the City of London. Better, surely, to travel to the very edge of the Latin world, the last border with the barbarians, the furthermost, outermost, uttermost boundary of civilisation, beyond which were nothing but dangerous savages, wild mountains, snow, ice and winter darkness—I mean, of course, to go to Hadrian's Wall, where Parnesius, Kipling's Centurion of the Thirtieth, served with such noted distinction.

The Great Wall, commanded into being by the Emperor Hadrian during his visit to Britain in the year 122, was the most extensive and elaborate defensive structure ever built by the Romans. Fifteen feet high and ten feet wide—wide enough to take a standard war chariot—it stretched for seventy-three miles right across the country from Bowness on the Solway Firth in the west to Wallsend on the River Tyne in the east. It was always more than just a wall, with forts every Roman mile, turrets between them and a deep ditch on the enemy side. Like many grandiose engineering projects of the past and of our own day, the initial cost estimate and even the design—perhaps sketched out by the Emperor himself together with his newly appointed governor of Britain Platorius Nepos—proved unrealistic. Constant redesign in the course of its six years of building, including the eventual construction of the Vallum—a huge trench running along the entire length of the Empire side of the wall, twenty feet wide and ten feet deep with twenty-foot mounds set back thirty feet on either side—sent the costs escalating ever upwards. Hardly surprising, then, that Governor Nepos eventually came under the emperor's disfavour and was ultimately dismissed.

Kipling suggested in his *Puck of Pook's Hill* story—on what evidence is unclear—that a great long, narrow, raucous and turbulent town had grown up along the whole length of the Roman side of the Wall. Maybe, though if so, we have not yet uncovered most of the remains. What is more certain is that individual garrison towns definitely did flourish, with their bars, fast-food stalls, brothels, armourers, undertakers, craftspeople, merchants and camp followers of every kind—the usual facilities, in fact, which seem to spring up out of the ground wherever military men gather in large numbers. And among these must be included their places of divine worship, for Roman soldiers were notoriously superstitious and—far away from home and security, surrounded by unfriendly barbarians—the legionaries must have felt in pressing need of whatever supernatural help they could get. In the third century, the cult of Mithras was the most popular religion of the imperial forces. Three Mithraic temples have been discovered by the Wall and yet others probably still lie under the windswept and rain-lashed turf. The best preserved was near the fort they called Brocolita, what is now Carrawburgh, where a first temple building proved too small and had subsequently to be rebuilt and enlarged, not once but twice, to accommodate an ever-growing congregation. So, armed with the extensive information provided by the Newcastle Museum of Antiquities website, with its splendid virtual reality reconstruction of the Carrawburgh site and temple interior, I set off for Pons Aelius or Aelius's Bridge, as they called Newcastle in those days—in honour of the Emperor Hadrian, whose clan name it was.

I had intended to take a train from Newcastle to Hexham and walk the four miles to the ruins along the Wall to Carrawburgh. This would, I thought, put me in the right romantic mood for viewing Mithraic remains. But, in the event, it was snowing heavily, so I allowed discretion to be the better part of valour, and hired a taxi from Hexham instead. I am glad that I did, for the driver had been taking tourists on the Hadrian's Wall run for so many years that, though entirely self-educated in Roman history, there was little that he didn't know about this part, or most other parts, of Roman Britain. Did I realise, he asked, when I commented on the weather, that the Romans were so cold up here in the north of the country that they imported the Roman nettle—a plant not native to Britain—for rubbing on and stinging their skin in a vain effort to get warm?

He himself was a Geordie, a native of Tyneside, like his family for many generations before. But heaven knows where they originally came from, he shrugged, speaking with that strong Tyneside accent that still sings like the Scandinavian speech of the Danes who ruled here in the ninth, tenth and eleventh centuries. For he would not allow me to imagine that when the Germanic invaders arrived, the Romano-British simply disappeared. Not at all; the incomers' numbers were far too few to people the whole region by themselves. No, new and old obviously mixed and intermarried until there was but a single uniform population that called itself English. And even the Romano-British themselves were a mixture. The indigenous Celts in these parts were mostly from the great tribal federation called the Brigantes, but much of the population was military in origin, the families of soldiers stationed along the Wall. And since Roman policy was to transfer recruits from their homelands to far distant parts of the empire, the legionaries of the Wall would have been Thracians and Dacians, Batavians and Germans and who-knows-what other nationalities.

I was startled to hear the taxi driver mention Sarmatians in passing. They were from a tribe called Iazygians—Iranians from the steppes beyond the Danube. They had been defeated by the emperor—Marcus Aurelius as I later discovered—who had first intended their total extermination, but was distracted from that course by a crisis elsewhere in the empire. Instead, he summarily recruited the eight thousand Sarmatian heavy cavalry into the imperial forces and sent more than five thousand of them to Britain to man the Wall. They never went home again, and were eventually settled permanently in the Ribble valley in Lancashire. With wives and children, and perhaps personal slaves, they must have numbered near to fifteen thousand, a substantial presence in an underpopulated land. Ever in search of any Zarathustrian connection, I asked the driver whether he thought the presence of Iranians could have had something to do with the popularity of Mithras, an Iranian god after all, along the Wall. Again he shrugged.

"The Roman soldiers were so scared and so far from home, they'd believe in just about anything and everything," he said. "Right next to the Mithras temple we're driving to, there's the ruin of something called Coventina's spring; it was probably a shrine to a Celtic water spirit. The Romans went on throwing coins into it right up to the end, and it wasn't even their own goddess."

But then, I thought, people have always thrown money into wells and springs—even into pools in shopping malls, like the one near my home that has to be cleared of coins every month to stop them breaking the pumps. What spirit might be being propitiated there?

My taxi driver was intrigued by my description of the Sarmatian contribution to the medieval Gothic style and immediately suggested a connection with King Arthur, whom he knew to have been a Romano-British chieftain or warlord. He thought the Iranian connection might well support the claim, as local folklore insists, that Arthur lies buried somewhere in these parts.

"Not so very long ago this local chap was wandering blind drunk round the fields near Housesteads, where the Roman fort is, when he falls into a hole. He crawls along a long tunnel till he comes to a blank rock-face where he sees a handwritten sign which says: POUR ME A DRINK AND BANG ON THE ROCK. Well, there's a bottle of Newcastle Brown in his pocket, but he doesn't fancy pouring it away, so he takes a great swig of it instead and bangs on the rock with the empty. The rock opens and there's a furious King Arthur standing there. 'You were supposed to pour me a drink,' he says. 'Too bad,' says the bloke. 'Too bad for you,' says King Arthur. 'If you'd have poured me that drink, I'd have come right out of here and saved Britain.' "

"Saved Britain from what?" I wanted to know.

"From the bloody European Union, of course."

Yet more snow was swirling out of the sky in the gusty wind as we skidded into the Carrawburgh temple car park on the main road that runs across the country from Newcastle to Carlisle. Turning up my collar against the weather, I got out of the taxi and tried, initially unsuccessfully, to find the signposted footpath which was supposed to lead first around the great field where the Brocolita fort itself had once stood, and then around another even larger field, the location of the original *vicus,* or civilian settlement. The whole landscape of rolling Northumbrian moorland was white, with no sign of the Mithraeum to be seen, and it wasn't until I had suddenly sunk knee deep into the frozen mud of a shallow ditch marking the fort's outline that I was able to orient myself and pick my way, much more carefully now, down a shallow slope. Only then did the ruined temple come into view. And what a temple!

Though abandoned for seventeen hundred years or so, the stone walls still rise to waist height, the pillars which once separated the central aisle from the side benches are still in situ, broken off some four feet above the ground, the side platforms that once bore the dining couches are also still there, with the unmistakable impression of their original wattle and brushwood facings still clearly visible. Three altars still stand at the sacred end ready and waiting for libations, or whatever other ritual the worshippers are at any moment about to perform in front of them. It strikes me as odd that while groups of druids or witches or other retro-religious folk seem ever ready to resurrect other long forgotten and now reinvented faiths from oblivion, prepared to dance naked around stone circles at sunrise on the solstice, or perambulate invisible ley-lines over deserted downs, none have attempted to bring back into use this temple of Mithras, which was, after all, dedicated to the god of the unconquered sun. Perhaps Brocolita fort is simply too bitterly cold, windswept and far from anywhere, still as remote an outpost today as it was to the Roman legionaries who manned it, longing for home, almost two thousand years ago.

Or maybe the Carrawburgh Mithraeum is just not mysterious enough. On close examination, these concrete-cast altars (the originals are now in the Newcastle Museum of Antiquities) prove to be crudely sculpted and the lettered dedications uneven, with the marking-out lines still visible: "To Mithras the invincible God, Lucius Antonius Proculus, Prefect of the First Cohort of Batavians, 'Antoninus's Own,' willingly and worthily fulfilled his vow." "Sacred to the Invincible God Mithras, Aulus Cluentius Habitus, Prefect of the First Cohort of Batavians, of the Ultinian voting tribe, from Colonia Septima Aurelia Larinum, willingly and worthily fulfilled his vow." The image of Mithras on the left-hand pedestal looks more like a Celtic fertility spirit than a classical divinity; it can only be the handiwork of a local craftsman, untutored in the arts of metropolitan Rome, as different as can be imagined from the work of the original Pergamon master. One feature is almost childish. Mithras is crowned—as usual—with sun rays. Here, the rays have been punched right through the stone, to meet a space hollowed-out from behind, so that a lamp or candle placed at the back would send light flickering through the apertures as if to simulate a weak and unsteady sun.

Yet the very crassness of the workmanship, its surprising ordinariness, actually brings the Mithraic community much closer to me. We may not know exactly what rites they performed here, but these were obviously ordinary men, with whom one could have enjoyed a drink and a laugh. And, as I imagined sharing one of the ritual Mithraic meals described by St. Justin Martyr in the second century, I suddenly realised the significance of the dining couches. As well as the occasional military prefect, perhaps the odd magistrate, maybe one or two small landowners, we include among our number private soldiers, traders, freedmen and slaves. Roman dining rules were clear: in their own homes, women sat in chairs, men reclined. In the presence of their superiors, the lower classes were only permitted to sit; slaves never reclined to eat. The fact that Mithraic feasts were *lectisternia*, reclining dinners, rather than *sellisternia*, sitting meals, had profound implications of equality and freedom. To this day, during the festival of Passover, Jews—who ritualised their religion in Roman times—are still supposed to eat the celebratory Seder meal while reclining rather than sitting. One of the formal questions asked by the youngest child present is why this is so. "Today we are slaves, next year we will be freeborn," is the answer recited in Aramaic. To the worshippers of Mithras the Mediator, patron of contracts, of friendship, of courage, probity, honesty, justice and fair-dealing, special friend of soldiers, petty traders, freedmen and slaves, the liberty, equality and fraternity hinted at by their dining arrangements may have been among its most important features.

There is an air of deep sadness about this abandoned temple. Other older British ruins—like stone circles, megaliths and dolmens, or even the rare remains of prehistoric villages—are merely mysterious. We have no idea of who attended or inhabited them and so cannot easily invest their former occupants with human motives and emotions; the remains have become part of the mute and unrevealing landscape. But here at Brocolita, where we can still read the names of some of the congregation who took part in the convivial fellowship of Mithras, I can't help wondering what became of Lucius Antonius Proculus and Aulus Cluentius Habitus. Such contact, at the same time close and very distant, underlines the desolation of the temple's present surroundings and the totality with which belief in Mithras was abandoned.

For, as we know, the cult was destined for oblivion. And its end was to be just as sudden and mysterious as its beginning. Archaeology tells us that Mithraic temples everywhere fell into disuse in the course of the fourth century, sometimes converted to other—though still pagan—purposes, as if the god's former congregation had turned to other faiths. There is only occasional evidence of purposeful destruction, of attacks perhaps by Christians, followers of the one new creed that could not and would not tolerate any of the old beliefs.

The London Mithraeum by the Walbrook was converted, its colonnades and dining benches removed, its sacred images carefully and respectfully buried under the floor. For a time it seems to have been used as a temple of Bacchus, god of wine and good fellowship, "who gives life to wandering men," says the inscription on a marble sculpture found on the site, or "that limb-loosener and effeminate creature," as Theodoret, a fifth-century Bishop of Cyrrhus, called him. After that, the building was abandoned and left to decay: the roof fell in, the walls sagged and began to crumble. As the English Heritage report suggests, it probably still survived as a ruin into post-Roman times, one of the many Roman remains "which would have remained visible amid the undergrowth in the walled city during the Saxon period." Here at Carrawburgh the fate of the Mithraeum is more uncertain. It seems to have suffered attack on a number of occasions, but whether by Christians out of religious zeal, or by local Britons in the course of anti-colonial agitation, is not known.

Yet though discarded by its former congregations, the cult that Mithraic temples were built to house did not vanish without trace. Belief in the "Capped One" does seem to have left a residue behind, a small number of bequests to the future whose traces can still be noted today, like the use of his Phrygian headgear to symbolise liberty, equality and fraternity to the French revolutionaries of the eighteenth century.

Another relic may be the date of Christmas. Mithras, as the Unconquered Sun, was naturally said to have been born on the winter solstice, around 21 or 22 December, when the days begin to grow longer again. The celebration of Jesus's birth, for which no date is given in the Gospels, was fixed in the late fourth century, the very time of Mithraism's rapid decline. Many scholars believe that Christmas took over the day of the older festival. After all, the birth of the Son of God (the Prophet Malachi's "Sun of Righteousness") and the birth of the Unconquered Sun, had much in common.

Historians of architecture, too, have found a Mithraic residue in the design of Christian churches. Ancient gods, they point out, were worshipped al fresco. But the secret cult of Mithras demanded privacy, so an entirely new kind of sacred building was devised for the purpose. The long, narrow ship shape (nave is from the Latin for ship) of the typical early North European church is provocatively similar to that of the structure designed to shelter the devotees of Mithras, with its central aisle and side colonnades dedicated to dining.

Many further examples could be given of features of European culture which have in their time been ascribed to the influence of Mithraism—Franz Cumont believed that our millennial obsession with astrology was one of them—but the link I would most like to be true is perhaps the most unexpected of all.

Six thousand feet up on Nemrud Dagh, a spur of the Taurus Mountains in south-eastern Turkey, not too far from the banks of the Euphrates, moulders the site of an extraordinary religious sanctuary. Carved out of the mountainside in the middle of the first century BC by King Antiochus I of Commagene, one of the Hellenistic successors of Alexander the Great, as a *herothesion*, "a common dwelling place for all the gods," its unparalleled assembly of statues and bas-reliefs looks out in all directions over the long-dead king's former domains. Among the reliefs are scenes depicting Antiochus being invested with kingship by each of his gods in turn, and as a self-proclaimed descendant of the ancient Persian Zoroastrian kings, Antiochus ensured that Mithra the Mediator was prominent among them. It is the gesture of investiture that catches the eye. For Mithra and Antiochus are shown shaking hands, a gesture which signified to the followers of Zarathustra the transference of divine power from God to his earthly representative.

Hand-shaking, though now almost universal, was never a Greek, Roman, Babylonian or Hebrew habit. Other peoples salute, bow, hug, kiss or, as supposedly among the Inuit, rub noses; Tibetans raise their hats. Only in Europe is shaking hands the traditional form of greeting. Could it be significant that in the very earliest depiction of this act in history it is Mithra who is one of the parties? For shaking hands is not just a greeting. We shake hands to seal a bargain or to express our honesty and goodwill. It is as if, in our handshake, we still remember what the Persian Mediator, patron of contracts, of friendship, of honesty, and of justice stood for. If there really was a connection between the Iranian demigod and the Unconquered Sun of Rome, it might explain how the handshake became the European gesture of honest greeting.

All this is to describe what happened, rather than why. The complete disappearance of a religion once so widespread across an entire continent, and its replacement by an equally and literally exotic faith, is difficult to explain. Why did Mithraism disappear as quickly as it had arisen?

The decline of the cult paralleled the decline of Rome itself. At the start of the fourth century the Eternal City had ruled the greatest European empire ever; its army could muster many hundreds of thousands in the field. Soon enough all this was gone. By the year 410 the Emperor Honorius had been forced to pull the last remaining legions out of the province of Britain and tell the colonists to look to their own defences. In 446 the first Jutes landed in Kent, marking the beginning of English history. In 476 a German tribal chief deposed the last Roman emperor of the West.

In Britain at least, and probably elsewhere too, some semblance of Latin civilisation continued on for at least another century, yet the fast fading Roman provincials seem quickly to have turned from Mithraic to Christian worship. Did Mithras's followers lose confidence in a god who was no longer able to guarantee success? Was Mithraism simply the loser in competition with the runaway success of the Christian cult? There must have been a wholesale conversion to Christian belief (even though in Britain there are far fewer concrete remains of established Christian communities than of Mithraic congregations) for a "Celtic Church" survived in

Wales well into the eleventh century. Perhaps the fact that Mithraism was restricted to men only, while the worship of the Christian God had particular appeal to women, may have been a factor in its decline.

Moreover, after Emperor Constantine's conversion to Christianity at the start of the fourth century, and the proclamation of Christianity as the state religion of the empire at its end, believers in pagan faiths stood little chance: Christianity was unusually intolerant of other religious ideas.

The historian Noel Swerdlow has suggested one possible reason for Mithras's swift capitulation to Christ. In an entertaining article, "On the Cosmical Mysteries of Mithras," he points out that the silence of the Church Fathers on the subject of Mithraism suggests the battle was over even before it had begun. No Bishop ever fulminated against its foolish flock. No Christian authority ever called on the followers of Mithras to give up their bone-headed belief in a non-existent god. Perhaps, Swerdlow suggests, there never was a real conflict between what we have wrongly seen as two similar, even equivalent, secret mystery religions. Mithraism, in his view, was never a profound faith. "Yes, it had images of some now forgotten myth . . . of torches, keys, shovels, caps, zodiacs and planets. And, like other cults, it had names of deities imported from the exotic East, grades of initiation, secret rites, and doubtless a good deal of divination, magic and mumbo-jumbo . . . But that may be the whole of it, a cult and fraternity of soldiers as eclectic as freemasonry, and no more profound."

It's an attractive solution to the mystery, but offers no explanation of why the cult didn't simply disappear without trace, as completely forgotten as freemasonry would be, were it suddenly to vanish from our business, professional and social life. I have heard Christians say that their faith's victory over pagan religions was because it was true and the others were all false. Myself, I would guess that belief in Jesus as the Son of God triumphed because it insisted on an entirely novel teaching that it had inherited from the Jews, and which it now introduced to Europe for the very first time: the certainty that the events described in its basic myth had actually happened in history. Other religions told stories about their gods— much of Greek and Latin literature celebrates the many adventures of the divine residents of Mount Olympus. Mithraists too may have told a tale involving the sacrifice of a bull and a feast with the sun god. But nobody could say when, or even whether, these events had literally, truly happened as described. Christianity's God, however, had actually lived, suffered, died and risen from the dead—and almost within living memory. This was evidence of a kind with which no other faith could compete.

There is an irony in the victory of this new Roman religion and its expulsion of an Iranian-linked paganism. For while the novel idea of a God who reveals himself through history may have ultimately come from the Jews, another aspect of Christianity that singled it out from all other faiths was a conviction that its followers were living through the last days of creation. And though we may not know what connection Roman Mithras had with Iranian Mithra, we do know that it was unquestionably the Iranians who first put forward the belief that the end of the world was at hand.

6

The End of Time

To walk on the high, wide, tawny mounds which are all that remain of many of the great cities of Middle Eastern antiquity is a strange experience. If you take an ancient eye-witness as your guide, you can't help being struck by the stark contrast between the described glories of the distant past and the observed desolation of the immediate present. Your feet crunch on broken potsherds that may be as much as four thousand—though equally possibly they may also be only four hundred—years old; without an expert eye, it's impossible to tell. Supporting your feet is the crumbled brickwork of what were once splendid palaces, magnificent temples, offices, shops and simple private homes—all now, for this is the way of sun-dried clay brick, reduced to crumbly dust. Where archaeologists have dug among the fragments, you can make out the remains of walls, windows and doorways, sometimes rising to shoulder height, with stretches of paved street between, so well preserved that their empty abandonment seems quite eerie, like a landlocked Marie Celeste. Someone once slept or ate or sat chatting in these rooms, you tell yourself, as you look vainly for the footprints of long-dead inhabitants. On the surface is a litter of smashed marble and limestone; sections of drystone wall run from nowhere to nowhere; occasionally a mighty stairway leads pompously up out of the ground to end blankly in the empty air.

Ancient Ecbatana (Persian: Hakmataneh), modern Hamadan, some two hundred miles west-south-west of Tehran, was the first capital of the Medes and the Persians. As one of my guides I have taken the fifth-century BC Greek historian Herodotus, who informs me that Deioces, the legendary founder of the Median Empire had built for him those great strong walls that are now called Ecbatana, one circle of them inside the other. The building was so contrived that each circle of walls is higher than the next by the battlements only . . . The battlements of the first circle are white, the second black, the third scarlet, the fourth blue, the fifth orange. Thus the battlements of these five circles are painted with colours; but of the last two circles, the one had its battlements coated with silver, the other with gold. These walls, then, Deioces built for himself and about his own palace, but the rest of the people he ordered to build houses outside the walls.

The rest of the people's houses still surround the drab dun-coloured hill, on which the bright polychrome walls once stood with their enclosed royal palace and treasuries. (Oddly enough, according to a Persian guidebook, the large nondescript modern city surrounding the mound was built to the plans of a German architect, Karl Fritch.) The site lying behind today's Ekbatan Street must have looked stunning back then. Now the only magnificence is provided by nature: Hamadan is six thousand feet above sea level and the high snowy peaks of the Zagros Mountains back the scene majestically.

Few tourists come visiting here, there is so little to see. And as at so many other antique locations in Iran, where at least a thousand museums' worth of treasure must still lie buried in the lumpy acres, a combination of Persian politics, penury and paranoia has long driven the archaeologists away. Yet one historic landmark is worth the journey: a rare and touching personal relic of Alexander the Great himself.

You won't find it behind Ekbatan Street any more. It has been moved some way off, to the centre of a little tree-lined public open space among offices, shops and concrete apartment blocks, where old men sit on the sides of bare, raised flower-beds in the weak spring sunshine, drinking black tea, gossiping and telling their *tasbih* rosary beads.

It doesn't look like much. A pale rock, some eight feet long, rounded and pitted like an elongated boulder, or perhaps like a large meteorite whose outline has been softened by melting in its passage through the atmosphere. It takes an effort of the imagination to recognise in this rather shapeless lump the much-worn form of a crouching lion with a mournful, melancholy, downturned head. Today's Iranians call it the Shir-e-ghamgin, the sad lion or, more prosaically, Shir-e-sangi, the stone lion. It was sculpted, they say, in 322 BC on the orders of Alexander to commemorate his friend, protégé and, perhaps, lover, Hephaistion, much hated by the other men, who had drunk himself to death (or was maybe murdered) in some place now hidden in the depths of the Hakmataneh mound. The lion, the Iranians say, represents Alexander himself and its inconsolable mien expresses the conqueror's grief at his irreparable loss. In Parthian times, the sculpture stood by the city wall at the Bab-ol-Asad, the Lion Gate. A later invader, Ard Avij of Ziar, had the lion's paws smashed, convinced that the Alexandrian connection was providing supernatural protection to the city.

The convexities of the white stone are strangely blackened. I ask why. My Iranian friend looks abashed. "You see," he admits, "barren women come here to touch it in the hope that its spirit will help them conceive. The stain is from the oil of their skin."

Hamadan's stone lion is a rare indication of human feeling in a man called "the Great" for his personal contribution to human history: a saga of serial murder and mayhem, of savagery, thoughtless cruelty, uninhibited drunkenness and barbaric excess. No wonder the Persians—and later the Qur'an—thought Alexander had horns. But perhaps this was no more than was expected of a warrior in that heroic age. He was undoubtedly a great leader, but of an army of destroyers, not creators. When he died in 323 BC at the age of thirty-two, what he had done was not so much to create from scratch the greatest empire the world had ever known—a children's history-book view of his achievement—but rather to defeat the Shah of Iran in a series of battles, and by his victories add Macedonia and Greece to the giant area already efficiently and rather benignly controlled by the Persian Achaemenids. So how come, in an age before spin doctors, advertising agencies and PR executives, the exalted reputation? Why the idolisation? I had always supposed it could only be because history is always written by the winning side and the European story, as we have all been taught to believe, began with the ancient Greeks.

The question led me to look a little more closely at the revolution which Alexander's destruction of the Iranian *ancien régime* undoubtedly brought in its wake—the demise of West Asian antiquity and the birth of the classical, Hellenistic era, the name given to that period when the dominant culture was Hellenic—i.e., Greek—though the rulers were Syrians and Egyptians of Macedonian extraction. With greater knowledge, I couldn't avoid the conclusion that our own times still owe Alexander far more than I had first imagined, but in a rather different way from the one I had supposed. What I was looking for was the world out of which Mani and the other Gnostic preachers arose, to spread the Zoroastrian dualist word abroad. What I found was that long before Mani's time the destruction of the Persian Shahs' God-given order by a ruler whose mandate came not from heaven, but from the point of the sword, had already released the teachings of the Persians' sacred mentor Zarathustra from their national boundaries, to spread throughout the wider world in a liberation that was to have great consequences for us all.

To get the full measure of the impact of Alexander's conquest on the ancient world, we must return to the southern province of Fars and to another ancient site, but a very different one: to the extraordinary palace complex of Persepolis (Greek for City of the Persians), sited not far from the dynastic Achaemenid burial site at Naqsh-e-Rustam, the place where earlier we found the Sassanians recording their victories.

Persepolis plays an odd rôle in today's Iranian self-image. On the one hand, it is a relic of the time before, as a sign in English tells you, "Iran was honoured by receiving Islam" and in addition is fatally associated with the last Shah's megalomaniac 1971 celebration—the tents and canopies are still dustily preserved for family parties of Iranians to shuffle slowly round and roundly condemn. On the other hand, the ruin is one of world's greatest spectacles and rightly a source of huge Iranian pride.

Backed by the barren brown Koh-e-Rahmat (Mountain of Mercy) the complex sits on a thirty-five-acre platform built up to overlook what was then a fertile plain. Here, over a period of more than a hundred and fifty years, from 520 BC onwards, successive Shahanshahs built an ensemble of buildings that can have had few parallels in ancient times. On three different levels, the lowest for commoners, the next for aristocrats, and the highest for royalty, stood the many-pillared and colonnaded palaces of Darius, and Xerxes, with their throne rooms, audience halls and treasury. The brilliant embroidered canopies, glittering gilded and silvered wooden entablatures, and the brightly painted and tiled sun-dried brick walls have long gone, leaving behind merely the stonework: the columns, some still standing with their bases and capitals intact, the door frames and the window casements. Some are charmingly labelled with a sort of ancient brand logo in cuneiform writing: "Stone window-frame, made in the house of King Darius."

What stonework this is. Every inch is covered in bas-relief decoration and the huge capitals that supported the roofs are sculpted in the shape of bulls, lions and eagles of exquisite design. The monumental ceremonial double staircase leading up to the main platform, cut from twenty-four-foot blocks and rising some fifty feet to the first terrace level, has steps shallow enough to ride horses up, or for notables in long robes to climb while protecting their dignity—or their angina. For here was the ceremonial capital, the religious focus of the Achaemenian Empire, the place to which foreign ambassadors and supplicants would come for an audience with the King of Kings, bringing gifts and tribute during Noruz, the Persian New Year, the festival which yearly reaffirmed the Great King's rule as viceroy of God on earth.

Noruz is still a ten-day festival holiday in Iran, just as it was two and a half millennia ago in Zoroastrian times, but as I look at the sightseers thronging Persepolis at this time of year, the men in shirtsleeves and jeans, the women covered all over in black *chadors,* I can't help finding them a very dull and repressed crowd compared to the ancient tribute-bearers whose magnificent procession is sculpted with loving detail all along the low walls lining the steps and passageways. Though two thousand years have washed away the colour—ancient sculpture seems always to have been brightly painted—it is not hard to imagine the scene into life. The emissaries would have ceremonially climbed the outer stairs and passed, first, between the giant cedarwood doors at the top and then on through the Gate of All Nations, a sixty-foot-high ante-room flanked by two huge standing stone bulls. They would eventually find themselves in a vast open square among a surging crowd of supplicants. In front of them is the audience hall, the Apadana, with its thirty-six grand columns, more than sixty feet high, supporting a wooden roof, the fabric of which sparkles with gold and silver and is decorated and picked out in red, blue, green and gold paint. This is a building which can accommodate as many as ten thousand representatives of the twenty-three different nations in the Achaemenids' federal empire. In its day, it was probably the most magnificent building in the entire world.

Over here Nubians in African robes, their leader's hand held like a schoolgirl's by a dignified Medean usher, bring the King of Kings a giraffe—or is it an okapi?—as well as elephants' tusks and a vase. On this side Indians in loincloths and sandals are guided by a Persian beadle with staff and dagger, bringing an ass, a pair of axes and something carried in baskets. On that side Scythians from the Central Asian steppelands approach, wearing the pointed hats Herodotus wrote of, bringing a horse, bolts of cloth, and what looks like a pair of long boots—perhaps those knee-length Parthian boots of red leather so favoured by later Roman emperors. Over there Elamites lead a lioness who snarls and turns her head, straining towards the two young cubs carried in the arms of the delegates behind her. There too are the Babylonians, the Arabs, the Thracians and the Greeks. But where, I wonder, are the Jews: a significant minority, after all, in the Achaemenian Empire. Can they be that group in the distance near the delegation from Babylon, carrying vases and ornaments and leading a chariot drawn by two small Arab horses? Pictured with hooked noses and curly beards, all but two are wearing strange tall, conical, spirally-wound turban hats, from under which hang long earlocks of hair, just like today's orthodox Jews. The guidebook describes them as Assyrians or Phoenicians but I wonder if that's right.

In fact, as we stand in Persepolis, we are surrounded by representative delegations from every one of the Persians' subject peoples, each with its own costume, its own particular headgear, its unique hair and beard style, and its special gifts for the king on this auspicious New Year's Day. A stone tablet found in the ruins lists them:

> Xerxes the King says: By the favour of Ahuramazda these are the countries of which I was king; Media, Elam, Arachosia, Armenia, Drangiana, Parthia, Aria, Bactria, Sogdiana, Chorasmia, Babylonia, Assyria, Sattagydia, Sardis, Egypt, Ionians—those who dwell by the sea and those who dwell across the sea, men of Maka, Arabia, Gandhara, Sind, Cappadocia, Dahae, Amyrgian Scythians, Pointed-Cap Scythians, Skudra, men of Akaufaka, Libyans, Carians, Ethiopians.

Persian and Medean guards, ushers and beadles protect the doorways. In a few places, the Shah himself is seen doing battle with a demon, killing a lion, or passing by in his magnificent robes, accompanied by a servant with a sunshade or a ceremonial fly-whisk. And over all hovers the winged symbol of Ahura Mazda, the "Wise Lord" who, as Zarathustra taught, is the one and only God, omniscient and omnipresent, and in whose name the king rules, maintaining the divine order and keeping the forces of chaos at bay. On an inscription over the Gate of All Nations we read:

> Ahura Mazda is the great God who created this Earth, who created the heavens, who created mankind, who created every good thing for mankind, who made Xerxes King, sole King of the many, sole Commander of the many.

And further:

> King Xerxes says: By the grace of Ahura Mazda I had this Gateway of All Nations built. Many other beautiful things that were built in Persia were built by me and my father. Everything that we have built that looks beautiful was built by the grace of Ahura Mazda.
>
> King Xerxes says: May Ahura Mazda protect me and my kingdom and whatever is built by me as well as what was built by my father.

The Achaemenid Empire was the greatest the world had ever known. "Darius the King says: This is the kingdom which I hold, from the Scythians who are beyond Sogdiana, thence to Ethiopia; from Sind thence to Sardis." It stretched from the Nile to the Indus, from the Caucasus Mountains to the Arabian Sea. But Ahura Mazda could not, would not, or at any rate did not, protect it against the ruthlessness of Alexander and his army, who arrived victorious in Persepolis on 30 January 330 BC. The Macedonians must have been dumbfounded by the city's magnificence, for nothing they had ever seen could possibly have matched it. They must also have been thunderstruck by the gold and treasure they found stored away. It was to take seven thousand pack animals to carry it all off—equivalent to three centuries' worth of the whole Athenian Empire's annual income.

The experience seems to have driven Alexander's men out of their senses. Even three hundred years later, the Greek historian Diodorus Siculus (Diodorus of Sicily) was scathing in his condemnation of what happened next. According to his account, after Alexander had told them that Persepolis was "the most hated city in Asia," the Macedonians gave themselves up to an orgy of plunder and destruction. Every Persian man was killed, the women and children dragged off for rape and slavery. The overpowering lust for loot was so great that Diodorus says Alexander's troops ended up fighting each other and many were killed or had their outstretched, grasping hands hacked off in the struggle.

But that was not all. For in late May or early June, at the end of a celebratory banquet, when everyone was much the worse for drink, an Athenian courtesan called Thaïs proposed that "it would be his crowning achievement in Asia, if Alexander would join them in a triumphal procession to set fire to the palaces, and let women's hands extinguish the glories of the Persians." So they all picked up torches and formed a victory procession. Diodorus wrote that as they conga'd around the city, Thaïs was the first, after Alexander, to fling her blazing torch into Xerxes's palace. Others followed suit and the entire palace was soon engulfed in flames. A hundred and fifty years earlier, Xerxes himself had attacked Athens and burned its temples. Now, Diodorus says, "it was most remarkable that the impious act of Xerxes, King of the Persians, should have been repaid in kind after so many years by one woman, a citizen of the land which had suffered it—and all in sport." When Persepolis was first excavated in the 1930s, high heaps of ash still covered the remains of the palace.

As we return down the monumental staircase to ground level, an Iranian guide tells me how differently Persians see the story. "Alexander hoped to receive the Noruz gifts as King of Kings here in Persepolis," he explains. "That is why he waited here so long, from January to June. But eventually he had to accept that we Iranians would never see him as our rightful ruler. That made him angry. His advisers warned him that unless Persepolis were destroyed, nobody would ever believe that the Persian king had been truly defeated. There would be constant uprisings; the city must be ruined for the sake of future peace. But it was to be a Greek peace only. Alexander wanted to make the whole world Greek, so he forced ten thousand of our Iranian women to marry his soldiers." He shook his head, mystified. "As if burning down our capital city and raping our women could prove Greek ways better than ours."

Then he brightened, gesturing towards a large family party coming towards us, two young men helping their venerable veiled grandmother up the steps. "But as you see: we are still here. Iran is still here, free and independent." His face broke into a wicked smile. "And what is Macedonia? Just a former Yugoslav republic."

The Greek peace never really happened. Seven years after the burning of Persepolis, Alexander was dead and thirty years of civil war inexorably followed before the fight over the Macedonian inheritance settled into a sort of belligerent stalemate, with the empire divided among the conqueror's generals and their successors. Even then, these new Greek or, properly, Hellenistic, rulers—the Ptolemies, Seleucuses and Antiochuses—continued to squabble, like rats fighting over scraps, failing to notice that a pair of large and ferocious dogs were approaching. These last, the powerful new polities of the Romans and the Parthians—the latter themselves descendants of nomadic Iranian barbarians from the steppes—eventually imposed order, driving Alexander's successor-princelings into the backwoods. Though the new lords of creation continued to fight viciously over the border territories between them, they did manage, after a century and a half or so, to give the region at least a semblance of stability.

For the many peoples of the Persian Empire, the fall of the Achaemenians did not merely mean a change of masters. It is no exaggeration to call it the end of their world. In ancient times, kingship was an aspect of the divine order. Though the Persian state was monotheist and believed only in Ahura Mazda, it did respect every nation's right to serve its own gods. In fact, the Achaemenids had taken care to encourage, even urge, their subject nations to follow their own spiritual traditions. Under Persian rule, the god Marduk was still enthroned in Babylon, and the Jerusalem Temple of the Jews had been rebuilt with active Persian support. Now all this was to be changed by a foreign ruling class, unsupported by divine sanction, who, having dethroned the ancient deities, expected everyone to take up Greek ways.

Economic hardship added to the agony. In classical times warfare was just another way of filling state coffers, and the wealth of newly conquered nations was ruthlessly stripped and shipped home. Ancient armies lived off the land, so herdsmen lost their animals and starved, peasants died of famine among their empty ravaged fields. Cities, the engines of the ancient economy, were destroyed, their walls torn down, their inhabitants put to the sword or taken into slavery. Thus prosperous ancient Iran was tipped overnight into poverty and destitution. Everywhere, like Victorian white settlers in Africa and India, new colonisers now set up new cities in the Greek mould, with Greek citizens, Greek constitutions and Greek appetites. The world culture of the new age was to be Greek, just as that of the nineteenth century was British.

Even when the Parthians took over colonial Persia, the new rulers still called themselves Philhellene (pro-Greek) on their coins, just as, in the twentieth century, freshly independent post-colonial one-party states unconvincingly and inappropriately claimed to be European-style democracies. For four hundred years Parthian rulers went on inscribing their money with legends in increasingly corrupt Greek lettering.

Judging by later developments, however, this Hellenism could have been no more than a superficial gloss, a surface layer. The rural populace, and probably the old nobility too, can't have given up their ancestral Zarathustrian beliefs so easily, for when the time came for the Sassanians to take their turn of power from the Parthians, they were able to restore Zoroastrianism as the state religion almost at once. If five hundred years of religious amnesia had really separated the era of Cyrus, Darius and Xerxes from that of Ardeshir and Shapur, the ruthless chief priest Kartir would hardly have found it so easy to impose orthodoxy.

Yet under the Hellenistic veneer, Zoroastrianism was indeed subtly changing. The shock of the conquest, the trauma of being reduced to a subject people by those they considered followers of Ahriman, the personification of evil—a.k.a. Angra Mainyu and the Lie—seems to have led the Iranians to concentrate heavily on one particular aspect of their ancient sage's message. Unlike other prophets of antiquity, Zarathustra had taught that history was neither cyclic nor eternal. The struggle he described between good and evil would one day be brought to a head in a great battle, and after many troubles and torments, the forces of good would be victorious under the leadership of a divine saviour called the Saoshyant (Future Benefactor): in the view of later Zoroastrian theologians, he would be a descendant of Zarathustra himself. Evil would be vanquished; history—the world as we know it—would come to an end. In what Zarathustra called *Frasho-kereti*, to which some translators give the splendid name "The Making Wonderful," the victorious Saoshyant and his helpers will restore the world to its pristine purity. As the hymn called the *Zamyad Yasht* has it:

> *which from that day on will never grow old and never die,*
> *will never decay and never be corrupted,*
> *ever living and ever increasing, and master of its wish;*
> *when the dead will rise,*
> *when life and immortality will come,*
> *and the world will be restored.*

In our own days, when shambling men with sandwich boards proclaiming that "The End of the World is Nigh" are a commonplace and comic sight, it is hard to grasp how revolutionary and powerful the idea of the End of History was in those turbulent times. Neither the Hebrews of Torah days, nor the Babylonians, nor the Greeks—nor, come to that, the Indians and Chinese—had ever developed a concept quite like it; no other tradition had declared that time was about to come to a full stop.

It was this fervent belief in the Saoshyant, the Zoroastrian Messiah, which came to the psychological rescue of the conquered Iranians, who convinced themselves that the horrific destruction of Ahura Mazda's ordered world and the triumph of the godless Greeks was just the first stage in a final battle whose ultimate outcome would be glorious. To be sure, good would triumph in the end.

How do we know what the Persians were thinking? The historical record of Hellenistic and even Parthian times is very sparse indeed. In fact, some of the Parthian rulers and their approximate dates are only known from the coins they left behind. Though literary activity surely continued, hardly any secular texts dating from the yawning six-hundred-year gap between the victory of Alexander and the age of Shapur have been preserved, let alone religious writings. But we know from later references that a series of Iranian oracles, modelled on those of the Sibyl, an ancient Greek prophetess, began to circulate among the inhabitants of the Hellenised Middle East, prophesying that the end of the world was at hand. One of these so-called Sibylline Oracles, the "Oracle of Hystaspes" (supposedly delivered by the Iranian monarch who was Zarathustra's first convert), is extensively quoted by Lactantius, a Church Father from third-century North Africa:

> Hystaspes says . . . that will be the age when justice is banished, when innocence is despised and the evil ones drag away good men as their prey. No laws, no order, no rigour of military discipline will survive. None will honour the aged, none will acknowledge the duty of piety, none will take pity on women and children: all will unite and conspire against the divine law, against the laws of nature. The whole earth will be despoiled, as though by a universal pillaging.

We are so familiar with prophesies of the End of Time from the last books of the Jewish and Christian Bible that most believers have always taken for granted that the Iranian Lore of Last Things—eschatology, to give it its proper title—had been learned from Jewish teachers. But that is unlikely to be true. The biblical Hebrews had no notion that time would one day come to an end, that the world was of finite duration. Their understanding of the future was rather different, if no less glorious. As they looked out at the increasingly dangerous world of the eighth century, prophets like Isaiah had warned of troubles to come.

> *Woe, the multitude of many peoples,*
> *which roar like the roaring of the seas;*

The End of Time

and the rushing of the nations,
that rush like the rushing of mighty waters!

After the destruction of the northern kingdom of Israel by the Assyrians in 721 BC, and the deportation of the upper class from the southern kingdom of Judah in 597, prophets of fire and brimstone, from Ezekiel to the second sage writing under the name of Isaiah, developed their own revanchist dreams and revenge fantasies, telling themselves that one day soon, a Messiah, an anointed descendant of the house of David, would be sent by God to defeat Israel's conquerors and force the whole world to recognise the Jews as its masters.

> I will lift up mine hand to the nations, and set up my standard to the people: and they shall bring thy sons in their arms, and thy daughters shall be carried upon their shoulders.
> And kings shall be thy foster fathers, and their queens thy nursing mothers: they shall bow down to thee with their face toward the earth, and lick up the dust of thy feet.

Such prophesies were still very much this-worldly. By contrast with Iranian beliefs, the Jews' last battle was not to be a transcendental event. It would be an earthly eternal kingdom that the Jews would inherit. Also it would not be universal. The Prophet Joel foresaw that the Jews would triumph and all other nations would be subject to God's chastisement.

> Egypt shall be a desolation, and Edom shall be a wilderness. But Judah shall dwell for ever.

Thus two different traditions about the future, one Iranian and the other Judaic, were developing independently among what were now merely two equal subject nations of the Hellenistic powers. Yet so close was the relationship between the pair that it was not very long before the two met and combined into a third and novel teaching, a message which was to prove of immense historical significance. That synthesis would be marked by the writings ascribed to a personality who was at the same time Persian and Jew, a prophet honoured in both of his own countries even into our own times. His name was Daniel, the last biblical prophet to be recognised by Jews and Christians. He lived, or at least dreamed that he lived, in Susa.

And I saw in a vision; and it came to pass, when I saw, that I was at Shushan in the palace, which is in the province of Elam.

THE PROPHET DANIEL

Shush, as the city is called in modern Persian, sprawls across the banks of the river now called the Shahoor, some ninety miles east of the Tigris. It was first settled by makers of painted pottery some time before 5000 BC, later becoming the capital seat of the Elamites. An Assyrian attack destroyed it in 639 BC. A century later, the Achaemenian kings made Susa their winter residence, and the city, with the huge and splendid Apadana audience hall—"Shushan the Palace" in the Hebrew Bible—survived Alexander's conquest, as well as Parthian and Sassanian dynastic rule. Visiting Susa in the twelfth century, Benjamin of Tudela, an itinerant Jewish rabbi who wrote a book about his travels, could still see "a large structure of great antiquity." A hundred years later, Susa was utterly annihilated by the Mongols.

Today Shush is just another huge dusty, dusky, mound, littered with stone fragments of long-gone buildings sweltering under a brassy sky. Though not as dramatic as the noble ruins of Persepolis, more of Susa's palace walls and processional pathways remain for the visitor to walk around than in many other locations of far less age. After some two and a half thousand years the baked brick wall footings still stand to waist height, clearly outlining the building's ground plan. Ancient paving stones, across which Achaemenian nobles once swept in their colourful robes, still delineate the streets. The broken-off lower section of a single gigantic fluted marble column, eight feet in diameter at least, with its typical Achaemenian decoration of drooping leaves around the base, suggests the extraordinary grandeur of what was lost here—though today the most spectacular construction on the ancient site is the Crusader-style "castle" built only a hundred years ago by a Persian master-builder on the instructions of a French archaeological team, supposedly to protect themselves from raids by local Arab tribesmen.

After climbing the steep roadway to the top of the ancient mound, past the usual soft drinks, postcard and trinket sellers, and exploring the scattered remains, I took time to look down on the town from the heights of the ancient Acropolis. Over towards the river, rising from behind the corrugated-iron shop roofs of the main street, I could see a strange stubby

white spiral like a large pine cone. The town map published by the munici-
pality claims that this "stepped pyramid" shape is "the typical kind of the
dome found in the area." I was thinking that I recognised the shape from
somewhere—an unlikely similarity, perhaps, to Chesterfield church's twisted
steeple—when I realised that the visual link was in fact with the head-
dresses of those earlocked Jews (or as the Iranians would now have it,
Phoenicians or Assyrians) whom I had seen parading in stone along the
walls of Persepolis. Here was the same shape again: like a spirally-wound
turban hat constructed in stone. It seemed to me a rather serendipitous
link, for this odd construction tops the tomb of the Prophet Daniel.

Daniel's tomb in Shush has a long history, though the present building
itself is not very old, probably built not much earlier than the nineteenth
century. Before then the prophet's remains had a complicated and rather
peculiar past. According to later Islamic sources, the invading Arabs discovered Daniel's remains when they occupied Susa's Apadana in the seventh century. Perhaps having heard tell of the famous burial of Alaric—the
Visigoth king who had sacked Rome two centuries earlier—in the bed of
the Busento river in Italy, Khalif 'Omar decreed that the River Shahoor
should be diverted, that Daniel be interred in the river-bed, and the water
allowed to return to its former course.

This seems an unlikely tale. Most Arabs had probably not even heard
of Daniel at that early stage in their religious history. More intriguing yet is
the supposedly eye-witness report by Benjamin of Tudela. According to his
twelfth-century account, Daniel was once buried on the side of the river
where the Jewish merchants lived. The burgeoning prosperity of this business community aroused the jealousy of those on the other side, and there
was fighting between the two settlements. Growing tired of the conflict,
both parties eventually agreed to alternate the prophet between the two
banks, to bury him one year on this side of the water, the next year on the
other.

"This they did," writes Rabbi Benjamin, "and both sides became rich.
But in the course of time, Sinjar Shah-ben-Shah, who ruled over the kingdom of Persia and had forty-five kings subject to his authority, came to this
place."

The great ruler was outraged by this *lèse-majesté* to the memory of a
great saint and commanded the citizens to measure the bridge and find its
exact centre-point. He then ordered them to take the wooden coffin of
Daniel and enclose it in another of crystal,

and to suspend this from the middle of the bridge by a chain of iron; at this spot you must build a synagogue for all comers, so that whoever wishes to pray there, be it Jew or Gentile, may do so. And to this very day, the coffin is suspended from the bridge. And the king commanded that out of respect for Daniel no fisherman should catch fish within a mile above or a mile below.

Nobody knows whether the good rabbi really saw what he claimed to have seen, though surely no pious Jew would have invented such a tale. But if he was telling the truth, it is equally unclear at what stage the coffin was removed from the bridge and taken to its present resting place.

We had missed the tomb with its white pine-cone dome when exploring the main street earlier in the day, for it hides itself behind a typical Iranian mosque archway. Even once inside, it is impossible to distinguish the court-yard from that of any other Iranian mosque or shrine, its arch-pierced façade decorated all over with geometrical patterns, Qur'anic texts, and the words God and Muhammad in stylised Arabic Kufic script inlaid into the tile-work in white, gold and shades of blue.

A crowd of Muslim devotees was pressing around the archway into the burial chamber itself. As I was taking my shoes off to go in, an attendant spotted my camera and demanded that I leave it outside with him—and buy some of his photographs instead. When I declared that I had no inter-est in photos, he rather lost interest and waved me through. I found an interior exactly like the mausoleum of any other Shi'ah saint or holy man: a hugely ornate metal cage surrounds the sarcophagus, surmounted by a blue, green and gold pitched cover, with gold plaques and goblets arrayed round the edge, under glass-crystal lampholders which break up the light into a myriad of dancing reflections. The *tout ensemble*—achieving what most Europeans would regard as the most baroque and kitsch-like of tastes—reminded me irresistibly of a 1950s ballroom; I'm afraid I couldn't help thinking of "Mecca Dancing." The Muslim visitors pressing their faces to the metal grille of the shrine, kissing it and whispering prayers, seemed particularly incongruous in this context.

On one wall, an illuminated Farsi text outlines the Daniel story: how he was taken prisoner by the forces of Nebuchadnezzar, how he worked hard to master Chaldean science and eventually rose to prominence in the Babylonian king's entourage. How he had been the only one able to inter-pret the king's dreams, and how he had finally travelled with a group of

Israelite refugees to Susa, where he remained until the end of his life. Nowhere does the document note that Daniel is not in any sense an Islamic figure, not mentioned in the Qur'an, and unknown to the Hadith, the traditions of the Prophet. That a Jewish sage should be so highly honoured among Iranian Shi'ah Muslims is far from expected. Might it be explained by Daniel's significance as the one who first united the prophetic traditions of Moses and of Zarathustra?

As I emerged, blinking, into the bright sunlight from the dim interior, the paradox of Daniel's double identity was underlined by the huge mural covering one whole wall of the courtyard. Using an extraordinary amalgam of the style of a Dublin IRA gable-end painting, with the stylised gestures and profiles of the antique Achaemenian reliefs, and the architectural abstraction of early Cubism, the muralist shows us two uniformed Iranian soldiers and two Palestinian guerrillas, masked by their checkered *keffiyehs*, tearing aside the iron bars imprisoning the Dome of the Rock in Jerusalem, while white doves of peace hover above and a slogan in English and Farsi proclaims: "Al Quds For Us." (Al Quds, "The Holy," is Islam's name for the Israeli capital.) Such murals are not uncommon in today's Islamic Republic of Iran, which has always worn its ideological heart on its sleeve, but the choice of this particular courtyard, at the shrine of an Israelite prophet, seemed to me to be too pointed to be accidental. It was time to go back to the Bible and remind myself of who Daniel was actually supposed to be.

The Book of Daniel is a strange work. To begin with, the text was composed in two languages, Hebrew and Aramaic, with no immediately obvious reason for the division. It consists of two sorts of materials. There are the stories about Daniel himself, his friends and associates, which purport to take place in Babylon during the reigns of Nebuchadnezzar and Belshazzar— familiar tales like that of Daniel in the lion's den, of Shadrach, Meshach and Abednego in the burning fiery furnace, and perhaps the best-known scene of all, Belshazzar's Feast, where a mystery hand appears and writes incomprehensible graffiti on the wall. In the other part of the book Daniel himself speaks of his visions in his own voice, and prophesies about the End Time, when God will overcome all evil and usher in a new and perfect world.

Aside from his book itself, there are other stories associated with Daniel, like that of Susannah and the Elders or Bel and the Dragon. These are now found in the additions to the Bible called Apocryphal by Jews and Protestants (and Deuterocanonical by Catholics), but were included in the quasi-canonical second-century BC Greek translation of the Bible called the Septuagint. Clearly, at that time in their history these other documents were considered as much Holy Writ as the chapters now accepted by Jews and Christians.

Holy Writ as it may be, Daniel turns out to be rather short on historical accuracy. Whoever compiled it had little clear idea of the chronology of the Babylonian Empire, which is the setting for the stories. Belshazzar, for instance, who is described as king, and as son of Nebuchadnezzar, was in fact neither. Nebuchadnezzar's real name was Nebuchadrezzar, with an "r." The last Babylonian ruler was Nabonidus, and he lost his empire not, as Daniel would have it, to Darius the Mede (there never was such a person) but to Cyrus the Persian. Belshazzar, Nabonidus's son, never became king. However, the writer or writers of Daniel must have heard tell of those times for, though distorted, there are hints of a Babylonian reality behind the book. Details like Daniel's court-name Belteshazzar, which means "May He Protect the Life of the King" in the old Akkadian language, have the ring of truth. Belshazzar, as crown prince, did often stand in and run the show for his father Nabonidus, who spent most of his time away from the capital, pursuing his passion—believe it or not—for archaeology. Though there is no evidence that Nebuchadnezzar ever went mad, there are indications that Nabonidus did suffer some years of serious illness.

These errors and deviations suggest that Daniel was written long enough after the events it describes for only the broad outlines of history to have been vaguely remembered when its petty details had faded from popular recall. Such factors, as well as close scrutiny of the language, lead students of the work to conclude that a later writer collected a number of traditional tales about the Judaeans' Babylonian exile and combined them with new material ascribed to an old, well-known, folk hero and saint. (This is not the first time the name Daniel appears in the Old Testament— King David had a son called Daniel, another Daniel figures in the Book of Nehemiah, and Ezekiel names a Daniel as a paragon of righteousness together with Noah and Job.)

When did this happen? In about 180 BC Ben Sira, author of the apocryphal book Ecclesiasticus, lists the famous men of Israel without mentioning Daniel. An Iranian Sibylline Oracle of about 140 BC alludes to one of the book's chapters, while the First Book of the Maccabees, written in about 100 BC, directly refers to its stories and characters. We can go further. Strong internal evidence helps pin down the date of composition to a remarkably narrow time-window. The Book of Daniel almost certainly took its present form after 167 BC. In that year Jerusalem was attacked and the Temple desecrated on the orders of Antiochus III, the king of the Syrian segment of Alexander's empire, who called himself Epiphanes (God made manifest) but was called by most others Epimanes (Mad). It was probably completed before Antiochus's death in 164 BC.

This was the greatest moment of crisis for the Jews since the captivity in Babylon more than four hundred years previously. The danger was even worse, for in Babylon, Jews had at least been allowed to follow their faith. Now the religion itself was seriously threatened.

Though they had lost the independence of their own kingdom, the Jews had largely weathered the storms of conflict that had swept over the region, as first Persia conquered Babylon, then Alexander conquered Persia, and then Alexander's successors fought between themselves over the remains. At one point Jerusalem changed masters seven times in twenty years, not unlike the experience of some Eastern European towns in the twentieth century. The Persians had allowed the Jews to go home to their own country and rebuild their Temple, but most had decided to remain in exile and had spread into a populous diaspora. One of the Persian Sibylline Oracles affirms to the Jews that "Every land and every sea is filled with thee." The historian Josephus claimed that "there is not a people in the world which does not contain a portion of our race." Their numbers in the whole of the Near East have been estimated at upwards of eight million, which must have been a sizeable proportion of the total population, perhaps as much as a quarter. Nearly everywhere they were permitted to administer their own affairs and live by their own religious laws. Whether for this reason, or because Jews were genuinely respected for their goodness and their worldly success in those international Hellenistic times, synagogues attracted around them large numbers of semi-detached and uncircumcised, but extremely enthusiastic, non-Jewish "God-fearers."

Given the strong opposition by today's orthodox to the very idea of conversion to Judaism, it seems surprising that in those days faith in YHWH attracted so many sympathisers. It seems that in classical times Jews were thought of as relentless proselytisers and missionaries. Even the Roman poet Horace referred to this widespread reputation: "When I have a moment to spare, I entertain myself by writing—it's just one of those minor sins. If you don't excuse it, a big band of poets will come to my rescue; for there are many of us and, like the Jews, we will force you to join our gang."

It would be wrong, however, to think of the Jews of the time as following the one orthodox faith we know now. There was no single mainstream form of Judaism then as there is today, but many different religious parties, ranging all the way from strict and pious fundamentalists of the Torah calling themselves Hasideans or Hasidim, through those who worshipped the Jewish God alongside his consort Asherah and other deities, all the way to the shameless Hellenisers, who in time even took over the High Priesthood and tried to turn Jerusalem into a fully Greek city, with baths, a gymnasium where young men exercised naked (an abomination to the prudishly pious), willingly underwent extreme pain in their attempts to undo the effects of their circumcision, and joined the Ephebeion, the "Young Men's Guild," donning its uniform of wide-brimmed hat, cloak fastened with brooches at the shoulders, and high lace-up boots. (I can't help mentally comparing this entertaining vision with the seventeenth-century Polish court costume of today's Hasidic Jews, with their wide fur hats, their long gabardines and their black breeches over white stockings.) At one stage Jerusalem was even given a new name: Antiocha.

This turbulent but survivable state came to an abrupt end when Antiochus Epiphanes was humiliated by the Romans in 168 BC, while attempting yet again to annex Egypt to the territories under his control. He and his army had paused in Eleusis, on the outskirts of Alexandria, when the Roman legate Gaius Popillius Laenas demanded to see him.

The two men squared up to each other in front of Antiochus's tent. Gaius Popillius ordered Antiochus to evacuate Egypt. Antiochus refused. The Roman threatened. The Greek prevaricated. In the end, the legate lost patience and presented the king with an ultimatum: Either you withdraw here and now, or Rome itself will declare war on you and your kingdom. Antiochus asked for time to consider. Whereupon the Roman rudely walked around the Greek king, drawing a line in the sand with his baton of office. Then he drew his sword. You will not leave this circle, he told the abashed Antiochus, until you have given me your answer.

Antiochus knew that he couldn't prevail against the power of Rome and had to agree to withdraw. It was during his disappointed journey back home to his Syrian capital that he apparently decided to reassert his lost dignity by the political equivalent of kicking the cat. At least he could show those damned Jews who was master. He sent his army off to attack Jerusalem. The general in command knew enough about Judaism to wait until the Sabbath, when he reckoned, rightly, that the orthodox wouldn't fight. The city was sacked, the walls broken, the buildings burned and much of the population slaughtered or taken into slavery. Further—and uniquely in the ancient world—Antiochus decreed that the Jews should no longer be permitted to observe their own religion. The Sabbath was prohibited, circumcision and the reading of the Torah were banned and the festivals were abolished—all under pain of death. Yet worse still, a statue of Olympian Zeus (Daniel's *abomination of desolation,* a distortion of the Hebrew words for *Lord of Heaven*) was put up in the Temple and pigs' flesh offered in sacrifice. This fearful moment, when it seemed that Judaism had no future left, was the context which called forth the Book of Daniel.

The series of stories with which it begins first establishes Daniel as a saintly and God-fearing man. Then, in a series of four visions experienced by the prophet himself, the meaning of recent history, of current political events and of their future outcome is revealed to the reader—of course in highly symbolic and allegorical language—in images strongly coloured by Zoroastrian ideas. Thus we read of the division of time into a series of "world-ages"; the giving of names to angels, a first for the Old Testament; the promise of resurrection after death for some, another first; the emphasis on fire in the great judgement scene of Chapter 7. A peppering of Persian loan words helps out its Hebrew vocabulary—words like *Raz,* meaning "mystery," which had no equivalent in the holy tongue. On the huge image in Nebuchadnezzar's dream, with "its head of fine gold, its breast and arms of silver, its thighs of brass and its legs of iron," what Norman Cohn, our leading historian of apocalyptic thought, calls the curious detail of its feet—"part of iron and part of clay"—was a description already found in a Zoroastrian text dating back to the time of Alexander the Great. And finally the Saviour, the "One like the Son of Man" who comes riding "on the clouds of heaven," an image which was to be so meaningful to Christian believers in later times, immediately brings to mind Zarathustra's teachings about the Saoshyant.

Yet the glorious future kingdom prophesied in the Book of Daniel, while accommodating the Zoroastrian belief in the End of Time, was still imagined as this-worldly, still rooted in the earth-bound Hebrew prophetic tradition which knew no other kind of existence.

"And the kingdom and the dominion, and the greatness of the kingdom under the whole heaven, shall be given to the people of the saints of the most High, whose kingdom is an everlasting kingdom, and all dominions shall serve and obey him."

Bad times would have to get even worse before the Jewish religious imagination was liberated from its earthly fixation, to seek out an entirely new dimension.

Religious oppression on Antiochus's grandiose scale could hardly fail to generate strong opposition, particularly from those more "zealous for the law" than for their own lives. Matters came to a head when Antiochus's agents arrived in a village called Modi'im, seventeen miles north of Jerusalem. As described both by the Jewish-Roman apologist historian Josephus as well as in the apocryphal First Book of the Maccabees, an old priest called Mattathias, leader of the community and father of five sons, was ordered to offer a sacrifice to the divine Antiochus. Mattathias of course refused, saying, "God forbid that we should forsake the law and the ordinances. We will not hearken to the king's words, to go from our religion, either on the right hand, or the left."

> Now when he had left speaking these words, there came one of the Jews in the sight of all to sacrifice on the altar which was at Modin, according to the king's commandment.
>
> Which thing when Mattathias saw, he was inflamed with zeal, and his reins trembled, neither could he forbear to shew his anger according to judgement: wherefore he ran, and slew him upon the altar.
>
> Also the king's commissioner, who compelled men to sacrifice, he killed at that time, and the altar he pulled down.

Mattathias fled to the hills and, though the old priest himself soon died, his sons launched a classic guerrilla war against Antiochus's Syrian rule. In two years the third son, Judas, known as Maccabee (the Hammer), recaptured the Temple and had it purified and rededicated, a victory still celebrated in the Jewish *Chanukkah*, the Festival of Lights. The following year he took advantage of Antiochus's death to wrest full religious freedom from the Seleucid regent. Nineteen years later, in 143 BC, Simon, the last brother to survive after each of the others in turn had come to a violent end, finally established Judaea's complete independence. He himself was assassinated in 134 BC, and the throne passed to his son John Hyrcanus, who continued to extend Jerusalem's control, from Samaria in the north to Idumaea in the south, forcibly converting their populations to Judaism, circumcising as he went. The irredentist dreams of prophets like Joel and Daniel seemed close to fulfilment. The prophesies of the final victory of the house of Israel seemed to be coming true.

But if the Jews began to believe that the Maccabean triumphs were in fulfilment of the foretold victory of God over the enemies of Israel, and that from now on Jerusalem would be the centre of earthly power among the nations, they were quickly disabused of that pleasant fantasy. As any cynic could have predicted, the Maccabean rulers fast turned themselves into a dynasty—the Hasmonean—and soon adopted the ways of typical Hellenistic princes in all their worldliness and wealth. Even the Syrian ambassador was taken aback: "So Athenobius the king's friend came to Jerusalem: and when he saw the glory of Simon, and the cupboards of gold and silver plate, and his great attendance, he was astonished," says the First Book of the Maccabees. John Hyrcanus's son went so far as to give himself the title Philhellene. Worse still, the new ruling family had taken the High Priesthood for themselves, a position reserved by God's command for the descendants of Aaron, brother of Moses—which the Hasmoneans definitely were not. Pious opinion was outraged and Judaean society divided into warring factions as never before.

By the start of the first century BC, under the rule of Alexander Jannaeus (Hebrew: Yannai)—a drunkard, a profligate, and the first Hasmonean to break all Jewish precedent and award himself the title of king, for he was not of Davidic descent—the public mood turned overtly revolutionary. While Yannaeus was officiating as High Priest at the Temple during the Festival of Tabernacles, a cry went up that he was unworthy of his office, the mood became ugly, and the congregation pelted him with the fruit they were carrying to use in the service. According to Josephus, he flew into a rage "and slew of them about six thousand." The nation thereupon descended into six years of civil war. Yannai hired foreign mercenaries, in response to which the insurgents backed a foreign invasion of Jerusalem. Though temporarily defeated, Yannaeus managed to survive and wreak terrible vengeance on his enemies. Josephus tells us that:

> when he had taken the city, and gotten the men into his power, he brought them to Jerusalem, and did one of the most barbarous actions in the world to them; for as he was feasting with his concubines, in the sight of all the city, he ordered about eight hundred of them to be crucified; and while they were living, he ordered the throats of their children and wives to be cut before their eyes.

As a contemporary text, one of the Dead Sea Scrolls, put it: "He hanged living men on wood . . . which was not formerly done in Israel."

Yannai died, to everyone's relief, in 76 BC. Thirteen years later, during the inevitable civil war between his sons, the powerful sect of the Pharisees, descendants of the pietist Hasidim, foreseeing no end to the suffering of the Jewish nation, approached the Roman general Pompey and begged him finally to depose the Hasmonean line. Can one imagine how great must have been their despair, for pious Jews to call for the ending of their own state?

Pompey's taking of Jerusalem left twelve thousand dead. And so it was that Jewish political and religious independence, the fond dream of centuries of longing, foundered in a sea of blood. The Hebrew tradition of eschatology, which predicted the victory of a pious God-fearing, Torah-observing Israel over the gentile nations, was in ruins. The way was now open for the triumph of the Iranian apocalyptic tradition, which foretold nothing less than the end of the world.

THE SECT AT THE DEAD SEA

The ancient, brown, stony, arid, wilderness of Judaea, between Jerusalem and the Dead Sea, the lowest point on earth, a landscape as sunburned as a Bedouin and as warted and wrinkled as a centenarian, was from earliest times a place of refuge and retreat. Far from the fleshpots of the coastal plain, beyond a day's walk from the holy heights of Jerusalem, the wilderness long provided a place for rebels, dissidents, separatists and hermits to be alone with their God. There, in the parched hills that were once the patrimony of the Israelite tribe of Judah, where John the Baptist preached and where Jesus was tempted by Satan, you can still persuade yourself that time has stood still for two millennia and some wild prophet may at any moment crest the nearest ridge and accost you about the approaching End of Time.

In the last decades of Hasmonean rule in the first century BC, this would really have been quite likely, for the Jewish kingdom seethed with such eccentric characters, entertainingly described in the Babylonian Talmud, the definitive collection of Jewish religious commentary completed between the fifth and sixth centuries. You might well, for example, stumble upon Chanina ben Dosa sitting by a snake's nest.

It happened somewhere there was a serpent who hurt creatures. They came and informed Rabbi Chanina ben Dosa.

He told them: "Point me to its hole."

When they did, he put his heel over the hole's mouth. The serpent came out, bit him and died. He hung it over his shoulder and brought it to the house of study.

He told them: "See, my sons! It is not the serpent that kills. Only sin kills."

With this they began to say: "Woe to the man who meets a serpent, but woe to the serpent who meets Rabbi Chanina ben Dosa."

Or, less alarmingly, you might run into Choni the Circle Drawer with his direct hot line to heaven, as described in the Mishna, the second-century compilation of rabbinic law.

It happened that they said to Choni the Circle Drawer:
"Pray for the rains to come!"
He prayed, but the rains did not come. What did he do?
He drew a circle, stood in it and said: "Lord of the world, your sons have turned their faces to me, for I am like a son of the house before you. I swear by your great name: I will not move from here, until you have compassion on your sons!"
It began to drizzle.
He said: "I didn't ask for rain like this, but for rain to fill cisterns, wells and caverns!"
A downpour threatened.
He said: "I didn't ask for rain like this, but for rain of good will, blessing and grace."
It rained as it was supposed to, until, on account of the rain, Israel had to go up from Jerusalem on to the Temple Mount . . .
Simeon ben Shetach sent for him and said: "If you were not Choni, I would have you excommunicated. But what can I do to you? You are presumptuous before the Creator and yet he does as you wish, like a son presumes on his father and he does whatever he wishes."

Rabbi Simeon's threat was for presumption, not heresy. There was no mainstream, "normative" Judaism in those days which heretics could be accused of abandoning. In fact the religion was divided as never before and never since. A rabbinic source tells us that apart from the well-known Pharisees and Sadducees (the Temple aristocracy), there were at least twenty-four groups of schismatics within Judaism before the Roman destruction of the Temple in the year 70. Among those we know about were Boethusians, Essenes, Hasidim, Hellenes, Herodians, Sicarii, Therapeutae and Zealots. Others not mentioned by the Talmudic rabbis, perhaps because they were associated with the Jewish-Christian cult, were those like John the Baptist who believed that the End was at hand and that they had been sent into the wilderness to prepare the way of the Lord—some scholars maintain that the Baptist was himself brought up by the Essenes. Or like the hermit Bannus, who preached a vigorous asceticism, and with whom Josephus says he himself spent three years from the age of sixteen.

Though we have long known many of these individuals and groups by name, what they believed, and precisely how they differed from other Jews, was a mystery until the middle of the last century, when a spectacular find of documents in a series of caves near the northern end of the Dead Sea shed new and unexpected light on the kinds of ideas which were circulating in Judaea just before the birth of Christ.

Some time, probably in the second century BC, a group of pious sectarians opposed to the Jerusalem hierarchy withdrew to a settlement on the cliffs above the dried-up river-bed called the Wadi Qumran, to wait, it seems, for the world to end. Some time, probably just before the destruction of the Jerusalem Temple by the Romans in the first century, an entire library of sacred books was secreted in the caves nearby—perhaps by these same sectarians, perhaps by somebody else. Some time in the twentieth century, probably in the 1940s but perhaps in the 30s, a Bedouin shepherd boy discovered the cache of documents in one of the caves and the modern age was presented with a window into the thought world of those expecting to experience the End of Time two thousand years before. Some of the documents proved to be the Hebrew or Aramaic originals of works previously known only in Greek or Coptic translations; some were found to be the very earliest manuscripts of biblical texts ever to be discovered; and some of the scrolls contained entirely new books, hitherto unknown to biblical scholars.

It strikes me as somehow appropriate that the details of the discovery of the so-called Dead Sea Scrolls, the remains of that two-thousand-year-old library, as well as the identity of their discoverer, are as vague and difficult to pin down as the identity of the dissident sect of Qumran and the details of who it was that hid the books. In *The Mystery and Meaning of the Dead Sea Scrolls*, Hershel Shanks, founder and editor of the *Biblical Archaeology Review*, has written an entertaining account of their discovery and significance, that should give pause to anyone who believes that the true facts of an event should be easy to pin down in the age of radio, newspapers and international communications.

The first finder of the scrolls was apparently a young member of the local Ta'amireh clan nicknamed Edh-Dhib, the Wolf. The well-known story of the find is that Edh-Dhib was tending his family's herd among the Qumran cliffs, when an animal disappeared into one of the many caves that honeycomb the terraces. To chase the beast out, the boy hurled a stone into the cave and heard the unexpected sound of breaking pottery. On investigation, he and his friends found some large earthenware jars, inside which, wrapped in crumbling ancient linen, were a number of scrolls.

But further than this broad-brush account it is impossible to go. As Shanks writes: "Was it a goat or a sheep that he was looking for? Was it one shepherd or two? Did they enter then or only the next day? And who was Edh-Dhib? Scholars have interviewed, inconclusively, several Bedouin who claim to be Edh-Dhib, and even the date when the scrolls were first found is uncertain." Furthermore, "what happened when the scrolls reached Bethlehem is as obscure as the circumstances of the initial discovery. In Bethlehem the Bedouin contacted one antiquities dealer, or perhaps two: Faidi Salahi or Faidi al-'Alami, who may have been the same man under different names, and possibly Khalil Iskander Shahin, better known as Kando." Given that the first attempts to establish what really happened took place within ten or fifteen years of the event, such confusion is a salutary lesson to those who believe that near-contemporary accounts, like those, say, of Jesus in the Gospels, are likely to be factually accurate.

However, while the full story of how and by whom the scrolls were discovered will now probably never be known, we do have the scrolls themselves. And the light they shed on religious belief during that dark age known as the Second Temple period—the time after the canon of the Old Testament was closed but before the New Testament was written—reveals just how far Jewish beliefs about the end of the world had accommodated themselves to the Persian teachings of Zarathustra in those heady days when everyone expected history to draw to a close within years if not months, and certainly within their own lifetime.

"A Man of Mockery arose who sprinkled upon Israel waters of Falsehood," says one of the documents. The reference is to a great enemy of the Qumran community who is commonly referred to in other passages as the Liar, immediately bringing to mind the Persian inscriptions of Darius and his successors. For in them Ahriman, the Power of Evil, often goes by the name of the Lie. "Darius the King says . . . may Ahura Mazda protect this country from hostile armies, from famine, from the Lie."

As among the Iranians, we find the principle of the two powers openly expressed: "The God of Knowledge has created man to govern the world, and has appointed for him two spirits in which to walk until the time of visitation: the spirits of truth and falsehood."

As among the Persians, the End of Time will be marked by a "War of the Sons of Light against the Sons of Darkness," when "affliction will come on earth and great carnage among the nations . . . "

As among the Zoroastrians, in the end, good will be victorious. It will be "a time of salvation for the people of God, an age of dominion for the members of His company, and of everlasting destruction for the company of Belial [Satan]."

Then "the heavens and the earth will listen to His Messiah . . . His spirit will hover and will renew the faithful with His Power . . . He liberates the captives, restores sight to the blind and straightens the bent."

A true golden age will be born, one which will last for ever and ever:

And the days will begin to grow many and increase amongst the
children of men,
Till their days draw nigh to one thousand years,
And to a greater number of years than before was the number of days.
And there will be no old man
Nor one who is full of days
For all will be as children and youths.

And all this was expected to happen at any moment, as Jewish state, nation, and religious unity rotted rapidly away.

One further detail took me by surprise: that the sectarians of the Dead Sea Scrolls used a different calendar from other Jewish groups. As a result, they were celebrating festivals and holy days at a different time from their co-religionists. Since their future, as well as the future of the world, was in their view so closely bound up with the proper fulfilment of God's commandments and the correct observance of his ordinances, adopting a different calendar was no small matter. The moon-based calendar of the Hebrews' most ancient inheritance—unlike settled tillers of the soil, desert nomads don't need to be able accurately to predict the seasons—was, and still is, so central to the daily, weekly and yearly round of Jewish custom, that the adoption of a new, sun-based calendar was tantamount to the adoption of a new Judaic faith. It is surely no accident that the new calendar was almost the same as that used in Persia under Achaemenid rule.

I was sitting on the stone footings of Xerxes's palace at Susa, looking up from Daniel's tomb past the rusty rooftops of the modern city of Shush, over the wide and fertile Mesopotamian plain, beyond which lies the Syrian desert, and beyond that, some eight hundred miles away, the Holy Land. For much of their earlier history, the plain, the desert beyond and the Holy Land itself had all been part of the Iranian world—in religion as well as politics. Now the border of Iraq runs close by and Mesopotamia is occupied by an Arab enemy. But the name Iraq itself is Persian—it means "lowlands"—and Baghdad was the name of the Iranian landowner (the Persian equivalent of Gift of God, or *Godiva* in Old English) on whose estate the capital city was founded. Even today, as in Iran, most of the Iraqi people are Shi'ah Muslims.

The story of the Messiah had begun so hopefully here, with Daniel, and had ended so sadly in disappointment over there, beyond the plain and the desert. But then it occurred to me that I was mistaken. The apocalyptic sectarians of the Dead Sea had been right, not wrong. The world did come to an end—their world, the ancient world. It was swept away by the new faith waiting in the wings, another Jewish sect which would quickly separate itself from its Judaic roots. For Jesus was born towards the end of these tragic and turbulent times and the Christian centuries were to be a radically new age.

Some writers have claimed that the incarnation of God in Jesus Christ was no more than a legend deriving from the Zoroastrian Saoshyant. But, as Norman Cohn elegantly puts it in his book *Cosmos, Chaos and the World to Come:* "Christianity was to change out of all recognition into something that was quite remote from both Judaism and Zoroastrianism. That Jesus's death on the cross was a redemptive act, by which God offered mankind the possibility of salvation from the consequences of sin, this was something wholly new . . ."

But Zarathustra's teachings had already done their work and made their mark on the world. For without that last pre-Christian century of religious ferment, without the conviction, learned from Persian eschatology, that these were the last days, Jesus's message would hardly have fallen upon such eager ears and spread so fast. Whether the first converts to faith in Jesus as the Christ, the anointed of God, were Jews, pagans, or—what is most likely—the throng of "God-fearers" still congregating around the synagogues of Asia Minor, Christianity conquered the Western world in so short a time and with such fervour because the message which it bore was so eagerly expected, awaited and longed for. In that respect Zarathustra's legacy was to give shape to the whole of the next two millennia—and, of course, is with us still.

The followers of Christ parted from Judaism and went their way. After the Roman destruction of the Jerusalem Temple in the year 70, the rabbis set about transforming Judaism also. True, Akiba, one of the greatest rabbis of the age, did back the final disastrous Jewish revolt of the second century, believing that its leader was the Messiah. But this ignominious failure, the more than half a million Judaean casualties, and the subsequent permanent expulsion of the Jews from their ancient capital, largely put an end to the conviction that God was directing the march of history. Not prepared to recognise Jesus as the Messiah, Judaism had little choice but to put all messianic hopes on the back burner. Out too went Zarathustra's dualist beliefs, though the Talmud, the anthology completed at the end of the sixth century, recalls that at least one first-century rabbi, Elisha ben Abuyah, was excommunicated for apostasy because he was still speculating that there might be not one, but two powers in heaven:

> The apostate cut down his own offspring. Of him scripture says: "Do not let your mouth make your flesh sin."
>
> He saw that Metatron [another name for Satan] happened to be granted authority to sit recording the merits of Israel; and he said:
>
> "It is a tradition that on high there is no sitting and no strife, no division and no toil. So perhaps there are two supreme Powers."

The rabbis of the Talmud believed that they were cleansing and purifying Jewish belief. Zarathustra's two supreme powers were an affront to Israel's One God. Yet to sit here in Susa, so close to the Persian tomb of a Jewish prophet, is to be forcibly reminded that the relationship between the two ancient nations had been so close for so long that many other Persian themes had successfully infiltrated Jewish thinking without being spotted. Without any sanction in the Torah, Jews had come to believe in heaven, angels and a life after death. And those teachings had come not from their own prophets but by the grace of Ahura Mazda.

7

By the Grace of Ahura Mazda

Very early in the morning, while the sky was still dark and sunrise only a low orange glow in the east, we came to Pasagard, site of the mausoleum of Cyrus II, known as the Great, first monarch of the ancient Persian Achaemenid Empire. Because of an unexpected eight-hour delay—our driver had been arrested at a police checkpoint for carrying a lump of opium in his wallet, put on trial that very evening and released, after bargaining, with a moderate fine ("Sir, I am a poor man, I cannot afford to pay so much." "What can you afford?" "Fifteen thousand Tumans." "So be it then.")—we had failed to arrive here as planned the afternoon before. So I was determined to make a virtue of necessity and drive the thirty-five miles north from the city of Shiraz early enough to witness the dawn rise over the tomb of the ruler who himself had presided over the dawn of a brand-new "Empire of the Medes and Persians."

My long search for Zarathustra was now on its final approach, for it is with Cyrus that the Persian story, and with it the story of Persia's prophet, emerges from the shadows of prehistory, myth and legend, into the sunlight of recorded times. It was under Cyrus, in the sixth century BC, that Iran became the core of the first universal, multiracial, multi-faith empire, stretching from the Mediterranean Sea to the Hindu Kush Mountains—the largest, most prosperous, most enlightened and longest-lasting empire of the ancient pre-classical world, a record not equalled until Roman times five centuries later. I believe that it was through Cyrus's example that Zarathustra's teachings about Ahura Mazda, the Lord Wisdom, and his eternal opponent Angra Mainyu, the Power of Evil, spilled out from their homeland and from their own time to influence religious thinking right across the world for the next twenty-five centuries.

Having wanted to visit this place ever since, as a schoolboy, I first learned of Cyrus from his Greek biographers, I had expected to be uplifted and moved. What I had not anticipated was that the entire area would be closed off with a high wire fence, the gates through which were firmly padlocked. After we had wandered around for some time, looking unsuccessfully for a way to bypass the barrier, the door of the shabby caravan parked next to the entrance suddenly opened and an elderly man, wearing pyjamas incongruously decorated with yellow daisies, stepped down, rubbing sleep from his eyes. He was not pleased to have been woken so early. "Are you mad people?" he demanded. "The tomb doesn't open till ten o'clock." The time was then just after six.

My Iranian companion tried to bend the truth a little: "I am from the Ministry of Antiquities in Tehran," he said grandly, waving a grubby scrap of paper in front of the man's nose.

"Oh no you're not," said the man with total conviction.

My companion was rather taken aback. "Why do you say that?"

"No government official from Tehran ever got up so early in the morning."

Seeing my companion now reach into his pocket and bring out an American ten-dollar bill, he shook his head pre-emptively. "And, by the way, bribery is illegal and un-Islamic. Come back at the proper time." He turned to go back into his caravan and, presumably, back to bed.

I made one last effort. "I have travelled a very long way to visit Cyrus's tomb," I pleaded.

"Where have you come from?"

"From London, England. And my schedule doesn't allow us time to wait four hours. If you don't let us in now, I really won't be able to come back again. That would be a great loss to me."

Perhaps my submissive tone mollified the man. "What do you want here?"

"To pay my respects to the burial place of the first and greatest of Iranian rulers."

"Are you Zoroastrian?" he now wanted to know.

"No, but I am a fan of Iranian history."

After an internal mental struggle lasting some seconds, he appeared to come to an executive decision, said "Wait," went back into the caravan, returned with a bunch of keys and unlocked the gate. After ushering us through he firmly locked them again behind us.

"Call me when you want to leave," he said.

"What if you're asleep?" my Iranian friend asked.

"I heard you before, didn't I?"

Pasagardae, as the Greeks called it, originally Pasragarda in Old Persian (perhaps meaning Camp of the Persians—long before Cyrus's day, this was already a gathering place for Iranian nomads), is quite different from other archaeological locations in Iran. No great mound squats here, signalling the disappearance of a former large city, and there is little to remind today's visitor of the teeming crowds which once gathered around the royal buildings. You get no feeling in Pasagardae, as you do in Persepolis, that the departed shades of the former Lords of Asia are hovering unseen over the stage of their former glory. Only a few broken white columns of simple plain design mark the site of Cyrus's private palace. Of a once elaborate gatehouse, a single door jamb remains standing, decorated with the bas-relief of a four-winged beneficent spirit or angel, wearing a long Assyrian robe and an odd, Egyptian-style three-pronged head-dress. According to the guidebooks, this is the oldest known complete Achaemenid work of monumental sculpture. It is striking to see a piece of such immense historical significance abandoned here in the Persian badlands. Since it was almost certainly the Persians who introduced to the world the belief in heavenly angels as we now imagine them, this could be the first model, the prototype, of every subsequent angelic figure depicted in the history of art—the start of the tradition by which angels are always shown with wings. Scholars used to think the angel represented Cyrus himself, for above it was once an inscription in Persian, Elamite and Babylonian, copied down by an eighteenth-century traveller: "I am Kurosh [Cyrus] the King, son of Kambujiya [Cambyses] the King, descendant of Hakhamanish [Achaemenes]." Today most archaeologists prefer to interpret the bas-relief as displaying the idea or spirit of the great king's rule—ancient Zoroastrian belief often embodied abstract notions in concrete representations. The empire is not mentioned in the inscription. Its lettering was almost certainly carved when Cyrus was still merely ruler of the district of Anshan, before he became overlord of the Medes, Persians, Babylonians, Lydians and the many other peoples shown paying tribute to the Achaemenian kings at Persepolis. No trace of the inscription remains today.

Close by, all that remains of the king's audience hall is a single tall column, tapering elegantly towards the top, a vivid demonstration of how high the roof once rose above the scene. A little further off stands one window-pierced wall of what may have been a temple. Yet further on a pair of eroded stone fire-altars peep out of the sandy ground.

All around, excavation has revealed channels and drains, unmistakable marks of an irrigated garden—a "paradise" in the Persian language—separated from the dry and dusty outside world by the foundations of an enclosing wall. Like Saudi Arabians today, who fondly recall the time before they exchanged their black goat-hair tents for concrete bungalows and their camels for Toyota Land Cruisers, Cyrus probably still felt close enough to his people's nomadic past for his capital to have been a moveable tent city. Only the private palace, audience hall and temple were permanently built of stone, brick and wood—perhaps as a gesture towards his settled, town-dwelling Elamite and Babylonian subjects, inheritors of a long tradition of civilisation. Even the design of the private palace, insofar as it can be reconstructed, suggests that a large central area between gatehouse and palace portico was once covered by a wide awning, protecting the supplicant crowd from the burning sun, and effectively extending the building into the garden, the garden into the building. One can imagine the king in his richly embroidered robe, his golden and bejewelled bracelets and anklets sparkling in the dappled sunlight, seated on a fine wool carpet surrounded by his courtiers, much as—a full two thousand years later—Persian and Moghul miniatures showed poets, musicians and dancing girls entertaining their Shah in a green park of flowers and singing birds. Both India's Moghuls and Persia's later Turkish rulers were, like Cyrus in his day, still nostalgic for the ways of their nomadic past.

But it is Cyrus's final resting place that we, like Alexander the Great before us, have come here to see. And it is worth the journey: an immensely dignified gabled white stone cube, set upon a monumental base, recalling the form of a ziggurat, a Mesopotamian step-temple. The whole ensemble is today some thirty-five feet (ten metres) high. One side is pierced by a doorway, above which there seems once to have been another opening, now filled in. The building stands all alone, isolated in a wide expanse of scrubby plain with only purple thistles as decoration, over which, in this season, the wind whistles across from the khaki-coloured mountain escarpments in the distance, the only features that break the monotonous view. According to Michael Wood, who came here to make a television film in the 1990s, Luri nomads on their annual trek from the plains to the high pastures of the

Zagros Mountains would until recently circle the building singing, and smear the steps with honey and mare's milk.

Standing before this simple and graceful building you know that you are on the very spot where Alexander himself stood in the year 330 BC. The tomb had originally been richly furnished; the embalmed body of the king had been laid in a golden sarcophagus on a golden couch, with a golden table by its side, on which treasures were placed: ancient swords, a shield and Cyrus's personal bow. Stationed all about the tomb was a permanent guard of Magi, the priestly clan of the Medes. Arriving two hundred and fifty years later, Alexander found the tomb plundered of its royal ornaments and the body lying on the floor. He ordered it restored to its place and the tomb closed up.

According to Greek historians, the following inscription surmounted the doorway: "O man, whoever you are and from wherever you come—for surely you will come—know that I am Cyrus who founded the Empire of the Persians. Grudge me not, therefore, this little earth that covers my body."

No writing remains on the building today, and scholars of the past have judged that this text owes more to the romantic Greek imagination than to actual eye-witness report. In 1970, however, careful examination of the stonework revealed for the first time the lower half of a much-eroded rayed disc carved over the doorway. This may well be the last remnant of the original inscription. If, as seems most likely, it once formed part of the divine symbol of Ahura Mazda, the *faravahar* (sign of divine glory) found inscribed all over Persepolis and other ancient sites, and called *farohar* by today's Zoroastrians, it suggests that Cyrus was indeed a follower of Zarathustra, a proposition hitherto much disputed among historians.

Alexander was said to have returned to this spot many times, almost as if his intention of founding a new multinational empire depended on the posthumous approval of the first founder of imperial rule in Western Asia. But there could hardly be a greater contrast between the young Macedonian adventurer and the Persian empire-builder. For while even Alexander's strongest supporters and apologists couldn't—and didn't even try to—hide their hero's ruthlessness, savagery and general excess, Cyrus the Great has gone down in history—even in Greek history—as a paragon of everything a good ruler should be.

We are so used to later Greek anti-Persian propaganda, contrasting Western democracy with Oriental despotism, that it is surprising to find Cyrus treated as a paragon of kingly virtue by near-contemporaries like

Herodotus. The Greek soldier and author Xenophon, writing a little later, at the end of the fourth century BC, even dedicated an entire book to a brilliant novelistic account of Cyrus's life, the "Cyropaedia" or "Education of Cyrus," setting up the Persian monarch as the ideal model for all rulers to emulate.

Lingering here in Pasagardae, as the sun comes up over the brown hills and washes the white tomb's roof with the colour of pink Persian roses, I try to bring to mind those verses of unmatched beauty in which the biblical prophet—the third to write under the name Isaiah—calls Cyrus the Lord's anointed, his "Messiah" (the first so designated in the Old Testament), and declares him to be the instrument of God:

> *Behold my servant, whom I uphold;*
> *mine elect, in whom my soul delighteth;*
> *I have put my spirit upon him:*
> *he shall bring forth judgement upon the nations.*

It seems strange for a Persian empire-builder to receive such flattering notices from Greek and Jew alike, but even to his own people he seems quickly to have become an almost mythical figure. The story of Cyrus's origins as told by Herodotus—with no sign of his tongue in his cheek—could only have been heard from Persian lips. Less than a century after the Persian king's death, the worldly Greek historian gives us a tale worthy of a fairy story, as fanciful as those of the biblical patriarchs or of Homer's legends—a superhuman hero's life-story, reminiscent of tales told about the origins of Moses, of Sargon of Akkad (conqueror of Sumer in the third pre-Christian millennium) and even of Zarathustra himself.

It all began with Astyages (Ishtumegu in Akkadian), King of the Medes, then the leading Iranian nation, who had taken control of the Iranian plateau and extended his rule over most of Anatolia. Astyages had a daughter, Mandane. "When Mandane was ripe for a man," Herodotus tells us, he married her off and, fearing insurrection, chose not a Median noble but "a Persian called Cambyses (Kambujiya in Old Persian), whom he found to be a man of good house and peaceable temper; though he considered this Persian to be much below a Mede even of middle class." Mandane quickly became pregnant and in a terrifying dream, Astyages saw a vine grow from between her legs that came to overshadow the whole of Asia. The Magian court soothsayers told the king the meaning of the dream: that Mandane's child would come to rule the world in his place.

When a baby boy was born to Mandane, Astyages knew that he must be eliminated, lest one day he take the kingdom from him. Too cowardly to perform the act himself, Astyages called on his kinsman Harpagus, "the faithfullest of the Medes and steward of all that he had," to take the child away and destroy him. But Harpagus couldn't bring himself to murder a baby, let alone a royal prince for whose blood he might some day have to answer. He gave the child to a poor herdsman in his retinue, with instructions to expose him on a distant hillside known to be frequented by savage wild beasts. But that very day the herdsman's wife bore a stillborn child, so the poor couple kept the live princeling as their own and exposed the dead baby in its stead. In the herdsman's family the child grew up healthy and strong. So far, so mythical.

One day, when he had reached ten years old and was playing with his friends in the village, the other children chose him to be king of their game. Among his playmates was the son of Artembares, a high Medean noble.

> This boy refused to obey one of Cyrus's orders, at which Cyrus commanded the other children to arrest him; and when they had done so, he treated the rebel very severely and had him whipped.

Artembares, the boy's father, was furious at the insult to his family and complained to King Astyages, who called Cyrus, the poor herdsman's child, to account for his actions.

> "You are the son of such a father, and yet you dared so shamefully to chastise the son of a man whom I honour among the first of my kingdom?"
>
> The boy answered: "Lord, I indeed did this to him, and was justified in doing so. For the children of the village, of whom he was one, acclaimed me King in their play, judging that I was best suited to the office. All the other boys did as I commanded, but this one was deaf to my orders and would not obey them. So finally he was punished for it. If I deserve to suffer for this, well, here I am to accept the penalty."

King Astyages was dumbfounded by this confident, George Washington–like, reply. Becoming increasingly suspicious of a strong resemblance the child seemed to bear to himself, he forced the herdsman, Cyrus's alleged father, to tell the truth about the boy's real origin. Now the whole story was revealed. The Medean king was furious, not so much with the herdsman, who was beneath his contempt, but with Harpagus, his supposedly loyal courtier. He planned a terrible vengeance. He told Harpagus how happy he was to have found his grandson again, alive and well, for:

> it was no small matter for me to be estranged from my daughter. Now, since things have turned out so well, please send your son here to join the newcomer among us and do you yourself come to dinner. For I intend to celebrate with a sacrifice to the gods to whom honour is due for saving the life of my grandchild.

When Harpagus's thirteen-year-old son arrived at the palace, the king had his throat cut, the corpse chopped up and had part roasted and part stewed, "all except for the head, the hands and the feet; these were kept separate, covered up in a basket."

Harpagus arrived for dinner and while the king and the other guests ate mutton, he was served the special dish the king had prepared for him.

> When it seemed that Harpagus had eaten enough of the meat, Astyages asked him how he had enjoyed the feast. "Very much indeed," said Harpagus. And then servants brought in the head, hands and feet of his son, still covered up. They stood in front of Harpagus and told him to uncover the dish and take what he pleased from it. Harpagus did so and, taking off the cover, saw it was the remains of his son. When he realised what he had been eating, he gave no sign of disturbance and remained quite calm. Astyages asked him if he knew what wild creature's flesh he had consumed. "Yes," said Harpagus, "I know. But whatever my Lord the King does is pleasing to me." With this answer he took up what was left of the flesh and went home, resolved, I suppose [says Herodotus] to gather it all together and bury it.

If Astyages was pleased with his day's work, with his terrible punishment of Harpagus's disobedience, he was badly mistaken. Of course Harpagus was determined to be revenged. But he didn't dream, as others might have done, of murder or mutilation, of blinding the king or slicing him, still living, into pieces. He was concerned that in his revenge he should retain his dignity and not descend to Astyages's level of bestial savagery. Justice and retribution for what the ruler had done to his son would be best served by depriving Astyages of what he valued above all else: his kingship. And as revenge, so the proverb has it, is a dish best eaten cold, he was prepared to wait long for the right moment.

Years later, when Cyrus was a man, some time between his thirtieth and fortieth birthday, and had already united the various clans and tribes of the Persians under his sole rule, Harpagus approached him—Herodotus tells us in another story with details as fanciful as the first—and promised to rally the Medean nobility in support of the young Persian if Cyrus rebelled from his overlord and struck out for the throne. Cyrus saw this as his opportunity to lead an army of Persians against the Medean capital. His troops were foot-soldiers, armed with swords and spears, in theory no match for the massed horsemen of Astyages's cavalry.

But when he received the news of the Persian rising, Astyages, whose character seems to have combined cruelty with faulty memory, an ill-starred mixture, appointed Harpagus general officer at the head of the Medean forces. It was that which cost him the throne, for Harpagus promptly led the Medean army over to Cyrus's side. According to Herodotus, Astyages, in an action reminiscent of Hitler's last stand in 1945, "armed what was left of his Medes in the city, the youths and old men, and led them out to fight the Persians. He was beaten and captured and lost his army." And so it was that Cyrus II, known to history as "The Great," became Emperor of Achaemenid Iran. The year was 550 BC.

THE CONQUEST OF BABYLON

It is tempting to dismiss Herodotus's account of Cyrus's life out of hand—and generations of hard-bitten and hard-headed historians have done just that. But remembering that the world and the values of the sixth pre-Christian century were very different from our own, one should perhaps be a little sceptical about the sceptics. In an entertaining lecture about Cyrus, delivered in the United States in 1874, the Reverend Charles Kingsley, author of the now largely forgotten children's classic *The Water Babies*, has fun with the notion, taken for granted by nineteenth-century historians, that Herodotus was not so much the "Father of History" as the "Father of Lies": "Did any of you ever read—if you have not you should read—

Archbishop Whately's 'Historic Doubts about the Emperor Napoleon the First'?" asked Kingsley of his audience.

Therein the learned and witty Archbishop proved, as early as 1819, by fair use of the criticism of Mr. Hume and the Sceptic School, that the whole history of the great Napoleon ought to be treated by wise men as a myth and a romance, that there is little or no evidence of his having existed at all; and that the story of his strange successes and strange defeats was probably invented by our Government in order to pander to the vanity of the English nation.

Whatever the truth behind the Greek historian's story, independent contemporary testimony affirms what came next: Cyrus's conquest and unification, first of the remaining Iranian peoples of the highlands, next of the Lydian kingdom in Anatolia, and finally—the greatest prize of all, this—of Babylon (Bab-el, the Gate of God), the magnificent metropolis of Mesopotamia, at that time the wealthiest, the most beautiful and the most sophisticated city in the whole of the Western Orient. "On the third day of the month of Arahsamnu, Cyrus entered Babylon," says the laconic Babylonian *Nabonidus Chronicle*. "They filled the street with palm branches in front of him. The king's peace was placed over the city. Cyrus's proclamation was read to all of Babylon." The year was 539 BC.

The great mud-brick town, with its multistorey houses and grid of straight streets sprawling over a bend in the River Euphrates, where it was crossed by the first known passenger bridge (whose ruined piers still stand in the dried-up river-bed, for the Euphrates has shifted its course since those days), surrounded and segmented by wide canals, and protected by twin fortified walls, was taken without serious resistance. Its area of some six square miles (16 square kilometres) was so large that, as Herodotus tells us, "owing to the huge size of the place, the inhabitants of the central parts, as the residents of Babylon declare, long after the outer portions of the town were taken, knew nothing of what had happened, but as they were engaged in a festival, continued dancing and revelling until they learned of their capture . . . "

When Cyrus himself arrived some time later—as a liberator, for the conquered city had first been given the usual sack, rape and pillage treatment by the army of the Persians' Gutian allies—the streets would have been crowded with onlookers, anxious to be among the first to cast eyes on their new overlord. The Great King would have been dressed like a peacock—or a rock musician. Xenophon described the royal costume as a long purple robe, wide-sleeved and encrusted with gold-thread embroidery, over a striped tunic and crimson trousers, perhaps, even back then, of silk, and leather boots. He would have worn a flat-topped cap of felt, decorated with scented blue and white ribbons. He would have been heavily made up and perfumed. Gold and silver jewellery would have weighed down his neck, ears, wrists and ankles—Plutarch, the first-century historian, tells us that a later Achaemenid monarch wore some three million pounds' worth of gold on his body. The cheering crowds, the frightened, the inquisitive, the jubilant, the priests chanting prayers to Marduk, the city's god, lined the processional route, its walls magnificently decorated with glazed-tile lions, all the way from the city temple precinct, dominated by the huge three-hundred-foot-high (90-metre) stepped tower or ziggurat, called by the Babylonians E-temen-an-ki (House of the Foundation of Heaven and Earth) and by the Bible the Tower of Babel, past the world-famous "Hanging Gardens of Babylon," built by a former ruler to remind his homesick Medean wife of the forested hills of her homeland, and finally through the magnificent sixty-foot-high (18-metre) Ishtar Gate with its crenellated bastions, their glittering blue façades decorated with bulls and dragons in white and ochre and with a long inscription in Babylonian cuneiform (wedge-shaped) writing, under the name of Nabu-Kudurri-us-ur (Nebuchadnezzar):

> King of Babylon, pious prince appointed by the will of Marduk, highest priestly prince, beloved of Nabu, of prudent deliberation, who has learned to embrace wisdom . . .
>
> This street of Babylon having become increasingly lower, I pulled down the gates and relaid their foundations at the water table with asphalt and bricks. I had them remade of bricks with blue stone on which wonderful bulls and dragons were depicted. I covered their roofs by laying majestic cedars lengthwise over them. I fixed doors of cedar wood trimmed with bronze in all the gates. I placed wild bulls and ferocious dragons in the gateways and thus adorned them with luxurious splendour so that Mankind might gaze on them in wonder.

Two and a half thousand years later, one still gazes in wonder as one walks where Cyrus rode in triumph between the lions of the processional way and under the Ishtar Gate's bulls and dragons, or places one's hand on Nebuchadnezzar's cuneiform inscription. But not in Babylon, nor anywhere in the Middle East. Nowadays the entire assembly has been re-erected on an island in Berlin, in the Pergamon Museum, together with the façade of Nebuchadnezzar's throne room, with its decoration of lions, stylised palm trees and flower borders. For when the excavation of the greatest city of antiquity was undertaken by German archaeologists at the turn of the last century, the discoveries were shipped out with the approval of the Ottoman authorities, and a museum was built around the reconstructed buildings in the capital of the Reich.

The brilliant colours still vibrate with life. Passing between the lions, the bulls and the dragons, and imagining the fabulous processions that had once paraded through the magnificent portal, I could still hear shouts and chants—though they proved to be coming from a party of foreign school-children visiting the Greek temple in the adjacent gallery—for I was expecting the roar of an ancient multiracial crowd. The Babylonian policy, borrowed from the Assyrians, of deporting the citizens of conquered peoples to swell the numbers in their own capital had ensured that almost every nation of the ancient Middle East was represented on the streets of Babylon that historic day. If the biblical story is anything to go by, most of them will have welcomed Cyrus into his newest and most splendid acquisition.

Among those celebrating the new monarch's arrival were, of course, the Jews. Or rather the "not yet" Jews, for the Judaeans, or Hebrews, or whatever one wishes to call them at that stage of their history (being from Judaea, one can't sensibly call them Israelites), were only starting on their way to becoming Jews—and it was Cyrus and his Persians who played an important rôle in that becoming. The Judaeans had been residents in Babylon since being deported into exile by Nebuchadnezzar sixty years before. Many who had made the journey would still have been living and sorrowing witnesses to the destruction of their sacred state and their holy Temple. Yet they had taken Jeremiah's advice to make themselves a new home on the Euphrates and, judging by their later reluctance to leave, had settled into a comfortable existence. Among the Persian king's first acts was to have a famous proclamation issued, allowing the not-quite-yet-Jewish exiles to return to their homeland. As the Book of Ezra records:

> Thus says Cyrus, king of Persia: All the kingdoms of the earth the
> Lord, the God of heaven, has given to me, and he has also charged

me to build him a house in Jerusalem, which is in Judah. Whoever, therefore, among you belongs to any part of his people, let him go up, and may his God be with him! Let everyone who has survived, in whatever place he may have dwelt, be assisted by the people of that place with silver, gold, and goods, together with free will offerings for the house of God in Jerusalem.

What the writer of the Book of Ezra thought it better to keep silent about, or perhaps what he genuinely didn't know—for his work was written many years later—was that Cyrus didn't single out the Jews alone, but accorded the same freedom of departure and worship to all the exiles of Babylon. And he showed equal liberality to those who stayed, recording his magnanimity on a cylinder of baked clay which once called out to the nations, but was found, millennia later, under the tumbled ruins of the city, and today sits mutely in a glass case in the British Museum:

I am Cyrus, King of the World, Great King, Legitimate King, King of Babylon . . . When I entered Babylon as a friend and when I established the seat of the government in the ruler's palace with jubilation and rejoicing, Marduk, the great god, induced the magnanimous inhabitants of Babylon to love me, and I daily endeavoured to worship him . . . I returned to the sacred cities on the other side of the Tigris, the sanctuaries which have long lain in ruins, as well as the images which used to live in them . . . I also gathered all their former inhabitants and returned them to their homes.

The conquered monarchs were treated with similar generosity. Greek historians were amazed to learn that Cyrus did not order them put to death as expected, but housed them and hosted their retinues, making them advisers to his officials in matters dealing with their former lands. The fate of the last native ruler of Babylon is not entirely clear, nor is that of Croesus, King of Lydia—different versions of history tell different tales. Some claimed that Nabonidus (Nabu-na'id in his own language) committed suicide, some believed that he perished among the flames of his burning palace, but others, including Herodotus, asserted that he and Croesus lived on in Cyrus's court as the king's valued confidants. It is certain that Cyrus kept his grandfather Astyages by him for as long as the old man lived, even though the former Medean king had attempted his murder. All in all, Cyrus was famed, even among the Persians' Greek enemies, for his justice, his mercy, his magnanimity, and the stability and generosity of his rule. The Persians called him the Father of their nation.

I had assumed that Cyrus's exemplary noble behaviour was the result of his Zarathustrian beliefs, his efforts to remain true to the principles of the one true God Ahura Mazda, and to avoid the traps set by the Power of Evil, the Lie, personified as Angra Mainyu or Ahriman. On looking further into the details of what we know about him, however, I discover that scholars have found no evidence that he was a Zoroastrian by religion. Nowhere is Cyrus recorded as having acclaimed Ahura Mazda as sole God, or even mentioned him. Where other Achaemenid rulers invariably invoke the name of the deity to justify their acts, Cyrus remains silent about his personal faith. And where his later successors actively deprecated the worship of other gods and attacked their temples and their idolatry, Cyrus's religious declarations seem to have been a matter of state policy rather than personal conviction. He appears always to have been happy to pay appropriate respect to whichever divine power was recognised by the foreign peoples he had to deal with and rule.

Yet the Jews—as, for want of a better name, I shall have to call them— would surely not have welcomed as Messiah a king who habitually "worshipped idols." Their positive response to Cyrus's rule could only have been based on what they understood of Persian religious belief and saw of Persian religious practice, both of which must have resonated strongly with their own theology. Herodotus tells us that:

> the Persians have no images of the Gods, no temples nor altars, and consider their use a sign of folly. This comes, I think, from their not believing the Gods to have the same nature as men, as imagined by the Greeks.

Though somewhat oversimplified, Herodotus's claim suggests that the Persians were rather more self-confident in their faith than the Jews, who abominated and violently denounced the worship of any divinity other than YHWH. The Torah's insistence that YHWH is a jealous God who will not tolerate infidelity by His chosen people actually implies that other gods do exist. After all, praying to a non-existent deity is no more wicked, and just as pointless, as adultery with a non-existent partner or theft of non-existent goods. Whereas to Cyrus's Persians, who regarded other nations' religious beliefs as at best misguided, at worst ludicrous, paying politically expedient homage to Marduk, Nabu, Ishtar or the moon god, Sin, must have seemed a matter of no great significance—and certainly no insult to the Wise Lord whom they knew to be the one and only true God reigning over all creation.

This is a point worth noting, for throughout their history, as the Old Testament frequently makes plain, the people of YHWH had long been divided between those who worshipped Him among several other divinities, and those whom the American scholar Morton Smith has called the "YHWH-Alone Party," a movement which ascribed all the ills of Israel's tempestuous past to syncretism, the mixing of worship of YHWH with that of other gods. Even these purists, however, had never before claimed that the others didn't exist; only that they must not be worshipped. It is the Second Isaiah, writing in Cyrus's times, who is the first to be told by God: "I am the Lord and there is none else, there is no God beside me." But Zarathustra had also recognised Angra Mainyu or Ahriman, the Power of Evil, as an opposing force to God. Isaiah must have known this well, for in an implicit recognition of, and explicit denial of, Persian belief, God goes on to assure him that: "I form the light, and create darkness: I make peace, and create evil." Some scholars have gone so far as to suggest it was under Persian tutelage that the Jews moved from henotheism (the belief that only one god of many is worthy of worship) to true monotheism (the belief that there is only one God to worship). At the very least, it has to be true that the support of a ruling power who believed that there was only one true God must have strengthened the hand of those who supported the worship of YHWH alone, and helped them ultimately to win the battle for the hearts and minds of the chosen people. The beautiful deathbed speech invented for Cyrus by Xenophon, could have been made by any of the Hebrew patriarchs:

> The everlasting God above, who beholds all things, with whom is all power, who upholds the order of this universe, unmarred, unageing, unerring, unfathomable in beauty and in splendour, fear Him my sons, and never yield to sin or wickedness, in thought, in word, or in deed. And after the Almighty, I would have you revere the whole race of man, as it renews itself for ever; for God has not hidden you in the darkness, and your deeds will be manifest in the eyes of all mankind. If they be righteous and free from iniquity, they will blazen forth your power; but if you meditate evil against each other you will forfeit the confidence of every man.

THE HOUSE OF DARIUS

There may be academic doubt about Cyrus's religious allegiance but there is none about his successor. "Ahura Mazda bestowed the kingdom upon me; Ahura Mazda bore me aid until I took possession of the kingdom; by the favour of Ahura Mazda I hold the kingdom." These words of King Darius, the next Achaemenian after Cyrus to establish stable rule over the Iranian Empire, were cut into a cliff-face, some time soon after 522 BC, three hundred feet (100 metres) above the main road linking two of the kingdom's most important cities, next to a depiction of the victories which gave Darius the throne.

Under the winged symbol of Ahura Mazda, the sole true God, Darius stretches out his arm, one foot placed on a fallen enemy; two nobles—his spear carrier and his bow carrier—stand behind him, while before him stand nine defeated rebels, roped together by the neck, their hands tied behind their backs. The site of this rock-relief—the location of the final battle—was to be my next port of call in Iran, a long way to the north-west from Pasagardae and Persepolis, at the place known to archaeologists as Behistun.

The monument at Behistun has been called the most important historical document surviving in Asia, a personal explanation by the ruler himself of how he won and secured the throne, in three languages: Babylonian, Old Persian and Elamite, speaking to us directly from a distance of two and a half thousand years—as if Darius understood how cavalierly time and history treats reputations and wanted to make sure that he got his story in first.

Actually, though these are the ruler's own words, they were of course merely carved in his name. In pre-literate times it was scribes who did the writing and other scribes who read out the text at the receiving end. This convention was still new enough not to be taken for granted, so letters were written explicitly from one scribe to another: "Tell the King that so-and-so-says . . . ," "Tell so-and-so that the King replies . . . ," and the same went for monumental inscriptions. Thus each paragraph incised on the cliff is prefaced with the words: "Darius the King says." Yet the huge memorandum was clearly a message to posterity, intended for later generations rather than Darius's own. After the work had been completed, the ledge on which the stonemasons had perilously perched to carve the cuneiform letters into the rock was cut away. Nobody could now approach the monument, nor could anyone read it from so far below—even if the Achaemenian age had been generally literate. All that could be made out from the highway was the giant bas-relief showing the King of Kings trampling his enemy, with a line of foreign kings queuing up to surrender.

What an odd feeling it is to visit a location described in antiquity and still recognisable today. When Ctesias of Cnidus, a Greek physician, came to the site then known as Bagastana (the Place of God) in 400 BC, he found a pool and a garden beneath a monument which for some reason he thought had been dedicated to Zeus by the legendary Assyrian Queen Semiramis. When I arrived nearly two and a half millennia later, the name had been corrupted to Bisotun (meaning Without Pillars) or Behistun (meaning the Good Place) but both pool and garden were still to be found below, now crowded with Iranian holidaymakers eating ice-creams, their children running riot around the base of the rocks. Five hundred years after Ctesias, the Roman historian Tacitus referred to an altar here, dedicated to Hercules and, sure enough, there by the side of the road, eroded by wind, sand and time, is the white limestone figure of the divine strong man, reclining comfortably on his side under a monstrously ugly and rusty twentieth-century corrugated-iron shelter.

I had greatly looked forward to seeing for myself just what Darius's stone memoir looked like from down below and we had driven the short distance from the north-west Iranian town of Kermanshah with eager anticipation. But on arrival at the foot of the mountain on whose lowest face the bas-relief was carved, we found that "the most important historical document surviving in Asia," indeed the whole area of the monument—the entire cleft in the cliffside on which Darius had commanded that his story be told—was completely obscured by a dense rat's nest of scaffolding and wooden planks. It was a huge disappointment.

I stepped up to the metal gate which gave on to the cat's cradle of steel tubing but it was firmly padlocked and, judging by the encrusting rust, had been so for a very long time. There might have been a way to clamber over the rocks and bypass the wire fence altogether, reaching the scaffolding from the side, but apart from the serious danger of falling from the sheer cliff walls, an Iranian in uniform standing down on the road was eyeing me suspiciously, and after the experience of our driver's arrest, I was keen to avoid spending yet more hours answering questions in a police station. So I scrambled up and perched myself on a ledge as high and as close to the ancient relic as I could get, looking down over Ctesias's pool, rather green with algae today, and across the wide valley carpeted in patches with closely sheep-cropped grass, to where the dust-coloured Zagros Mountains con-tinue their rise into the cloudless sky behind outlines as jagged as torn paper. I wondered whether the scene would have been very different in Darius's day as, just above where I sat, the stonemasons chipped away at their tremendous—and today infuriatingly invisible—work.

I tried to imagine the good modern tarmac road below, with its effi-cient white kerbsides and centre markings, as it might have been in the sixth century BC. It was then a main route, running between the empire's second city Babylon and the already ancient Medean capital at Ecbatana, and would have seen considerable traffic. This was the road that features in the apocryphal Book of Tobit. "Can you go with me to Rhages?" asks Tobias in Nineveh of the man he doesn't know to be the angel Raphael. (Rhages was an ancient town near the gap in the Elburz Mountains called the Caspian Gates. It is now a suburb of Tehran.) "Do you know those places well?" "Yes," replies the angel, "I do know the road well for I have often been there to stay with our brother Gabael." The two travellers would have passed right underneath the place where I am sitting.

Persian royal roads were famous in antiquity for their security, speed and splendid accommodation—Herodotus tells us that in his day "all along it are royal stages and excellent places to lodge"—supporting a postal sys-tem based on relay stations a day's ride apart, said to have been able to deliver letters from distant provinces in less time than it takes today. "No mortal travels as fast as these messengers," writes the Greek historian in a passage curiously reminiscent of the indefatigable and unstoppable Mister Stork, deliverer of baby elephants in Walt Disney's film *Dumbo*, "and noth-ing may hinder these men from covering the distance at the highest speed, neither snow, nor rain, nor heat, nor dark of night."

Thus thousands of travellers, official and private, military and civilian, would have had the opportunity to gaze up at Darius's spectacular relief as they hastened beneath it, though its meaning, significance, and even its author, must quickly have been lost to memory, to judge by Ctesias's incomprehension less than two hundred years later.

The good Greek doctor may have been the first, but he was far from the last Western writer to misunderstand the meaning of the monument. In 1598 Abel Pinson, French servant to a British diplomat, saw it as "the ascension of our Lord" with an inscription in Greek; in 1808 another French traveller recognised the twelve apostles standing under the Cross; while in 1818, the British scholar Sir Robert Ker Porter, who made the first drawing of the bas-relief, thought it represented the ten tribes of Israel taken captive by the Assyrian king. Perhaps these enthusiastic Christian travellers should be forgiven their mistake, for the symbol of Ahura Mazda, the *Faravahar,* really does look something like a cross from a distance, and the very last person in the world who would have been able to read the cuneiform writing died some time during the first century of our era. The last person, that is, until the scholars of our own times, for it was this very monument that was instrumental in the decipherment of the ancient writing system, and opened up the libraries of Assyria and Babylon to modern inspection.

I was sitting on my rock looking at the landscape below when it occurred to me that the isolation of this spot must have been far greater in the nineteenth century than it had been in the sixth century BC. The two great cities which the road had linked were now no more than mounds of dust, the fertile valley's cultivators long since driven off by sheep, Iran itself no longer the richest empire in the known world, but a poor Middle Eastern country struggling to gain the respect of the globe's industrial powers. I had taken out from my pocket the copy I had brought with me of the English translation of the inscription. On one page was an often published drawing that showed four tiny figures with horses labouring along an otherwise empty rough and narrow track squeezing between the pool and the mountain wall. One traveller turns in the saddle to peer up at the huge imperial announcement. What sense could he possibly have made of it? Even had he been able to read the writing, forgotten for two millennia, its language—Old Persian—was as dead as the Achaemenid kings themselves. Ironically enough, it had taken the interest and industry of Europeans to bring Darius's message, and his greatness, to life again.

In 1835, curiosity overtook the sense of self-preservation of a young British army officer called Henry Rawlinson, who climbed the cliff-face a number of times that summer, to make from the engraved signs a papiermâché imprint of the first few lines of the then unintelligible text. This kind of copy is given the resounding German technical name *Abklatch.* "I used frequently to scale the rock three or four times a day without the aid of a rope or a ladder," Rawlinson later wrote, "without any assistance, in fact, whatever. During my late visits I have found it more convenient to ascend and descend by the help of ropes where the track lies up a precipitate cleft, and throw a plank over these chasms where a false step in leaping across would probably be fatal."

A German schoolmaster by the name of Grotefend had, without knowledge of the Persian language but spurred on by a drunken bet, made a little progress in deciphering Persian cuneiform writing, recognising the word "king" and the names "Darius" and "Xerxes" among the collections of wedge-shaped signs copied from Persepolis inscriptions. Now, in a classic piece of code-breaking, Rawlinson was able to make further progress and, working from his *Abklatch,* managed to decode the first two paragraphs of the Old Persian inscription. He knew he was on the right track when the beginning of the text yielded a genealogy for Darius:

> I am Darayavaush the King, son of Vishtaspa, of the Hakha-manisiya dynasty, King of Kings. I am King in Parsa. My father was Vishtaspa, Vishtaspa's father was Arshama, Arshama's father was Aryaramna, Aryaramna's father was Chishpish, and Chishpish's father was Hakhamanish.

which was almost identical to the genealogy ascribed to Darius by Herodotus:

> Darius (Darayavaush), son of Hystaspes (Vishtaspa), son of Arsames (Arshama), son of Ariamnes (Aryaramna), son of Teispes (Chishpish), son of Achaemenes (Hakhamanish).

Rawlinson then returned to the site and, helped by a young Kurdish assistant, spent a year in a dazzling display of rock-climbing skill, risking life and limb on the sheer face, making a further impression of the whole of the Persian text. While the young officer was destined to go down in linguistic history for his later copying and deciphering of the Babylonian version of Darius's memoir and thus of Babylonian cuneiform, what he found in the Old Persian text caused a small sensation. For here, truly engraved in stone, was confirmation of one of Herodotus's wilder romances, one which had been dismissed by generations of historians as pure fantasy. Here was proof that Kingsley and Archbishop Whately were right: that it is easy but misguided to dismiss the ancient historian's tales as flights of his fevered Greek imagination. Here was evidence that in that distant heroic era, men and women really did behave in ways unfamiliar to our more mundane and prosaic times.

At the advanced age, for that era, of about seventy years, Cyrus the Great had died in 580 BC, fighting the nomadic Massagetai of Central Asia—already in those days led by a warrior-queen. He left two sons: the unstable Cambyses (Kambujiya) and Bardiya (for some reason known to the Greeks as Smerdis). Cambyses inherited the kingdom and went off to spend the first years of his rule subduing Egypt in a particularly brutal fashion—Herodotus tells us that at times his behaviour was quite mad. One of his battles has gone down in history as a unique victory for cats as, fearing defeat, Cambyses ordered his men to collect as many cats as they were able and to advance, holding the struggling and spitting felines in their arms. The Egyptians apparently refused to attack, fearing to injure the sacred creatures, and were roundly beaten. At some point in the course of this campaign, he supposedly had Bardiya secretly assassinated, fearing that his brother would usurp the throne while he was otherwise occupied, but not daring to allow the murder to become public knowledge.

"When Cambyses had gone off to Egypt," Darius announces in his cliff inscription, "the people became evil. After that, the Lie waxed great in the country, both in Persia and in Media and in the other provinces." We remember that the Lie was another way of personifying Zarathustra's Power of Evil, which undermines and corrupts God-desired stability and good governance.

"Darius the King says: Afterwards, there came a Magian named Gaumata . . . He lied to the people saying: 'I am Bardiya, the son of Cyrus, brother of Cambyses.' Then all the people rebelled against Cambyses, and went over to Bardiya, both in Persia and Media and the other provinces. He seized the kingdom . . . After that, Cambyses died by his own hand." Though Darius's phrase suggests suicide, Herodotus wrote that Cambyses died in an accident with his own sword.

The Behistun inscription goes on to describe how nobody would stand up against this false Bardiya, for "the people feared him greatly. He would slay in great number those who had previously known Bardiya . . . 'lest they know me, that I am not really Bardiya the son of Cyrus.' " Nobody said a word about the imposture, Darius continues, "until I came. After that, I sought the help of Ahuramazda and Ahuramazda bore me aid. Ten days had passed in the month of Bagayadi, when I with a few men killed Gaumata the Magian and his principal followers . . . I took the kingdom from him. By the favour of Ahuramazda I became king. Ahuramazda bestowed the kingdom upon me."

Darius, though not a son of Cyrus, did belong to a collateral, cadet branch of the royal Achaemenid family, so he could claim a right to the kingdom. But if he thought that his troubles were now over, he was much mistaken, for the Persian Empire was now visited by a positive plague of doppelgängers. Lookalike false pretenders to the thrones of the imperial provinces sprang up all over Greater Iran like mushrooms in the night:

> Darius the King says: This is what I did by favour of Ahuramazda in the year after I became king. I fought nineteen battles. By favour of Ahuramazda I smote them and took nine kings prisoner. One was named Gaumata, a Magian; he lied and said, "I am Bardiya, the son of Cyrus." He made Persia rebel. One, named Asina, an Elamite, lied and said, "I am king in Elam"; he made Elam rebel against me. One, named Nidintu-Bel, a Babylonian, lied and said, "I am Nebuchadrezzar, the son of Nabonidus." He made Babylon rebel. One, named Martiya, a Persian, lied and said, "I am Imanish, king in Elam." He made Elam rebel. One, named Phraortes, a Mede, lied and said, "I am Khshathrita, of the family of Cyaxares." He made Media rebel. One named Cisantakhma, a Sagartian, lied and said, "I am king in Sagartia, of the family of Cyaxares." He made Sagartia rebel. One, named Frada, a Margian, lied and said, "I am king in Margiana." He made Margiana rebel. One, named Vahyazdata, a Persian, lied and said, "I am Bardiya, the son of Cyrus." He made Persia rebel. One, named Arakha, an Armenian, lied and said: "I am Nebuchadrezzar, the son of Nabonidus." He made Babylon rebel.

Somewhere up behind me, looking through the rusty scaffolding and rotting boards out over the main road from Ecbatana to Babylon, there they still stand in bas-relief, all bound together in a row: Asina the Elamite, Nidintu-Bel the Babylonian, Martiya the Persian, Phraortes the Mede, Cisantakhma the Sagartian, Frada of Margiana, Vahyazdata the Persian, Arakha the Armenian, with Gaumata the Magian shown trampled under Darius's feet and, added some time later to the end of the line, Skunkha of the Pointed-cap Scythians, wearing—you guessed it—a pointed cap, making him look like the dunce standing at the back of the class.

Of course in a world without photography or portrait painting, where the crude image of the king on his coins gave the populace their only idea of what their ruler might look like, pretending to be someone who had a right to the throne by birth was a perfectly rational way of trying to seize power. Remember how long it took, even in the twentieth century, to uncover the real identity of "Anastasia," the false claimant to the Russian inheritance of the Romanovs. We have no way of knowing, nor did the travellers who passed by this cliff back in those days, whether Darius's version of events was true, or whether, as many historians believe, the saga he had inscribed on the rock at Behistun was a face-saving fiction, designed to cover up an illegitimate coup against the true Bardiya, the real son of Cyrus, rightful heir to the Persian throne.

Doth the Great King protest too much? He certainly does repeat the assertion that he is telling the truth over and over again. "You who shall hereafter read this inscription, let that which has been done by me convince you. Do not think it a lie." And: "Darius the King says: I turn myself quickly to Ahura Mazda, that it is true, not false, that I did this in one and the same year"; and on and on in the same vein. This is a long text—the English translation I have brought with me runs to nearly five thousand words. And just in case the reader might suspect that Darius takes falsehood as a small matter, we are reminded that the Lie is a powerful evil force, not just an evasion of truth: "You who shall be king hereafter, protect yourself vigorously from the Lie. Punish severely any man who follows the Lie, if your hope is: 'May my country be secure.'"

Whether or not Darius really was telling the truth and Bardiya really was an impostor, I find myself wondering if there might have been more to the conflict than the usual power struggle between rival claimants to the Achaemenid throne. The constant invocation of Ahura Mazda and the repeated attacks on "followers of the Lie" suggest a possible subtext, in which the identification of Gaumata, the false Bardiya, as a Magian is significant.

For the Magi, or Magians, had originally been a Medean priestly tribe or caste, perhaps like the Levites among the Hebrews or the Hindu Brahmins, inheriting by birth a monopoly on the conduct of all religious activities. In the united kingdom of the Medes and Persians, they took over the rôle of ritual specialists to the new nation, expert in prayer and libation alike. But scholars believe that their origins date back to a time before Zarathustra had reformed the Iranians' ancestral paganism with his spiritual teachings, and that they long kept up a conservative reaction against his progressive message. They would have been strongly opposed to Zarathustra's downgrading of their many gods into metaphorical demons, merely representing the worst aspects of human nature. They would have loudly supported the sacramental use of the sacred plant Haoma (the Iranian equivalent of Indian Soma), of which Zarathustra disapproved. Though Zarathustra's reforming age was long past, the Magi still surely hankered after their previous religious ways. Later they were to smuggle some of their old beliefs back into the Zoroastrian religion. Thus, a hundred and fifty years after Darius, his great-great-grandson would no longer invoke Ahura Mazda alone. "Artaxerxes the Great King says . . . " he ordered carved into the bases of four stone columns. "May Ahuramazda, Anahita, and Mithra protect me from all evil." Against all Zoroastrian precedent, he was even said to have commissioned a golden statue of Anahita, the Great Goddess, mistress of the waters.

On Cyrus's death, the Magi would surely have planned and plotted to ensure that the throne went to the claimant most likely to support their ancient traditions and would have opposed any ruler who intended to demand worship for Ahura Mazda alone—as Darius did. "Darius the King says: You who shall be king hereafter, do not befriend the man who follows the Lie or who is a wrongdoer. Punish them well."

Cyrus's religious loyalties are unknown, as no dedication to any divinity has ever been found under his name. But the tolerance he showed towards his subjects' many and varied religions suggests that he was no puritan in spiritual matters. Darius's inscriptions, on the other hand, never stop invoking his God. What is more, gold tablets unearthed from the mound at Ecbatana bear dedications in the name of his grandfather Arsames and his great-grandfather Ariamnes. In both, the Great God Ahura Mazda figures prominently—and alone. Could it be that the struggle after Cyrus's death was between a Magi-influenced house of Cyrus, who tried to restore traditional Iranian polytheism, and the branch of the family to which Darius belonged, who followed Zarathustra in recognising Ahura Mazda alone? Was the conflict a trial run for the much later Priest Kartir's onslaught on the "*daeva*-worshippers" of his own time? Pure speculation, of course, but not impossible, for there is other evidence of the house of Darius's special devotion to Ahura Mazda. When his son Xerxes burned the temples at Athens, it was not necessarily, as the Greeks saw it, an attack on their civilisation, but an assault on their idolatry.

HEAVEN, HELL AND THE DEVIL

The suggestion that Darius was a committed Zoroastrian might shed some light on the otherwise mysterious process by which a number of Zarathustra's key concepts had already infiltrated the Jewish religion long before a belief in the imminent End of Time and the coming of the Messiah so altered the fate of the Roman world.

Unfortunately the only record we have of relations between the Judaean exiles and their Achaemenid rulers is contained in the biblical books of Ezra and Nehemiah, a rather tortured account of the re-establishment of a Jewish homeland in Jerusalem, so badly confusing dates and names of kings that generations of scholars have argued about whether Ezra or Nehemiah came first and when and how the walls of Jerusalem were repaired and the Temple rebuilt. What does seem clear is that both Ezra and Nehemiah were important personages in the Persian royal court in the fifth century BC—Nehemiah was cup-bearer to the king—and that they received permission—and financial support—to return to the land of their fathers and carry out a religious revolution, forcibly imposing their version of true Judaism on an astonished population. From now on, only those who had been in exile were to be counted as true Jews. It would be surprising if they hadn't, even unconsciously, absorbed Iranian ideas while serving their Persian masters. The consequences were to be great, for Ezra is thought by most scholars to have been the one responsible for editing together the traditional texts preserved by the Judaean exiles, thus creating the Hebrew Bible.

Far below me I now see my Iranian companion gesticulating and pointing at his watch. Where we had left our car by itself at the side of the road earlier in the day, there is now a long line of dusty, rusty vehicles, parked tightly nose to tail. In spite of there being nothing to see but scaffolding, the site still clearly exercises its magic on today's citizens of the Islamic Republic. I climbed carefully down, wondering how much history's course would have changed if Bardiya or Gaumata—whichever it really was—had survived. It seemed to me that Darius's victory over the Magi cast a very long shadow, enshrining Zarathustra's teachings at the very centre of the ancient Persian state and allowing the Zoroastrian vision of the workings of the universe to lay its influence over all the subject peoples of the empire, and so to become—transmitted first through Jewish, then Christian theology—part of the patrimony both of the Western and Islamic worlds.

We extricated our car with some difficulty and set off again along the road once taken by Tobias and the Angel, aiming for one last site said to date from Achaemenian times, one which literally embodies the close relationship between the house of Darius and the Jews. Near the end of the road, which now leads close to the busy commercial centre of modern Hamadan not far from the mound that was once Ecbatana, behind a high metal gate, through which a gatekeeper nervously responds to enquiries via a door phone, stands a structure housing the shrine of Esther and Mordecai: two biblical figures, Jews from the reign of Darius's son Xerxes (Akhayarshaya in Persian, Akhashverosh in Hebrew, Ahasuerus in the King James Bible). Like Daniel's tomb in Susa, there is nothing at all Achaemenian about either the building or the sarcophagi it contains, draped as they are in voluminous embroidered coverings in the Islamic style and resting on an elaborately carved ebony pedestal. The whole ensemble is clearly medieval in date. These days nobody but the occasional Jewish foreigner visits the shrine, but it was formerly a favoured pilgrimage site, for there were once many who agreed with the twelfth-century philosopher Maimonides that the story in which the two feature, the Book of Esther, was the next most important book of the Bible after the Five Books of Moses.

Most scholars now believe, however, that the book is one of the first known novels, based on the same tradition as that of the Persian story of Princess Scheherezade, *The Thousand and One Nights,* and written long after the period in which it is set, to explain the meaning and purpose of the newly introduced Jewish festival of Purim. There must have been Babylonian influence too, for the principal Jewish protagonists are named after Babylonian gods: Esther is Ishtar, Mordecai is *Marduk khai!* (Marduk lives).

But the very fact that the Book of Esther was written at all means that the close relations between the Persian court and its Jewish subjects were well and long remembered. Esther's original Hebrew name is given as Hadassah, meaning myrtle, a plant with a special significance to Zoroastrians as well as Jews, and no writer would have had Xerxes marry Esther if his readers had found it unbelievable, whether or not it was true—which, according to Herodotus, it wasn't. Moreover, the cordiality must have continued for many centuries—perhaps even after the Islamic conquest, given the obviously late provenance of the tomb and its contents. Local experts have identified one of the mausoleum's occupants as Shushan-Dokht (daughter of Susa), Jewish queen of the fourth-century Sassanian Emperor Yazdegird I.

Inside Esther and Mordecai's shrine, the crooked whitewashed walls are adorned with lines of curiously corrupt Hebrew lettering, so corrupt, in fact, as to be illegible—obviously repainted many times over the centuries by decorators with no knowledge of the language. I asked the attendant what they had originally said. He looked suspiciously at my Iranian companion—on this very day some Jews were on trial in the southern city of Shiraz for treason and espionage—and asked me if I spoke French. He then told me in that language that these were magic symbols, known to the ancient rabbis, but which no living person could any longer decipher. When I asked about the age of the coffins, he assured me that they were two and a half thousand years old. He was there to promote the story of Esther and Mordecai and wouldn't be deflected.

I returned to the modern Iranian street, noisy with mini-vans and motor scooters, pausing only to satisfy the doorman's demand for a "present" with my remaining ballpoint pen. The blank metal door clanged shut behind us. How sad, I thought, that the historic warm relationship between Jews and Iranians should have so badly broken down. For it was during that thousand years or so of close association between the two peoples, before the arrival of Islam, that many originally Zarathustrian notions became part of the mainstream of universal religious thinking—beliefs which had been noticeably absent from those books of the Old Testament dating from before the exile to Babylon and the encounter with Iran.

The Torah, the Five Books of Moses, and the other pre-exilic biblical books, had it that after death both sinful and righteous souls descend for ever to a gloomy place under the ground called Sheol. Even as saintly a figure as the Prophet Samuel, whom the Witch of Endor consulted on behalf of King Saul, ascended "out of the earth." Life after death, resurrection, eternal reward and punishment, and the existence of heaven, imagined as a garden—*Paradise* is the Persian word for a garden or park—these ideas were all first revealed to Zarathustra's followers. Mainstream Judaism has remained somewhat ambivalent about them, Christianity much less so—though nowhere in the New Testament is heaven explicitly described.

As with paradise, so with hell and its ruler the Devil. In original Hebrew belief, there was no independent force of evil, as there was in Zarathustra's theology; each individual was solely responsible for his or her own acts. The idea of a second, equal, evil, power would have been an unacceptable affront to those sternly trying to establish the sole worship of YHWH. But after the Persian victory, the notion was so persuasive, explaining so much to any ancient observer of—or sufferer under—Middle Eastern history and power politics, that it stimulated an extensive development of Jewish tradition. In God's celestial court, there now appears a sort of divine public prosecutor or heavenly policeman, who comes before God's tribunal to ensure the punishment of wrongdoers. He was called the

Antagonist, the Enemy, or the Opponent—the English rendering of the Hebrew word Satan. A being with the name Satan first turns up in the books of Job and Zechariah, both passages written during the Babylonian captivity or after the Persian liberation. But, as we know only too well, it is not far from being a policeman to becoming an *agent provocateur.* We see the process of conversion under way in the later Book of Chronicles. Rewriting a story that has already appeared in the much earlier Second Book of Samuel, in which the Lord purposely leads King David astray, the author now puts the blame on Satan rather than God—the very first time in the Bible that Satan appears as a wicked force. Now, in the Second Temple period, between Achaemenian and Roman times, the Devil and all his works begin to play an ever greater part first in Jewish, then in Jewish-Christian, religious thought.

At first there was great opposition among the Jews to belief in resurrection, heaven, hell and the devil, evidence of what many at the time saw as the importation of foreign religious ideas into the Jewish faith. This was one of the issues over which the Pharisees and Sadducees of Jesus's day were still divided. As the Acts of the Apostles tells us: "the Sadducees say that there is no resurrection, neither angel nor spirit: but the Pharisees confess both." Though much in the minority, it was the Pharisees who survived the Romans and whose beliefs therefore became the Jewish mainstream.

In the end the Jews never took wholeheartedly to heaven and hell. It was their Christian and Muslim inheritors who built most enthusiastically on Persian foundations and made the Devil a major symbol of evil and falsehood. The Book of Revelation, composed near the end of the first century, prescribes Ahriman's rôle in history:

And when the thousand years are expired, Satan shall be loosed out of his prison, and shall go out to deceive the nations which are in the four quarters of the earth—Gog, and Magog—to gather them together to battle, their number being as the sand of the sea.

And it was left to Islam's Holy Qur'an, revealed to the Prophet Muhammad in the seventh century, to paint paradise in its full Persian colours when describing the final destination of faithful souls:

they shall feast on fruit and be honoured in the gardens of delight. Reclining face to face upon soft couches, they shall be served with a goblet filled at a gushing fountain. Their drink shall neither dull nor befuddle their senses. And by their side shall sit bashful, dark-eyed virgins, as chaste as the sheltered eggs of ostriches.

Thus Muhammad, the final Messenger of God, confirmed the vision of Zarathustra, the First Prophet. With this full circle, my journey is almost complete. Having mapped the Persian seer's influence back through the two and a half millennia that separate our own era from the dawn of Persian civilisation, what remains is to seek out the traces of a time before Islam, before Christianity, before Judaism, before Cyrus and the Achaemenids, a time before recorded Iranian history began—the days of the First Prophet himself.

8

The First Prophet

The Lonely Planet Guide says: "You should seriously consider avoiding Iran altogether for about ten days before and after Noruz, the chaotic Iranian New Year which starts on or about 21 March," so that was the time I had specifically chosen for my final foray in search of the mark of Zoroaster, the Persian prophet.

Noruz is not Muslim at all—it has been an Iranian holiday at least since Cyrus's day, if not before. And in spite of its much flaunted Muslim piety, the Islamic Republic of Iran still celebrates this Zoroastrian festival as the biggest occasion of the year for serious merry-making. If the parallel with Christmas in Europe immediately comes to mind, the differences are significant. Though the way we celebrate Christmas, or Yule as the Germanic peoples originally knew it, may have its roots in pagan or even Mithraic rites, two millennia have thoroughly Christianised "Christ's Mass," making one of the central events of the Christian sacred drama—the birth of Jesus—its rationale. Not so Iranian Noruz, which never acquired Islamic ritual or Muslim meaning.

Perhaps Noruz is just an antidote to the usual Shi'ah mood of pessimism, self-flagellation and mourning. On the New Year the whole nation wakes in joyful spirit with, it seems, the compulsion to travel. Driving on Iranian roads, dangerous enough at the best of times, now becomes almost suicidal. Hotels in the more popular holiday destinations are booked up weeks in advance, for this is the time when families gather together from the far ends of the country. It is the season for colleagues to gift each other with trinkets and passers-by to offer sticky sweetmeats to complete strangers; a favourite season, too, for marriages. In the evenings, particularly in a tourist town like Shiraz, festive crowds press along the decorated streets, while gaily clad wedding parties crammed on to the backs of lorries—the women's black *chadors* flapping open to reveal brightly coloured party dresses—parade rowdily through the city centre, shouting and hooting and blaring raucous wind instruments.

In many homes, a secret supply of wine suddenly makes its appearance—brewed up from pomegranates and honey rather than the grape, either to avoid suspicion from the religious authorities or so as not to sin against Islamic prohibition. Shops and restaurants hang out bunches of cypress, myrtle or rue, plants with special meaning for Zoroastrians, and in every business premises and hotel lobby stands a *"haft sin"* (seven "s") table, a sort of religious Kim's Game, on which are arrayed seven items whose Farsi name begins with the letter *s*. Among them might be apples *(sib)*, coins *(sekkeh)*, garlic *(sir)*, vinegar *(serkeh)*, greens *(sabzi)*, ears of grain *(somboleh)*, sumach (*somaq*, a spice) and anything coloured red *(surkh)*. The symbolism is mysterious. What could possibly link vinegar to coins? In addition, perhaps to Islamise the custom, a copy of the Qur'an is usually displayed, though it neither begins with "s" nor adds anything to the *haft sin* table's hidden meaning.

A *haft sin* table was displayed in the foyer of my Tehran hotel when I arrived there on the eve of the celebrations. I asked the doorman what it meant, but all he could tell me was: Noruz. The cashier was no more helpful. A young clergyman waiting for a friend by the reception desk told me that whatever the symbolism might be, Islam frowned on it, but had so far not succeeded in weaning Iranians from the comforting practice of an age-old tradition. Such objects, he wrinkled his nose as he admitted it, have been laid out at Noruz since before Islamic times.

Indeed, the history books tell us that Noruz is quite astonishingly age-old. It is nothing less than the modern version of the New Year ceremony immortalised in stone by Darius at Persepolis. Under today's less autocratic rule—the Ayatollahs, in spite of their bad press, are no match for the tyrants of old—it is a feast for all the people rather than just the king. Perhaps it was the same in Achaemenian times too, but the peasantry just didn't get pictures of their parties sculpted on the wall.

Whatever life was really like for commoners in Cyrus's and Darius's day, or later in the Sassanian era of Ardashir and Yazdegird, today's Iranians—workers and the educated, poor and rich alike—are proud at this time of year to remember the details of their pre-Muslim civilisation. In spite of more than thirteen centuries of Islam, the remaining fire temples in and near Yazd, where much of the surviving Zoroastrian community still lives, are thronged with visitors. Hundreds of tourists, dressed inappropriately in their holiday best, crawl over the archaeological sites of Elamite, Achaemenid and Sassanian times. For anyone not accustomed to Persian religious schizophrenia—the personality split between awareness of having been one of the ancient world's superpowers under the protection of their very own God Ahura Mazda, and dedication to the much more recent faith in the Allah of the Arabs—the Noruz atmosphere seems rather surprising. Yet the immense popularity in this season of the national epic, Ferdowsi's majestic poem the *Shah-nameh,* supposedly a chronicle of Persian history before the Muslim conquest, suggests that the direction in which the Iranian heart naturally turns remains uncertain—and not always towards Mecca.

Being an outsider while the rest of the country was partying, I felt rather isolated, like an awkward teenage boy lurking at the back of the dance-hall waiting to be asked on to the floor. But it did at least allow me to take a more objective look at the merry-making than I might otherwise have done. Conscious that this was the very closest I had so far come to seeing the influence of Zarathustra's ancient inspiration on a modern society, I was hoping to discover what role the teachings of Zarathustra played in the celebrations. But in reading whatever I could lay my hands on about the origins of the festival, I quickly found that all is not as it appears.

Noruz, it seems, is not Zoroastrian in origin at all, but borrowed from neighbouring Babylon. Among the Semitic peoples of the Middle East, the most important festival marked the annual Enthronement of God. In Babylon, the statue of Marduk, the national divinity, was taken out and paraded through the streets of the city before being returned to his temple next to the great Ziggurat—the stepped man-made mountain that the Bible knew as the Tower of Babel. If this reminds one of the Easter celebrations around the Mediterranean, as in Malta, where the Virgin's image is taken in procession from the church and around the town, that may be no coincidence. Even today's Jews—who of course allow no images, let alone statues, of God—none the less regard their New Year, *Rosh Hashanah,* as marking God's annual symbolic coronation. Back in ancient Babylon, Nabonidus, the last king, who was deposed by Cyrus the Great, was blamed for the downfall of his empire because he had absented himself from the capital during his later years. Without his presence, the New Year rites could not be celebrated and Marduk could no longer protect his people from conquest. It appears almost certain that it was Cyrus himself who imported this foreign practice to secure his seat on the throne, establishing it in the process as the signature of Iranian nationhood.

If Noruz was not Zarathustrian in origin, what of the stories in the *Shah-nameh,* so eagerly read and recited by modern Iranians as an outline of their pre-Islamic history? On close examination, the events recounted in Ferdowsi's masterpiece took place, not in the Persian heartland but, judging by the names of the people and places, somewhere off to the north-east, in the neighbourhood of the legendary land of Turan. (Modern Persian schoolchildren are taught that Turan was the country of their traditional Turkish enemies and conquerors, but the Turks didn't actually arrive until many centuries after the memory of real prehistoric events had faded to legend.) To conclude my search for the Persian prophet, I would have to look not in Iran itself, but in Central Asia. By chance, the very place most often suggested as the location both for the *Shah-nameh*'s stories and Zarathustra's mission is one that I myself had visited some years before. I still remember it well.

We had parked the Toyota Land Cruiser on a bluff overlooking the river and got out to have a look. Below us, the glistening blue-green ribbon of water meandered greasily between crumbling banks where small patches of green struggle against the overwhelming wind-blown dust. The sun beat down unmercifully. Our Turkmen driver unexpectedly crawled under the vehicle, pulled a shovel from the emergency toolkit, and proceeded to bury himself up to the neck in the dark sand. "For the rheumatism," he responded to my amazed look—the sound muffled by the handkerchief placed protectively over his face—in a tone of voice suggesting that I should have known better than to ask.

This was the most famous river of the ancient Orient, called the Oxus by the Greeks (and the Amu Darya today), which flows a thousand miles from the frosted heights of the Pamir plateau on the borders of Afghanistan up into the—now rapidly shrinking—Aral Sea. To the south-west of the watercourse stretches the Kara Kum, the Black Sand, which becomes, on the other side of the Kopet Dagh Mountains, the Dasht-e-Kabir, the Great Desert of Iran. To the south-east lie the Afghan cities of Balkh, Mother of Cities, and Mazar-i-Sharif (the Noble Tomb, claimed as the burial site of 'Ali, the fourth Caliph of Islam), while off to the north-east are the Qyzyl Kum, the Red Sand, and the fabled Central Asian cities of

Bokhara and Samarkand. Somewhere near here, as far as I could judge, Alexander the Great crossed over with his army, the men floating over on rafts made by stuffing their animal-hide tents with straw.

Places writ so large in the annals of history all too often disappoint— such high expectations can rarely be satisfied. I am not exactly sure what I had hoped to find, but I should have known that the view over the Oxus could never have matched up to the way I had imagined it. There was nothing about this scene to suggest that the waters below featured in any important event of antiquity or, come to that, of any other time. The Amu Darya is a river flowing between two deserts, that is all.

These are not, however, deserts in Sahara style. By the banks a few fields, showing sparse green shoots of wheat or rice, huddle at the water's edge. And the surrounding terrain is not completely barren. Here and there scrubby bushes survive and clumps of spiky grass bind the sand together, for these are the southern margins of the Eurasian Steppe, that great transcontinental highway which stretches all the way from the Balkans to Mongolia. Once these banks were much more fertile; fields of grain and plots of vegetables supported communities of semi-nomadic cattle herders. Until the Turks arrived during the first millennium of our era, they would have been speakers of Iranian languages, who had controlled these lands from time immemorial. They belonged to an extensive ethnic group of many tribes and clans, trundling with their huge herds across the steppe-land in ox-drawn carts, camping in round felt-covered tents, planting gardens of vegetables and grain to which they would return in season. They eventually became wealthy enough to support a craftsman class which created a unique and original art form: the "animal style" of the steppe, with its curls and tendrils, its mannered elaboration of realistic form into decorative distortion, a style that would profoundly influence Celtic, Viking and medieval design and resurface at the end of the nineteenth century under the title "art nouveau." We have noted some of this people's tribal names in later times: Alans, Sarmatians, Scythians, Cimmerians. A thousand years before them, it was this wandering life that Cyrus's Parsa clansmen had only recently left behind when they descended on southern Iran to oust the Medes, earlier Iranian migrants from the steppe, and to found the Persian Empire.

Now the only life that could be seen was an old Soviet-built truck in the extreme distance, sending up a cloud of dust as it ground its way, like a slow-moving khaki-coloured beetle, up a far-off sand-hill. Its faint growling came and went as the direction of the slight breeze changed. Though this river may once have watered a cradle of civilisations, it was impossible to mentally repopulate the desolate and barren scene with any image of its former inhabitants.

That visit to the Amu Darya is now ten years in the past and in quite another context. Maybe, however, the river made more of an impression on me than I thought at the time. As I try to unpeel the very last layer of history from the Zarathustrian story, that river-bank comes immediately back to mind and I can again smell the sun-baked dust and the hot oil from the Land Cruiser's engine. For I now read that this river, dividing the ancient countries called Bactria and Chorasmia (or Khwarazm), the territory between the Amu Darya and the Hindu Kush Mountains, may well have flowed through the original homeland of Zarathustra, prophet to the Persians, and, "arguably," as scholars in less politically correct days were wont to say, "the only religious prophet to arise from the Aryan race."

There isn't much to go on. After tumbling back through the ages, tracking the spoor of Zarathustra in reverse through the European Enlightenment, the Middle Ages, the Dark Ages, late antiquity, the end of the classical and beginning of the Christian worlds, way back to the fifth-century BC start of written history, far from getting closer to the prophet, he seems to become ever more faint, the nearer we approach. There are two sources to consult: scholarly research and Zoroastrian tradition. As all too often, religious tales conflict with scholarly opinion, and the scholars are themselves divided. There isn't even any agreement on the exact historical period to which we should look to find Zarathustra's traces.

Zoroastrians say that their prophet made his first convert "258 years before Alexander." If that means Alexander's conquest—the Macedonians destroyed Persepolis in 330 BC—this would have been in 588 BC, which seems suspiciously close to the birth date of Cyrus the Great, founder of the Achaemenids, the first imperial Persian dynasty, who was born between 590 and 580 BC. Zarathustra's first and most important convert was said to be King Hystaspes, as the Greeks called him—in Persian, Vishtaspa or Gushtasp (which literally, if disconcertingly, would mean something like "horsemeat" in modern Farsi). Zoroastrian tradition equates this ruler either with the Vishtaspa who was father to Darius the Great or with the Vishtaspa who was governor of Persepolis in Cyrus's and Darius's day. But we now know that both Darius's grandfather and his great-grandfather left inscriptions praising Ahura Mazda as the one and only god. Since Zoroastrian tradition also credits their Prophet Zarathustra as the one who first introduced monotheism to Iran, "258 years before Alexander" seems far too late a date. In any case, scholarly investigation has now traced this particular number back to a late Greek, rather than Iranian, source and a fiction at that.

For the location of Zarathustra's birth, tradition would have us look to Rhages, the old city of Rayy, now a dreary suburb of Tehran, or else to Medea in the north-west of Iran, today largely Turkish-speaking. In Afghanistan, local people talk of the prophet's preaching outside the now crumbled walls of Balkh, and in the former Soviet Union yet other experts propose that his homeland was Central Asia or even as far away as what we call Kazakhstan today.

Where even the learned cannot agree, outsiders to the argument are free to make up their own minds. But the evidence is sparse—thick layers of myth and legend have collected around the figure of Zarathustra, as they do around all giant personalities of history. Stories once told about unknowns tend to migrate and attach themselves to well-celebrated names. Archaeology cannot help here either—the ideas and beliefs of pre-literate and pre-urbanised societies leave little physical trace. It is true that oral tradition, the cultural patrimony of non-writing peoples, passes down surprisingly accurately between the generations until eventually written down. But we have lost 90 per cent even of the works of Greece and Rome, and ancient Persian Zarathustrian texts are very few. Of the sacred literature of the Zoroastrians, a handful of hymns ascribed to the prophet himself remain; the rest is mostly commentary—the accumulation of more than two millennia of religious development under the many influences to which the Iranian people have been subject—and has left the ideas and beliefs of the prophet far behind.

Zoroastrians tell us that most of their ancient sacred literature was lost when Alexander the Great burned their books and killed their priests. But other nations too were conquered in antiquity, and many—like the ancestors of the Jews—more than once. Yet these others succeeded in preserving a library of texts which we can still read today—the Bible is the best example. Why Iranians should have so easily lost the major part of their spiritual canon is a mystery, unless it was the result of that common ancient antipathy to writing down matters of importance which was felt even by civilised Greeks like Socrates. In fact, unlike Hebrew speakers who came from the very area which had cradled the alphabet and, if the Bible is to be believed, already had books in King David's time (c. 1000 BC), the Persians of Cyrus's day had no writing system of their own. The cuneiform of the inscriptions that the founder of the empire and his successors ordered to be carved on roadside cliff-faces was a recent borrowing from Mesopotamia, simplified and adapted for Persian use. It was not long before this attractive but cumbersome writing system was first joined, and then replaced, by the alphabet devised for the non-Persian, Semitic language, Aramaic, the second language of the Assyrian and Babylonian empires. In the Persian chancery, too, Aramaic soon became the *lingua franca,* the official language of the multicultural empire. Palace bas-reliefs often show two scribes standing side by side as they take down the king's words: one with clay tablet and stylus for inscribing Persian in cuneiform, the other with a leaf of leather or papyrus and a pen for Aramaic alphabetic writing.

Aramaic rather than Persian was to remain the universal language of the whole Middle East for the next thousand years. So although there is no reason to doubt that the ancestral Persians had a rich culture, they were, perhaps, a nation primarily of the spoken, rather than the written, word. After all, Iranians today write in the adopted Arabic script, not wholly suited to their language, and remain a nation of composers and quoters of poetry—even taxi drivers commonly regale the visitor with phrases and quatrains from the works of the great figures of Persian literary history—often vulgar or obscene. Maybe declaiming verse from memory is, and always has been, more in keeping with the country's cultural tradition than reading or writing it. If so, we should count ourselves lucky to retain even a few fragments of Zarathustra's original hymn-book.

Or perhaps there may be another explanation. Oral tradition is usually only written down as text when seriously threatened. Though annals and chronicles may have been compiled in King David's Israel, it was the experience of conquest and exile in Babylon that led the scribe Ezra (if indeed it was he, as many scholars now believe) to take up his pen as *redactor*—collator and editor—of the library that we know as the Old Testament. The elaborate rules of the Jewish religion were not committed to papyrus and parchment until after the Romans' destruction of the Second Temple in Jerusalem. Only then was the academy founded that would inscribe the first pages of what would become the Talmud. Not until those who had memorised the separate sections of the Holy Qur'an—the *Hufaz*—began to be decimated in the fratricidal battles that followed the death of the Prophet of Islam, were steps taken to produce a definitive text of the Muslim revelation.

Could it be that, even under the Hellenistic rule of Alexander and his successors, the teachings of Zarathustra were never actually faced with an abrupt collapse of tradition? Rather that they slowly lost their adherents and followers over the centuries, the old traditions becoming unfashionable and neglected, so that there was never occasion to write them down in detail until long after much of the memory had faded?

The first steps in assembling a Zoroastrian literature were taken by the Sassanian ruler Ardashir in the third century. Kartir, the great enemy of Mani, was not the only Zoroastrian priest to be remembered from this time. Another priest, Tansar, less given to rock-carved self-publicity than Kartir, is recorded as having been ordered by the Shah to collect all the scattered sacred texts and fix a Zoroastrian "canon." It was only then, six centuries after Alexander, that the religion became for the first time a strict orthodoxy, to which the whole nation had to subscribe on pain of punishment. Orthodoxy develops, as the scholar Haym Soloveitchik has pointed out, "when what was a matter of course, what was once absorbed and habitual, has become subject to rules, formal teaching, and scrupulous attention to textual authority . . . Performance is no longer, as in a traditional society, replication of what one has seen, but implementation of what one knows." Ardashir and his descendants' orthodoxy may have been a response to the decay of their faith rather than its overthrow.

What, then, can we know or guess about the Prophet Zarathustra, from the writings and from the religion itself? Most scholars and Zoroastrians alike are convinced that in the *Gathas,* the liturgical hymns that now form part of the *Avesta,* the Zoroastrian texts, we hear the authentic voice of Zarathustra the man:

To what land shall I flee, whither to flee?
From the nobles and from my peers I am cut off, nor do the people love me, nor the Liar rulers of the land.
How am I to please thee, Mazda Ahura?
I know wherefore, O Mazda, I have been unable to succeed.
Only a few herds are mine and I have but few people.
I cry unto thee, O Ahura, grant me the support a friend gives to a friend.

In its original tongue, this tragic petition to God does point us to a place and a time. The language is very archaic, a dialect associated with the north-eastern end of Old Persian's range, with the lands around the Oxus. It is also very close indeed to the oldest layer of Sanskrit, the language of the *Vedas,* the sacred texts of the Hindus. The similarities are apparent even to those who know nothing of either language.

A line in Gathic Persian from the *Avesta:*

Tem amavangtem zazatem surem damohu sevishtem mithrem zazai zaothrabyo.

Word for word in Sanskrit this would be:

Tam amavantam yajatam shuram dhamasu shavistham mitram yajai hotrabhyah.

(With libations will I worship Mithra, that strong and mighty angel, most bountiful to all creatures.)

The two languages—little more than dialects of one tongue—are so close that not many centuries can have separated them from their common origin, at the time just before the ancestors of the Persians and the Indian Aryans split into two camps, concentrated around the Oxus and the Indus rivers. Since most researchers date the oldest of the *Vedas* to between 1500 and 1200 BC, the *Gathas* of Zarathustra are unlikely to originate from much later.

This suggests that the prophet lived some time around 1200 BC, a period traditionally ascribed to Moses at the other end of the Middle East, making Zarathustra, like Moses, a prophet of the late Bronze Age. Some, though, put him even earlier, between 1700 and 1500 B.C., which would align him rather with Abraham, in the middle of the Bronze. Both were times of economic and technological change with its consequent movements of peoples and the resulting social strains.

It may be easy enough to dream ourselves back into the nineteenth century or even early modern Europe. It may not be much harder, particularly for fans of "sword and sorcery" romance, to fantasise living during the European Middle and Dark Ages. Roman and Greek ways were much closer to ours than we often think and, because of familiarity with the Old Testament, its characters and its anecdotes, even life in biblical times is not beyond our power to imagine. (Though the one thing we can never leave behind, in our mental journeyings, is the knowledge of what was to come after.) But with Zarathustra, even the prophets of Israel are far in the future. We have arrived back at a period in human history whose mind-set is very hard for us to fathom, so different from ours are its accepted beliefs, ethics and values.

To us, such times seem at the very beginnings of history, but of course to the people who lived in those days, they had just as long a past to look back on as we do. Nabonidus of Babylon is said to have been as fascinated by archaeological digs as any television viewer today. They certainly must have told tales about their wanderings and the adventures they had on the way. Perhaps, like the Hebrews who long remembered their father Abraham's origins in "Ur of the Chaldees," they still had a dim recollection of the far distant time when their remote agricultural ancestors had cut their moorings and left village life behind in exchange for a nomadic existence on the steppe.

RELIGION IS A LIVING THING

Memories live long in Central Asia. Trying to conjure an image of what life may have been like among the ancestral Persians of Zarathustra's day, before they arrived in the land to which they would eventually give their name, my thoughts turned again to the trip which had taken me to the banks of the Oxus. There I had witnessed a wedding party which clearly showed how even now one can still sometimes catch a glimpse of the very bottom of that deep well that is the past. On the way to the river we had travelled by a former station on the Silk Road leading west from earth-walled Balkh. Ten years ago the Gissar fort still bore its Soviet name. (Hesar is Persian for castle, but Russian has no letter H, so substitutes a G, as in Gitler and Gemingway.) The fortress squats over the highway just after it skirts the border with Afghanistan and widens before it sweeps off over the mountains towards Samarkand. The castle was built on a low hill overlooking the remains of what was once an important stopping point on the major trade route across Asia. A great caravanserai once flourished here, with a pool, a mosque, a madraseh—a Muslim religious school—many shops and teahouses. Archaeology suggests that there was a travellers' rest here at least a thousand years before Islam, if not earlier.

Now all is ruin and decay, though buses do still stop, putting down and taking up passengers from the local villages. There is also a hideous and brutal Soviet war memorial. But it is the long abandoned remains of the fort which strike the eye. A great arch links two towers, like round-topped café sugar shakers, that once supported a huge wooden door—now gone. A high earth-brick enclosure stretches away on either side, protecting . . . nothing. Inside there is only a grassy mound, the remains of crumbled walls and foundations lifting the earth into bumps and ridges. Outside, steps lead up into the gaping entrance. And by the steps: a tree.

It is a willow, leafless in winter when I saw it. The trunk, massively thick and gnarled, leaned heavily to one side; the limbs, crabbed and knotted, swept the ground. On every branch and twig were tied hundreds, perhaps thousands, of strips of cloth, some quite new and still brightly coloured, some aged into greyness, some weathered into no more than bunches of threads. Next to the tree, like a primeval guardian, sat an old man with a stick, in white *chapan*—the Central Asian coat—white turban, white beard and, over his baggy Muslim trousers, black knee-high boots with rubber galoshes. Behind him lurked a dance band.

A bearded elder in a grey track suit struck up a rhythm on a big bass drum; a halting, slipping, insistent rhythm that quickly had everybody's feet tapping. Then two young boys wearing identical blue shell suits joined in with wasp-waisted thin-necked lutes, strumming them like manic mandolins. Finally the flute player sent a writhing, tumbling, burbling melody sailing over the top of the ensemble and everybody started singing.

Today's wedding party had arrived straight from the mosque. As the music urged them on, some fifty people gathered around the memorial to the comrades fallen in the Great Patriotic War. Communism may have collapsed, the Union unravelled, the Warsaw Pact wasted away, but old habits die hard. All over what was once the Soviet Union, anniversaries, birthdays and weddings are still not complete without a visit to one of the System's secular shrines.

The dancing started. The young men in ill-cut dark blue or grey Soviet suits and—in spite of the bitter wind—open-necked crackly white nylon shirts, at first looked slightly ill at ease, as if the tradition somehow compromised their modernity and Western tastes. Not so the women, who threw themselves into the festivities with gusto, saucily displaying their gaudy undertrousers to the knee, their multicoloured dresses and headscarves, in dazzling purple, red, green, blue and gold, flashing like a swarm of brilliant dragonflies in the weak December sun.

The party danced in line away from the memorial, up the sandy slope towards the tree. The bride stepped forward and drew from her belt a footlong strip of shiny red silk an inch or so wide. Her new husband took her by the waist and lifted her as high as he could. She reached up and tied her piece of cloth around one of the upper branches—a message, wish, a petition, to the *genius loci*, the spirit of the place.

The music turned into a march and the dance became a procession, moving away from the memorial, up the steepening slope towards a spot higher on the hillside, where a long narrow pit had been dug in which a fire had been laid. With music and chanting, the bride and groom would celebrate their union by jumping together backwards and forwards over the blazing coals.

Darkness was falling as the wedding party moved off up the hill for the fire ceremony. Having in short order remembered Muhammad and Marx, it was time for the bride and groom to propitiate a much more ancient power. As we returned to our vehicle and prepared to move on, I wondered which of all the rituals of that day meant most to the newly-weds. The Soviet era would fade from memory, the war memorial would weather away like most other relics of Central Asia's troubled history but, I guessed, in a hundred, even two hundred years, their descendants would surely still be tying petitions to the tree and performing the fire ceremony. For the veneration of fire is very, very ancient in these parts, from even before the time of Zarathustra, perhaps dating right back to the days when our pre-human, *Homo erectus*, ancestors first domesticated the dangerous but life-saving flames. Zoroastrians—like Moses who saw God in the Burning Bush—teach that fire is a symbol of the divine. Before Zarathustra's time, it may well have been worshipped as a god.

The late Bronze Age, during which Zarathustra probably lived and worked, was the era of the "heroic" society, the time of Homer's warriors when, among many peoples, honour, bravery and physical strength were valued above all else. Among the settled, clan preyed upon clan and tribe raided tribe, stealing treasure, cattle, slaves and wives: consider the conquest of Canaan by the Hebrews, or the abduction and rape of the Sabine women by Romulus, the founder of Rome. The full-time and part-time nomads, though they could preserve their safety by moving, could not always avoid the depredations of envious neighbours equipped with the new military technology of wheeled chariots and bronze swords.

It seems to have been a very simple life materially. In one of his hymns, Zarathustra prays that God will reward him for his righteousness with ten mares, a stallion and a camel. Such a simple, practical, boon compared with the choirs of angels and everlasting joy of Christian theology or the heavenly houris of Islam. I find myself rather moved by the contrast between the prophet's naïve, not to say poverty-stricken, request and the majesty of his spiritual vision. For one cannot doubt that Zarathustra was a deeply radical figure in the religious history of antiquity. Only for that reason could his fame have spread so widely in the following centuries among all the peoples of his world, friends and enemies alike. Only an extraordinary personality with an extraordinary impact on society, a Moses, a Jesus, a Muhammad, would still be remembered by name so long after his death, yet he left us no extensive revelation and his disciples bequeathed us no detailed accounts of his life.

Zarathustra addressed a nation who venerated fire and worshipped the ancestral deities of the Indo-Europeans, the gods of sky and earth, Asman and Zam, the gods of sun and moon, Mithra and Mah, the god of war Indra, and the host of *daevas*, spirits and demons by which all pre-scientific peoples explain the events of their world. Probably, as Herodotus said of the Greeks, they believed their gods to have similar natures to themselves, for this was the way of all Indo-European nations. But Zarathustra didn't threaten his people with supernatural powers that must be propitiated. He proclaimed that there is only one true God, Ahura Mazda, and he identified the source of all evil in the world as the Lie *(Druj)*—later to be personified as Angra Mainyu or Ahriman. He reduced all other divinities to the status of attributes, mere partial glimpses, of the glorious totality of his God. He rejected worship of the *daevas* altogether, teaching that the spirits of war, destruction, greed and acquisition were mere reflections of the amoral aspect of humanity.

That was just the beginning. According to Zoroastrian tradition, as well as hints in the hymns themselves, the prophet taught that each individual had a free choice between good and evil, and that following the path of *asha*, righteousness, would lead to salvation, even for lay worshippers. Until then, only priests and aristocrats had been imagined as having an immortal soul—heaven was the preserve of the upper classes, hell reserved for the laity. He condemned animal sacrifice as cruel and denounced the priestly cult of Haoma, probably a hallucinogenic plant and presumably related to the Soma of Hindu scripture (possibly cannabis, the hemp, which Herodotus claimed that the steppe nomads put to ritual use). He did not preach the adoration of fire. His basic doctrine was rational, anti-ritual and anti-sacrifice, encouraging his followers to come to personal terms with their God.

The princes and warriors of his people, not to speak of the priests, reacted badly to Zarathustra's claims. Who was this crazy thirty-year-old who was threatening the age-old traditions of the tribe? Or rather, who did he think he was, for they knew him only too well. He was from the priestly caste himself, of the noble Spitama clan. He should have known better than to rock the religious boat. How could he, of all people, have been granted divine recognition over his elders and betters? He was denounced by the *karapans*, the traditional priests, expelled from the community, cut off from his family and clan, and forced into exile. He was the first, though hardly the last, prophet to lack honour in his own country.

> *To what land shall I flee, whither to flee?*
> *From the nobles and from my peers I am cut off, nor do the people love me, nor*
> *the Liar rulers of the land.*

Eventually Zarathustra came to the court of King Gushtasp, ruler of a north-east Iranian people, perhaps in that ancient city we know as Balkh, in today's Afghanistan. There he was welcomed and heard out, winning over first the queen and then the king and his court to his religious reforms. Established as court prophet, he taught, preached and wrote hymns, a remnant of which are now preserved in the *Avesta*, the Zoroastrian sacred text. The names of the king and his principal courtiers appear in the verses. Tradition says that he prospered, marrying three wives in succession, the last of whom was King Gushtasp's chief minister's daughter. He is said to have had six children. The last of the *Gathas*, the Avestan hymns, appears to have been written for the marriage of his youngest daughter, Pouruchista (Full of Wisdom) to Jamasp (He of the Sturdy Horses), another minister of the king.

Zoroastrian tradition tells that their prophet lived into old age. At seventy-seven—a suspiciously magic number—he is said to have died at the hands of a *karapan*, a priest, called Bradres, who crept up behind him and stabbed him in the back.

More than three thousand years later, in the Iranian desert oasis city of Yazd, hidden among the palaces and prisons, below a unique skyline of tall wind towers, designed to catch any faint breaths of summer breeze and funnel them down into secret retreats at the heart of the huddle of mud-brick houses, Iran's most important Zoroastrian fire temple still attracts a huge crush of visitors. At Noruz, tourists from all over Iran press seemingly inexhaustibly through the ragged and litter-strewn garden and up the steps, beneath the large *Farohar* (the winged symbol of the Godhead) fixed over the doorway, pushing and shoving to get into the entrance hall. Inside, they could gaze through a protective thick glass window at what must be the world's oldest sacred fire, the flames of which have been burning, so the attendant claims, since the year 470, though—shades of grandfather's axe (both handle and blade, you may remember, have been replaced many times; so in what sense is it still grandfather's axe?)—not in the same place. One elderly doorman tries to keep the crowd in order at the same time as giving information—in Farsi, English and French—and soliciting donations for maintenance of the temple. I noticed quite a lot of cash collected in his box. Though some of it was Iranian rials, most was in US dollar bills. The Great Satan was, it seems, still supporting the Good Religion of Ahura Mazda.

The crowd was such that there was no question of receiving answers to my many questions. Whatever I asked the doorman, he directed me to the same framed text, with some twenty lines about the excellence and antiquity of the Zoroastrian religion and the age of the sacred fire. There was no real chance here of learning any more about what Noruz means to Zoroastrians. I and my Iranian companion decided that we had better look elsewhere.

A few years ago, after a great wind storm, Yazdis were amazed to see the top of a dome peek out of the desert sands that surround the town. Much digging exposed an entire buried Zoroastrian village, perfectly preserved, complete with a fire temple of its own. The buildings were not so very old: the village had probably vanished under the sands some time in the nineteenth century, but the place was still an eerie anachronism, a piece of history frozen in time—like Pompeii but without the calcined corpses. As we were clambering over the adobe walls, peering into the long-deserted rooms, a local family party arrived: two men, three women and two teenage girls. The women were dressed up to the nines under their *roupushes,* the long, fawn, figure-hiding raincoats worn by higher-class Iranian women who disdain the low-class *chador.* The young girls had their flowered headscarves pushed back on their heads as far as they dared, well beyond the officially sanctioned two centimetres of hair. This was a festive outing.

One of the men was father to the girls, and seemed to be speaking with insider knowledge as he lectured his wife and daughters about Zoroastrianism in a wild exaggeration of the theatrical style Iranians use when reciting verse—drawling out the long vowels as if eating them, peppering each sentence with SUDDEN LOUD PHRASES or unexpectedly . . . slowing . . . right . . . down. I decided that this must be a schoolteacher by trade—only they and television weather forecasters can get away with speaking in so mannered a fashion. We offered each other sweets and chocolates and I asked him to explain the Zoroastrian symbolism of the *haft sin*, the seven "s," table.

There is none, he told me. The *haft sin* table is an ironic comment rather than a religious symbol.

"Before Islam, Noruz was celebrated with a *haft shin* not *sin* table. We put on seven things beginning with 'sh.' We put *sharab* (wine) for celebration, *shir* (milk) for nourishment, *sharbat* (sherbet) for enjoyment, *shamshir* (a sword) for security, *shemshad* (a box) for wealth, *sham* (a candle) for illumination, and *shahdaneh* (hemp seeds) for enlightenment. So that these things would be ours during the coming year."

Hemp seeds for enlightenment? My thoughts immediately went back to Herodotus's description of Scythian funerals, when the nomads threw hemp seeds on a fire and inhaled the smoke from under a blanket.

"You have studied linguistics, perhaps?" the schoolman asked me. He looked disappointed when I shook my head. "Well, if you did, you would know that 'sh' and 's' are nearly the same but also very different: 'sh' is a soft, generous, warm sound and 's' is hard, bitter and cold. Try. Hear the difference."

And we all stood there for a moment in the abandoned village, hissing and shhh-ing like parked steam trains.

"You hear it?"

We all agreed that we did.

"So when Iran accepted Islam, the people wanted to keep their customs. And it was allowed, because the table did not break any of the laws of Islam. And also because the Qur'an was added. But the seven 'sh' of the *haft shin* table became now the seven 's,' so that every year Zoroastrians would be reminded of how bitter, hard and cold was the loss. But the Muslims, who have not studied linguistics, would not know this."

"But what do the seven 's' objects actually symbolise?" I wanted to know.

"Nothing. Didn't you listen to what I said?" (Now I was convinced he was a schoolteacher.) "Just seven things beginning with 's.' "

He lost interest in us, jumped on to a fallen wall, took up a heroic pose and went back to lecturing his family about the abandoned fire temple. The women looked up at him adoringly while the girls giggled.

Was this all that remained of Zarathustra's teaching in the country which had followed in his footsteps for a millennium and a half, I wondered. Just seven meaningless items beginning with "s"? The *haft sin* or even *shin* table seemed to have little to do with God or the fight between good and evil. Come to think of it, even the visitors to the Yazd fire temple had reminded me more of big-city tourists visiting a native American reservation than pilgrims seeking contact with their ancestral faith.

"Religion is a living thing—it grows," the schoolteacher had said in one of his perorations. "You cannot expect it to stay the same way for thousands of years." It is true that, like revolutionaries, religious visionaries are singularly bad at seeing the ultimate outcome of their labours; the founders of every revealed religion would surely be surprised at what had become of their teachings in later centuries. Moses—if the person to whom the first five books of the Old Testament are ascribed ever really existed—would certainly be perplexed by Jewish synagogue services, with their ceremonies elaborated in circumstances unimaginable to him, more than a millennium after his lifetime. Nor can I begin to guess what Jesus would make of the Catholic cult of the Virgin and the saints, or even the Mass—though Christian theology and worship were formulated within a few hundred years of the Crucifixion. Even Islam has developed in unforeseen directions, though the founding Prophet lived in relatively recent historic times. The first definitive gulf between Sunni and Shi'ah visions of Muhammad's message—which have no place in the Qur'an—opened up soon after his death and has continued to widen ever since.

The clear simplicity of Zarathustra's message, his opposition to formalism and his injunction to worship only the one God, seek happiness in this life, and choose good over evil, were soon enveloped in the accretions of history, like a precious jewel dropped in the sea and lost to sight under a thick coating of barnacles and weed. Though it all happened so long ago that nobody can be certain of what occurred or when, most scholars now believe that after the prophet died, his old enemies, the traditional *karapan* tribal priests, succeeded in smuggling back into newly minted Zoroastrianism many of the practices that the Prophet himself had opposed. The many lesser gods and good and evil spirits that he tried to persuade his followers were mere reflections of human attributes and physical forces, to be seen as angels at most, regained much of their divine dominion. The ancient and traditional Aryan fire cult, nowhere promoted in Zarathustra's hymns, now once again took centre-stage in the rituals of the Zoroastrian religion.

Though the cult of the Haoma plant had been censured by Zarathustra, it features in Zoroastrian prayers to this day.

Through Achaemenid and Hellenistic times—from the beginning of the empire of the Medes and Persians through the conquest by Alexander and its aftermath—the rôle of keepers of the Zoroastrian flame seems to have fallen to the Magi, the priestly caste of the Medean people, who managed to restore to the reformed faith much traditional Iranian custom. We don't know how they regarded the founding prophet, or even what they knew of him. In spite of the ancient Persian kings' inclination to record their achievements and beliefs on rock walls, Zarathustra is nowhere mentioned. At first we find only praise to Ahura Mazda. Eventually "the other gods" occasionally make their appearance in inscriptions, and finally, under Artaxerxes II, who also broke the no-temple and no-statue rule, Mithra and Anahita are mentioned by name. The Magi were working their magic.

In *The Dawn and Twilight of Zoroastrianism*, one of the most respected studies of Zarathustrian history, Oxford Professor R. C. Zaehner suggested that, in any case, with Alexander the Great, the glory days of the faith were over. The next thirteen hundred years have been no more than twilight and darkness. Naturally, the Persians themselves don't see it that way. According to the ninth-century work called the *Dinkart* (Acts of Religion),

> Daray, son of Daray [Darius III] commanded that two copies of all the *Avesta* and *Zand* [commentary] should be written down, even as Zoroaster had received them from Ohrmazd [Ahura Mazda], and that one should be preserved in the Royal Treasury and one in the National Archives.
>
> Valakhsh [Vologaises], the Arsacid [Parthian], commanded that a memorandum be sent to the provinces instructing them to preserve, in the state in which they had been found in each province, whatever of the *Avesta* and *Zand* had come to light and was genuine, and also any teaching deriving from it which, although scattered owing to the chaos and disruption that Alexander had brought in his wake and the pillage and looting of the Macedonians in the kingdom of Iran, either survived in writing or was preserved in an authoritative oral tradition.
>
> His Majesty, the King of Kings, Ardashir, son of Papak [founder of the Sassanian dynasty], following Tansar as his religious authority, commanded all those scattered teachings to be brought to the Court. Tansar set about his work, selected one ver-

sion and left the rest out of the canon: and he issued this decree: "The interpretation of all the teachings from the Religion of the worshippers of Mazdah is our responsibility: for now there is no lack of certain knowledge concerning them."

This was certainly wishful thinking, for by Sassanian times the key to the language of Zarathustra's *Gathas* had been lost and the *Zand* commentaries had become risible in their misunderstandings of the ancient verses. Not until modern linguistics demonstrated the link between Old Persian and Sanskrit would the full meaning of the text be recovered. Yet, as the above passage shows, doubt never deterred the Sassanian priests from turning the Good Religion of Ahura Mazda for the first time into a severe, puritanical and often persecuting orthodoxy—an officially imposed state religion with a hugely complicated set of purity laws, which have been likened to those of the Jewish rabbis. A few have even suggested a Zoroastrian origin for the Jewish laws of *kashruth*, the separation of clean from unclean foods. If anything, however, the dates of the respective lawbooks suggest just the reverse: that the Sassanian priests may have been influenced by the Jews' example of what a revealed religion ought to be like. Alas, centralisation of power in an official religious hierarchy usually leads to a proliferation of rules and the state-supported imposition of orthodoxy, and such an evolution may well have been an important factor in the faith's rout by Islam in the seventh century.

Not that Zoroastrianism disappeared overnight when the Arabs took over. Many centuries were to pass before the number of believers diminished to the present tiny minority. In Central Asia I was told stories of local Arab commanders paying unbelievers to attend the mosque on Fridays so as to make a good impression on those sent from the Umayyad capital Damascus, and later the Abbasid capital Baghdad, to ensure that the Qur'anic message was winning through.

A minority of Zoroastrians, however, found Muslim rule intolerable and, some time between the eighth and tenth centuries, emigrated first to Hormuz on the Persian Gulf and then to India. There they settled in the state of Gujarat to form a small quiet-living community of farmers and traders who called themselves Parsees (Persians). Contact between the Indian emigrants and their Iranian co-religionists seems quickly to have been lost and the two branches of Zoroastrianism remained out of touch with each other for some centuries. So much so, in fact, that when communications were restored at the end of the 1400s, the beliefs, rituals and even calendar of the two communities were found to have drifted quite far apart, a discovery that led to the split among the Indian Parsees, between traditionalists and reformers, from which Anquetil du Perron was later to profit.

It was the British who would change Parsee fortunes. When they established their trading posts in Gujarat in the early seventeenth century, they looked around for local allies who were neither Muslim like the Moghul ruling class, nor Hindu like the Indian majority, and found the Parsee community both open to European influence and keen to do business. When, later in the same century, the East India Company took control of Bombay, the enterprising Parsees soon began to move in. The city's rapid development in the eighteenth and nineteenth centuries has been attributed largely to the hard work and ability of Zarathustra's followers, who went on to found some of India's most important heavy industries—textiles, chemicals, steel, railways and shipbuilding.

Parsees exerted their influence in other fields too. One member of the community established the first printing press in India (1778), another founded India's oldest surviving newspaper (1822), yet others were active in the arts, education and sport. A Parsee captained the first Indian national cricket team to visit England (1886), which was also entirely composed of Zoroastrians—in fact, it was worshippers of Ahura Mazda who seem to have been largely responsible for turning cricket into what one Indian writer has called "an Indian game accidentally discovered by the British."

This keen interest in sport distinguishes the Parsees from the people they have most often been likened to: the Jews. Over the past two hundred years, they have spread, like the Jews, into a world-wide diaspora, making notable contributions to every society in which they have settled. In Britain, a Parsee was the first Indian undergraduate at Oxford, another was the first English Baronet of Indian origin, three Parsees were the first Indian-born members of the British House of Commons. More recently, Zoroastrians have distinguished themselves in the arts, drama, television management and music—who can forget the international orchestral conductor Zubin Mehta, or Freddie Mercury, lead singer of the stadium-rock-band Queen?

Back in Iran, however, as Zoroastrian numbers continued to shrink, the major impact of Zarathustra's vision turned out to be its effect on the version of Islam which evolved in the area which had once been the Persian Empire. Iran, Iraq, Central Asia, parts of Turkey and India all were once—and still are to a degree—dominated by Iranian culture. The marker of Iranian identity within the Islamic *Ummah*, the Muslim community, is the Shi'ah version of Islam, which—though it originated in a political struggle

for the succession to the Prophet Muhammad, a purely Arab dispute—
became in time the national religion of Iran.

Noruz is one of the two great annual occasions of Iran. Ashura is the other,
the tenth day of the Muslim month of Muharram, anniversary of the martyrdom of the Prophet Muhammad's grandson Hussein at Kerbala—now
in Iraq—in the year 680. It couldn't be a more different kind of event.
Where Noruz is all jollity, fun and relaxation, Ashura is a sober holy day of
deep mourning, publicly marked by processions of flagellants who walk
through city streets piercing their flesh with needles or whipping their own
backs bloody with chains set in wooden handles—items on sale to tourists
in the trinket shops. In the villages, the event is marked by the *Tazieh* (consolation), the sequence of passion plays that recounts Hussein's sad end
when, with his band of fewer than a hundred, he faced up to an army of
four thousand—and refused to surrender.

I once had the opportunity to watch Iranians celebrate—if that's the
right expression—this antique historical event. It was a striking experience.
Country people from miles around had assembled on the village sports
field, and were sitting themselves down in a large circle around the spot
where the yearly drama would play itself out. These are conservative folk
and the women were almost entirely concealed inside their black *chadors,*
only their eager eyes visible. The men had dressed in their Friday-best
mosque clothes, jackets and trousers—only the clergy wear traditional
gowns—and some carried guns. Many of the men would have been veter-
ans of the pitiless Iran-Iraq war, and many of the women widows or
bereaved mothers; for them, the martyrdom of Hussein has a more personal meaning. Unusually, there was no gossip or chatter. Even the many
children were quiet, the younger ones clinging to their mothers and looking about them wide-eyed. Everyone sat in silence, waiting for the play to
begin.

Suddenly a menacing black-turbaned figure armoured in painted card-
board, but with an iron (though thankfully blunt) sword and buckler, rides
through a gap and reins his horse in. The black beast rears and then circles
the ring, snorting impatiently. The audience flinches. The protagonist now
begins to recite a long speech in a singsong voice, his effect only slightly
spoiled—to the cynical Western eye—by having to glance at a prompt, a

scrap of paper in his hand, between every line. This is the personification of evil, the wicked Umayyad who will murder the Prophet's rightful successor.

The hero now appears on a white horse, clothed in a white surplice with a green turban and similarly armed to his enemy. He chants a ringing speech of his own, with much raising of the arms and looking up to heaven—as well as down at his crib sheet. This is Hussein, personification of all that is noble and good.

Others arrive, also on horseback and variously clad, then dismount, and a sort of balletic battle is joined, with much shouting and clashing of swords against shields. While the actors take great care not to inflict real injury on each other with their weapons, the public is at genuine risk from whirling blades and wheeling horses. Now the first martyr falls. The actor playing Ali Akbar, Hussein's son, wearing white and green, with strands of red wool sewn all over his tunic to signify bleeding wounds, drops his weapon and sinks to the ground—carefully looking down first, to make sure that he isn't about to fall painfully on a stone—and delivers his final interminable verses before laying his head on the dust and expiring theatrically.

I won't go on to describe the rest of the event in all its gory detail. The performance went on for more than three hours, until all of Hussein's party were lying on the ground playing dead—only occasionally stirring to make themselves more comfortable. Eventually Hussein himself, having washed his hands and arms in red-tinted water—standing in for that ubiquitous mystical Iranian liquid: martyr's blood—poured from a disgusting pink plastic teapot, lay down on a wooden trestle and delivered himself of a dying speech long enough to make the death aria of an operatic diva seem trivially brief.

But though mostly bored by the almost unintelligible and unending recitations, and also quietly amused by the grotesque and amateurish performances, I noticed something quite extraordinary: that many in the audience, both men and women, were crying bitterly, real tears streaming from their eyes, their shoulders heaving with sobs; burly men with rifles over their shoulders were wiping their damp, unshaven cheeks with huge bandana handkerchiefs. This was no play-acting, no demonstration of religious piety for the sake of the clergymen in the crowd. Nor was it the self-indulgent fantasy-mourning that these days erupts on the death of Western celebrities like Princess Diana. I was seeing real, genuine, unashamed weeping that could only possibly come from the heart.

The emotion cannot really be the response to a thirteen-century-old power struggle. This depth of sorrow cannot be felt for a man of whose reality these people actually know nothing. Their heartbreak can only be over their own lives and their own losses.

It was a very young but rather gloomy-looking village policeman, with an angry boil on his neck, who explained the paradox to me when the performance was over and the audience was dispersing—the children much more boisterous now.

"For us, the human being Imam Hussein (peace be on him) is not the subject. Yes, he was the grandson of the Prophet of Islam (peace and blessings be upon him), through 'Ali (peace be on him) his cousin and son-in-law and his daughter Fatimah (peace be to her), and so is a very holy person who should not be killed in such a way. But the story of Kerbala is more: it is the story of the battle between good and evil, between truth and lies. This battle never ends. That is why the play must be repeated every year. It is the battle every good Muslim must fight. These men and women who cried were not only mourning for Imam Hussein (peace be on him), they were sad for their own defeats in this war. But . . ." and suddenly he brightened up, " . . . when the hidden Imam comes back to us, the war will be over and good will have won. I pray it may be in my or my children's lifetime."

I might have been listening to the words of a Zoroastrian rather than a Muslim. While serious students of religion express many caveats, my impression is that much of Zarathustra's theology has been transferred straight over to Iranian Islam. Ultra-orthodox Muslims claim that the mourning rites for Hussein are not authentically Islamic, but were learned from Iran's neighbours. After all, the village policeman's eternal war of good against evil, central to Shi'ah consciousness, is not a feature of Sunni belief. In the Iranian imagination, behind the figure of 'Ali, murdered Arab successor to the Caliphate, one can see the shadowy presence of Zarathustra, the Persian prophet, himself. Many Shi'ites believe that 'Ali and his descendants the Shi'ah Imams, spiritual leaders of the community, are channels for the Primeval Light of God and the sole possessors of secret insights into the Qur'an. Indeed, with 'Ali, the Islamic prohibition of images is frequently broken, and icons of the sacred personality, with light blazing from the halo around his turban, are on sale everywhere. And the "Hidden Imam," the twelfth successor to 'Ali, who disappeared in the year 878 "—went into occlusion," as they tell you—and will one day return, is surely the Zoroastrian Messiah, the Saoshyant, in Muslim guise.

Iranian Shi'ahs see themselves as ideal Muslims and are horrified when orthodox Sunni critics accuse them, as they do, of secret Zoroastrian tendencies, pointing to the hierarchy of clergy with a Supreme Leader at its head, like some Zoroastrian *Mobed-e-mobedan*, Priest of Priests. But on one notable occasion the Shi'ah façade cracked and revealed something of what lies behind. This was Zoroastrianism's final throw. In the tenth century, a radical and energetic branch of the Shi'ahs in Bahrain, excited by an unusual astrological conjunction as well as the supposed 1,500th anniversary of Zarathustra's death, began by blockading the pilgrimage routes to Mecca and ended by capturing the holy city itself and carrying off the sacred Black Stone of the Ka'aba, one of the most revered objects in the entire Islamic world. Their leader, a young Persian who claimed descent from the Sassanian kings, was hailed as the awaited Muslim Messiah, or *Mahdi*, who would bring the Islamic era to an end. He abolished Islamic law and ordered the veneration of fire to be restored. According to the Ottoman historian Qutb ud-Din, he was eventually destroyed by God, who afflicted him with gangrenous sores and let his flesh be eaten away by worms. He lasted for eighty days before being assassinated. Twenty years later, the Black Stone was returned—broken—to Mecca. From then on Zarathustra's followers would work within, rather than against, the victorious Muslim faith.

GOOD WORDS, GOOD THOUGHTS, GOOD DEEDS

Near Yazd, but further from the city than the buried village, high above the road which runs up through crumbling sandy iron-stained cliffs before petering out at a thousand feet, leaving us to climb a final rough, boulder-strewn path on foot, an ancient Zoroastrian shrine survives and still remains in use.

It is a pretty sight, a holy place high in the hills, a little outbreak of greenery where a tiny grove of myrtle and cypress—two trees sacred to Zoroastrians: myrtle for joy, cypress for sorrow—retains a toehold amid the jagged tan-and-ochre sandstone. In among the shrubs, a mix of ancient and modern buildings clusters close to the rocks. Later we would be told that Princess Ashraf, the last Shah's sister, had ordered the restoration, refurbishment and rebuilding of the shrines, confirming my suspicion that the short-lived twentieth-century Pahlavi dynasty had been dangerously heterodox in its religious allegiances.

Even from far below we could see that a service was in progress. What immediately caught our attention was the sight of the Zoroastrian, *Zardushti,* women and girls, looking from this distance like a roosting flock of brightly coloured tropical birds. Though modestly headscarved, they were all in brilliant festive attire, having abandoned the shapeless black *chadors* and *roupushes* that the law demands they hide under when in public. Here they were in their own domain and could dress exactly as they wished. My Iranian companions suggested that we watch from down here and wait for them to finish before going up to meet them. They are very shy, I was told, and wary of outsiders. It would be better not to barge in and disturb their prayers.

We took the opportunity to park ourselves on a large boulder by the side of the path and eat our lunch of *lavash* bread with *sir,* Iranian cheese, washed down with ersatz Coca-Cola. The sound of melodious singing, rather different from the musical tradition of the mosque, reached us faintly on the even more faintly myrtle-scented warm breeze, sometimes the gruff voice of the priest sounding solo, sometimes the chorus of worshippers joining in.

The distance was somehow appropriate. These were hymns which would have included passages from the *Gathas* of Zarathustra himself. We were listening to the final reverberations of a spiritual explosion that happened more than three thousand years ago, the most ancient religious revolution of all. They were the words of the man who can truly be called the First Prophet.

Ancient Egyptian beliefs and praises of the gods are even older than the Zoroastrian texts. But the religion of the Pharaohs died with the end of the classical world. Moses—if that legendary national hero really existed— may have been a contemporary of the Persian sage, and his name is still held in awe by his remote descendants the Jews as well as by their Christian and Muslim cousins. But the Five Books of Moses contain history, genealogy and law and are reported speech rather than a direct personal response to divine revelation—orthodox believers say that they are words inspired by God Himself. They were collated and written down (or, some say, invented) a thousand years after Moses's time and no echo can be heard in them of his own voice. In any case, Hebrew concern was for obedience to God's commands and meticulous observance of His laws. The early books of the Bible do not concern themselves, as does Zarathustra's teaching, with moral choices and leading a good life.

Among the texts of still living religions, only the Hindu Scriptures, the

Vedas, vie with the Zoroastrian *Gathas* for antiquity. The Vedas, however, still reflect the cruelty of the heroic age, and of its many gods "with the same nature as men"—that is to say, with all their faults and shortcomings. Zarathustra's contemporaries would have recognised most Indian Aryan beliefs as similar, if not identical, to their own. Yet from this unpromising, conservative seedbed had sprung an entirely novel spiritual growth, embodied in a man with a completely new understanding of our relations and duties to each other, to the world around us and to God.

As I sat and listened to the distant voices, I couldn't help being profoundly moved by the thought that someone who lived in such a remote age, whose circumstances were so inconceivably different from those of our own times, who could not have even begun to imagine what people would make of the world in the following millennia, should none the less have had such a profound understanding of the human condition that his message still speaks directly to us today. Zarathustra had such a clear vision of humanity's moral choices that his counsel—good words, good thoughts, good deeds—is as applicable to our times as it was to his own.

Not only ours, but indeed every age has, in its own way, recognised the wisdom of Zarathustra's message. Looking back on my journey through time, following the First Prophet's trail down the ages, casting his reflection on Zoroastrians, Jews, Christians, Muslims, as well as adherents to other faiths that came, like Buddhism, more indirectly under his sway, the importance of his mission becomes clearer. At the root of it all was his solution to the question of Why: Why does evil exist in a God-ordained world? Every people who worshipped a single omnipresent, omnipotent God faced the same conundrum. Either God was not all-good or He was not all-powerful. As the Book of Amos asks: "Shall there be evil in a city, and the Lord hath not done it?" Each faith tried to solve it in its own way. Jews told themselves that it was all their own fault; Christians agreed and added that all Adam's progeny was corrupt; Muslims waited for recompense in another life. But none of these ways of coping with the reality of living has been convincing enough to stop believers being attracted to Zarathustra's alternative.

Zarathustra saw in the workings of the world a clear sign that evil was an independent force that must be combated. Open any daily newspaper on any morning three millennia later, and you are likely to find his perception amply endorsed by the headlines. The existence of evil as a power in the world is an easy leader-writer's explanation for any atrocity, crime or misdemeanour that shocks today's public. And hasn't the history of the twentieth century given us good cause to adopt that Zarathustrian view? I think back to Nietzsche's dictum that Zarathustra's "invention of morality" was the greatest philosophical error in human history, and then recall the catastrophe achieved by those who claimed to be inspired by Nietzsche's insight. The story of Hitler and Stalin, with their millions of victims, cannot be simply ascribed to greed, egotism, or the Seven Deadly Sins of Christian belief. If Nietzsche had known what the world would be like when Zarathustra's "invention" was abandoned, I doubt he would have looked forward with such passionate enthusiasm to the post-moral age.

Accounts of murder and mayhem are not the only daily reminders of journalism's debt to the Persian prophet. For it was he who also proposed that the world—and time itself—would one day come to an end. It has surprised me, who tends to smile, indulgently patronising, at the eschatological, End of Time, fantasies of earlier eras, to realise that we are just as obsessed with impending doom as were our ancestors in more credulous days. True, most of us don't take religious prophets very seriously any more, nor sandwich-board men with placards reading "The End of the World is Nigh," preferring to heed the words of New Age gurus, cult leaders, environmentalists, climatologists, physicists, astronomers and medical experts. But, taking popular television documentaries as a measure, it would be hard to argue that we are any less fixated on the End-of-the-World-as-We-Know-It than were those in the first century BC, when a Messiah was expected to bring time to a close at any moment.

Nor are heavenly visitors exactly unfamiliar in our days, either. It was Zoroastrianism that introduced named angels to us; even the Talmud admits that "the angels' names came from Babylon." But having learned all about angels from their Persian mentors, the Jews rapidly integrated the idea into their—and therefore our—beliefs. Sadly, we don't see angels any more, as thousands—like the poet William Blake—used regularly to see them, but surely enough time, energy and money has been spent on investigating UFOs and extra-terrestrial abductions, to suggest that visitations from another world are as common today as they were in medieval, Roman or Achaemenid times. Secular translations of religious motifs are a notable feature of our time. It is as if those who have abandoned religion are left with a residue of concepts that must now be justified by other means.

For those of us who still need spiritual support and cling to faith, a new sort of ecumenical religion has developed. In our Western, tolerant, multi-faith societies, we have managed to pool a basic common denominator of belief, shared by nearly everybody. When we strip off the particularities of Judaism with its detailed purity laws, of Christianity with its unfathomable Trinity, and of Islam with its claim that Muhammad is the Final Prophet, we are left with what the distinguished critic Harold Bloom has identified as the "American Religion"—but might better be called Universal than American. The universal religion comprises a belief in good and evil, angels, the Devil, heaven and hell, the coming of a Messiah, and an eventual end of the world. These are beliefs with which Jews, Christians and Muslims can all agree—as well as that majority who do not claim to believe in any particular religion. Every one of those ideas first appeared in Zarathustra's teaching long before the start of recorded history, a message as influential today as it ever was. As Professor Mary Boyce has put it, his is "a shadowy but powerful presence in the Judaeo-Christian world."

When the Zoroastrian service in the mountain grove was over, we climbed the path the rest of the way up to the shrine. The elderly man in charge—I never discovered whether he was a priest or a community leader—clean-shaven and very smartly turned out in a Western suit and black shoes polished as shiny as jet, was friendly and welcoming. Having mildly scolded us for not coming up earlier to witness the prayers—at which, he said, we would have been very welcome—he showed us enthusiastically around the grove. The trees, he pointed out, were very old indeed. These specimens— of the species *Cupressus Sempervirens*—are known to survive for up to five thousand years, and myrtles too can be very long-lived. The central building of the shrine had originally been put up in antiquity around a spot where a myrtle sprig sprang wild from a cleft in the rock. This sacred place, perhaps the goal of pilgrims even in Zarathustra's time, had been dedicated to Zoroastrian worship early in the Sassanian era, the third century perhaps— we were told a complicated and unbelievable story of three dead Sassanian sisters—and sacred fires have burned here continuously since a time as far back in history as anyone can imagine.

The rocky spot was enclosed and a small building erected around the myrtle, to shelter the pilgrims from summer sun and winter rain. The shrub was originally small. But, though myrtles like these grow slowly, particularly up here, high in the hills, the leafy aromatic growth eventually began to press against the imprisoning walls and threaten the clay-brick structure. Rather than pulling the building down and raising another, larger one, which might itself be outgrown one day, they pierced a window in one side of the little temple and fed the myrtle's main stem out through it. Today, the building is completely overwhelmed and invisibly hidden beneath a huge ball of shrubbery.

We passed from bright sunlight into the green-tinged gloom of the interior, our noses smarting with the combined scent of myrtle and wood-smoke. In the centre of the small room stood a pedestal supporting an iron basket in which the sacred fire burned. Realising that this was the very closest I had so far come to Zarathustra, I asked the temple-keeper if the core of his teaching could be simply expressed, maybe in a few sentences. I was slightly embarrassed at what I was demanding from an ancient, complex and sophisticated faith, and apologised for my typical Western crudity, but the old man was in no way disconcerted.

"Easily," he said. "Our basic beliefs are very simple. Choose truth and oppose lies. And always strive for good words, good thoughts and good deeds."

Simple beliefs they may be, but profound too, teachings as practical and as relevant for the post-religious modern world as they were for ancient times. Every writer, journalist or film-maker, every creative artist or scientist, every worker, business person or professional, indeed every individual can feel personally addressed by the perception that truth supports what is good, positive and creative, while falsehood leads to what is bad, negative and destructive. I thought, as I stood in the chamber of that little temple in the Iranian hills, that the message I had been given was a fitting final end to my long journey in search of Zarathustra.

I felt a deep and moving kinship with the old Zoroastrian. Two and a half thousand years ago my ancestors and his had encountered each other in a meeting that would shape our world. Through my ancestors, the exiled Judaeans of Cyrus's empire, the teachings of Zarathustra had passed to the Jews, and through them to the Christians and the Muslims, eventually to become an integral part of a universal spiritual world-view. Western culture is often said to have been erected on foundations of Hellenism and Judaism. From now on I would always have to add "and Zoroastrianism too."

Yet however much I thought I had finally come to grips with Zarathustra's ancient significance, his modern followers still had the power to spring surprises. I became aware of a tapping on my arm. Our driver, my Iranian companion's brother-in-law, was dying for a smoke and was signalling to me that he was about to step outside. But he quickly came back into the little shrine looking slightly abashed, and gestured to ask if I had a light. My Iranian companion didn't smoke and I too had run out of matches, so I shook my head and patted my pockets uselessly. As we stood there foolishly signalling to each other, the elderly Zoroastrian smiled, stepped towards the fire in the iron basket, picked up a twig, ignited it from the sacred flames and held it out to light Muhammad's cigarette.

From a Hymn of Zarathustra

Hear with your ears the Best; look upon it with clear thought. When deciding between the two beliefs, each for himself before the great consummation, think that it be accomplished to our pleasure.

The two primal Spirits, who reveal themselves in vision as twins, are the Better and the Bad, in thought and in word and in action. And between these two the wise choose aright, the foolish not so.

In the beginning, when those two Spirits came together, they created Life and Not-Life, and at the end, the followers of the Lie shall inherit Worst Existence, but Best Existence shall be for those who follow the Right.

Of the two Spirits, he that followed the Lie chose the Worst. The holier Spirit, he that clothes himself with the massy heavens as with a garment, chose the Right. So should do likewise they that would please Lord Mazda by dutiful action.

The Daevas also chose wrongly between the two. Infatuation came upon them as they took counsel together, so that they chose Worst Thought. Then together they rushed to Violence, that they might enfeeble the world of men.

If, O mortals, you shall hearken diligently unto those commandments which Mazda has commanded you, of happiness and pain, long punishment for the followers of the Lie, and blessings for the followers of the Right, then hereafter all shall be well.

(from the *Ahunavaiti Gatha*)

Notes and Acknowledgements

INTRODUCTION

p. xiii A short account of my Iranian trip, given the fanciful title "The Mark of Zoroaster" by the travel editor, was published in the *Guardian* in October 2000, and is—at the time of writing—available in a number of places on the Internet.

1 AN IDEA FOR NOW

p. 3 "The Golden Journey to Samarkand" is from James Elroy Flecker's (1884–1915) verse play *Hassan*.

p. 5 The production was the 1993 BBC2 series *Living Islam*. The presenter did later—briefly—become Pakistan High Commissioner in London.

p. 10 The verse is from Ferdowsi's *Shah-nameh*, the Book of Kings, in the section called "Isfandiyar." I have adapted the translation from that of Helen Zimmern, available on the Internet at http://classics.mit.edu/Ferdowsi/kings.html.

p. 15 A very clear and concise account of both the Iranian and the Afghan revolutions is in *Islamic Fundamentalism*, by Dilip Hiro, published by Paladin in 1988, and—as *Holy Wars: The Rise of Islamic Fundamentalism*—by Routledge in 1989.

p. 24 The production was the 1984 BBC2 series *Orchestra* and the young conductor was Dr. Jane Glover.

2 THE TRUE PHILOSOPHER

p. 28 The script of *The Little Man* is in *The Little Man and other Satires* by John Galsworthy, published by Charles Scribner's Sons, 1915.

p. 31 The clearest and most moving introduction to Nietzsche's work that I could find was not a book but a film: *Human—All Too Human*, a BBC/RM Arts co-production, produced and directed by Simon Chu in 1999 and transmitted on BBC2 the same year.

p. 37 An exhaustive survey in German of the European response to Zoroaster is in

Faszination Zarathustra by Michael Stausberg, published in two volumes by De Gruyter, Berlin, in 1998.

p. 38 The passage is from Voltaire's *Poème sur la loi naturelle*, 1751. In the original French:

> Cette loi souveraine, à la Chine, au Japon,
> Inspira Zoroastre, illumina Solon.
> D'un bout du monde à l'autre elle parle, elle crie:
> "Adore un Dieu, sois juste, et chéris ta patrie."

p. 39 I found many of the stories about Abraham Hyacynthe Anquetil du Perron in the brilliant novelistic *Vie d'Anquetil-duperron* by Raymond Schwab published by E. Leroux, Paris, in 1934. I don't understand why the French cinema industry has never made it into a movie—or perhaps I just never saw it.

p. 46 The famous philologist was the Danish Professor Rasmus Rask (1787–1832), whose researches laid the foundations for what would later be known as Grimm's Law. He wrote: "Eine Neidschrift voll Gift und Gall, und des Verfassers Namens durchaus unwördig."

p. 54 An abridged transcript in 375 pages of *Jung's Seminar on Nietzsche's Zarathustra*, edited by James L. Jarrett, from which I took many of the anecdotes in this chapter, was published by Princeton University Press in 1998.

3 THE GREAT HERESY

p. 57 The magnificent website at http://www.cathares.org, contains—at the time of writing—a complete gazetteer of all the important Cathar sites, pen portraits of all the major participants in the Albigensian Crusade, and much more.

p. 58 *Massacre at Montségur: A History of the Albigensian Crusade* by Zoé Oldenbourg was published by Weidenfeld & Nicolson in 1961.

p. 59 *Montaillou: Cathars and Catholics in a French Village 1294–1324* by Emmanuel Le Roy Ladurie was published by Penguin in 1980.

p. 61 The Provençal troubadour Raimbault de Vaqueyras died in 1207. He was said to have written the words to "Kalenda Maya" after hearing the tune of an *Estampie*, an up-tempo court dance, played on viols by a pair of *jongleurs* (itinerant minstrels) at the court of Montferrat, modern Monferrato, in Piedmont.

Chrétien de Troyes, who flourished between 1165–80, wrote five romances which established the Arthurian genre for all time.

p. 63 The dialogue about Pythagoras is between the Clown and Malvolio in *Twelfth Night*, Act IV, scene ii.

p. 69 *The Hidden Tradition in Europe*, the secret history of medieval Christian heresy, by Yuri Stoyanov, from which I learned much of the detail of Catharism, Bogomilism and Manichaeism, was published by Penguin in 1994.

p. 78 According to Yuri Stoyanov, the source claiming that Bogomilism lasted into the nineteenth century was Friedrich Heer in *The Medieval World*.

p. 82 For more on the travelling lifestyle of the Great Steppe, I greatly value *Tents, Architecture of the Nomads* by Torvald Faegre, published by John Murray in 1979.

p. 83 *The Black Sea* by Neal Ascherson, which introduced me to the world of the Sarmatians, was published by Jonathan Cape in 1995.

p. 85 An account of Gaiseric's ship order is in *The New Penguin Atlas of Medieval History* by Colin McEvedy, published by Penguin in 1992.

Europe: A History by Norman Davies, a major reference source for me, was published by Pimlico in 1996.

4 THE RELIGION OF LIGHT

p. 88 Muhammad Shams ud-Din Hafez lived *c*. 1325–89.

Abu abd-Allah Musharraf Ibn Muslih-ud-Din, known as Sa'adi, lived *c*. 1208–93.

In a statement by Kofi Annan, then UN General Secretary, his verse was translated as:

> The children of Adam are limbs of one another
>   and in their creation come from one substance.
> When the world gives pain to one member, the other members find no rest.
> Thou who are indifferent to the sufferings of others
>   do not deserve to be called a man.

p. 91 *The Medieval Manichee: A Study of the Christian Dualist Heresy* by Sir Stephen Runciman was published by Cambridge University Press in 1946.

p. 92 *The Gardens of Light* by Amin Maalouf, the beautiful and moving novel of Mani's life-story, was published by Quartet in 1996.

p. 94 I found the Talmudic references to *Habbars* in an article, "The Menorah and the Magi," by Professor Eliezer Segal of the University of Calgary, first published in the *Calgary Jewish Free Press* on 19 December 1997.

p. 96 For what follows, I am indebted to the compilation of *Manichaean Writings* by L. J. R. Ort in his 1967 thesis, published by E. J. Brill, Leiden.

p. 103 *Manichaeism in the Later Roman Empire and Medieval China* by Samuel N. C. Lieu was published by Manchester University Press in 1985.

5 THE MYSTERY OF MITHRAS

p. 116 *The Temple of Mithras, London* by John Shepherd was published by English Heritage in 1998.

p. 118 "If you wish to see building contractors cower and property developers turn pale, you need only whisper the words 'Temple of Mithras' " was said by Dr. Ralph Merrifield of the Museum of London in 1965.

p. 122 *The Dawn and Twilight of Zoroastrianism* by Professor R. C. Zaehner was published by Weidenfeld & Nicolson in 1961.

Translations from the Zoroastrian canon by Darmester and Mills from *Sacred Books of the East* are available on many Internet sites.

p. 123 A shorter account of Cumont's work on Mithraism is contained in *The Mysteries of Mithra* by Franz Cumont, published by Dover Books in 1956.

p. 127 The thesis that Mithraism had nothing to do with Iran and was an entirely new astrology-based religion was put forward in *The Origins of the Mithraic Mysteries* by David Ulansey, published by Oxford University Press in 1989.

p. 129 *Roman London,* by Jenny Hall and Ralph Merrifield, an excellent illustrated guide, was published by HMSO in 1986.

p. 132 A fascinating and very readable account of Hadrian's Wall, as well as much else in Roman Britain, is in *Roman Britain* by Peter Salway, published by Oxford University Press in 1981.

p. 133 At the time of writing, the Newcastle Museum of Antiquities website at http://www.ncl.ac.uk has a splendid virtual reality display of the Carrawburgh temple both as it is now and as it would have been in Roman times.

p. 138 At the time of writing, there is a remarkable virtual reality representation of the Nemrud Dagh *herothesion* at http://www.learningsites.com/NemrudDagi/.

p. 139 A novel which brilliantly brings to life the final days of Roman power in Britain, though with no mention of Mithraism, is *The Little Emperors* by Alfred Duggan, republished by Methven's Booksellers in 2001.

p. 140 Noel Swerdlow's review article "On the Cosmical Mysteries of Mithras" appeared in *Classical Philology* 86 (1991): 48–63.

For the following chapters, I have adapted the translations of Zoroastrian scripture from James Darmester, *Sacred Books of the East,* as well as from I. J. S. Taraporewala, *The Divine Songs of Zarathushtra.* The accuracy of the former work is questioned by some, but since my purpose was illustrative rather than scholarly it served me perfectly well. I adapted the translations of Achaemenid royal inscriptions from Joseph H. Peterson's *Old Persian Texts* page on the Internet at http://www.avesta.org. Biblical quotations are from the Authorised Version of the Bible.

My major historical resource for this period of Iranian history was the multi-volume *Cambridge History of Iran,* while for biblical commentary I turned to the volumes of *The New Clarendon Bible,* published by Oxford University Press, which combines religious and political history and their reflection in the religious canon clearly and concisely.

I enjoyed the version of *Herodotus* translated by David Grene and published by University of Chicago Press in 1987 and I would recommend the translation of Xenophon's *The Persian Expedition* by Rex Warner, and published by Penguin in 1972, as a rattling good adventure story.

6 THE END OF TIME

I found much of the background to this chapter in *The Jews in the Greek Age* by Elias J. Bickerman, published by Harvard University Press in 1988, as well as in *The Jewish Festivals* by Hayyim Schauss, published by Schocken in 1962. I also consulted *Readings in the Classical Historians,* by Michael Grant, published by Maxwell Macmillan in 1992.

The best Iranian travel guide I found, readable, informative and light of touch, was unquestionably *A Travel Guide to Iran* by M. T. Faramarzi, published in English by Yassaman Publications, Tehran, in 1997.

p. 155 *The Itinerary of Benjamin of Tudela,* translated by Marcus Nathan Adler, was published by Oxford University Press in 1907.

p. 159 I found the reference to Horace's satire in *Jews and Christians: Graeco-Roman Views* by Molly Whittaker, published by Cambridge University Press in 1984.

p. 161 The "curious detail of the feet" is referred to in *Cosmos, Chaos and the World to Come* by Norman Cohn, published by Yale University Press in 1993.

p. 164 The anecdotes from the Talmud were taken from Mahlon H. Smith's remarkable and extensive Internet resource, *Into His Own, Perspectives on the World of Jesus,* at http://religion.rutgers.edu/iho/, saved me many hours of Talmud study.

p. 166 *The Mystery and Meaning of the Dead Sea Scrolls* by Hershel Shanks was published by Random House in 1998.

7 BY THE GRACE OF AHURA MAZDA

p. 175 Michael Wood refers to the nomads blessing Cyrus's tomb in his book *In the Footsteps of Alexander the Great,* published by BBC Books in 1997.

p. 181 A beautifully illustrated guide to the Berlin Pergamon Museum's Babylon display is *The Ishtar Gate, The Processional Way, The New Year Festival of Babylon* by Joachim Marzahn, published (in English) by Philipp von Zabern, Mainz, in 1995.

p. 185 The convincing thesis that there had long been a YHWH-Alone Party was put in *Palestinian Parties and Politics that Shaped the Old Testament* by Morton Smith, published by Columbia University Press in 1971.

p. 190 At the time of writing one can see this and other illustrations of Behistun on the Internet at http://seminary.georgefox.edu/courses/bst550/reports/Jbartlett/.

p. 198 I took this Surah of the Qur'an from N. J. Dawood's translation, published by Penguin Classics in 1956.

8 THE FIRST PROPHET

p. 208 Haym Soloveitchik was quoted in the journal *Judaism,* Winter 1998.

I am indebted to http://www.iranianlanguages.com for the passage from the *Avesta* and its Sanskrit translation.

p. 218 The translation of the passage quoted from the ninth-century text, the *Dinkart,* is from Zaehner, op. cit.

p. 220 The writer who called cricket "an Indian game accidentally discovered by the British" was Professor Ashish Nandy, director of the Delhi Centre for the Study of Developing Societies, in his book *The Tao of Cricket.*

A list of Zoroastrian "firsts" is available on the Internet site of the World Zoroastrian Organisation at http://www.w-z-o.org/.

p. 228 The proposition that there is such a thing as the "American Religion" is put in *Omens of the Millennium* by Harold Bloom, published by Riverhead Books in 1996.

Index

Index

Index

Paul Kriwaczek was born in Vienna in 1937. At the age of two he fled Vienna and the Nazi threat with his parents, eventually arriving in England. He attended grammar school in London and studied at the London Hospital Medical School. After qualifying as a dental surgeon in 1962 and traveling extensively in Asia and Africa—including a two-year stint as the only European dentist in Kabul—he joined BBC External Services as a specialist in Central and South Asia affairs, later switching to BBC Television, where he enjoyed more than two decades of success as a program maker. He took up writing full-time in the 1990s. He is married and lives in north London.

A NOTE ON THE TYPE

This book was set in a modern adaptation of a type designed by the first William Caslon (1692–1766). The Caslon face, an artistic, easily read type, has enjoyed over two centuries of popularity in our own country. It is of interest to note that the first copies of the Declaration of Independence and the first paper currency distributed to the citizens of the newborn nation were printed in this typeface.

Composed by Creative Graphics
Allentown, Pennsylvania

Printed and bound by Berryville Graphics
Berryville, Virginia

Designed by Soonyoung Kwon